VIRGINIA BINDER is Associate Professor of Psychology at California State University, Long Beach.

ARNOLD BINDER is Professor of Social Ecology and Psychology at the University of California, Irvine.

BERNARD RIMLAND is Director of the Institute for Child Behavior Research in San Diego.

MODERN
THERAPIES

Edited by

Virginia Binder
Arnold Binder
Bernard Rimland

A SPECTRUM BOOK

PRENTICE-HALL, INC. *Englewood Cliffs, New Jersey*

Library of Congress Cataloging in Publication Data
Main entry under title:

Modern therapies.

    (A Spectrum Book)
    Includes bibliographies and index.
    1. Psychotherapy.   I. Binder, Virginia.
II. Binder, Arnold.   III. Rimland, Bernard, 1928
RC480.M64   616.8 '914   76-20652
ISBN 0-13-599001-7
ISBN 0-13-598995-7 pbk.

© 1976 by PRENTICE-HALL, INC.
ENGLEWOOD CLIFFS, NEW JERSEY

A SPECTRUM BOOK

10   9   8   7   6

Printed in the United States of America

Prentice-Hall International, Inc., *London*
Prentice-Hall of Australia Pty. Limited, *Sydney*
Prentice-Hall of Canada, Ltd., *Toronto*
Prentice-Hall of India Private Limited, *New Delhi*
Prentice-Hall of Japan, Inc., *Tokyo*
Prentice-Hall of Southeast Asia Pte. Ltd., *Singapore*

Contents

Preface

Several years ago a course called the Survey of the New Therapies was presented at the University of California, Irvine. Each week a therapist representing a different orientation described and demonstrated his own system. The response of the students (and there were 380 of them) was overwhelmingly enthusiastic and seemed to reflect the broader interest of many lay people in the therapeutic movement. An effort to choose a text revealed that most collections of therapies were outdated or written by a single author who could not convey the style and philosophical idiosyncrasies of each approach. Short of assigning a book for each orientation, there was no way students could be exposed to the writings of major practicing therapists. Though collections of works by different therapists have since appeared, there are still no edited volumes directed toward the beginning student or lay reader. This book presents twelve major therapy systems from the perspective of the founder or a major therapist of the system. Each author was given the freedom to describe his approach in the way he thought best represented it. The book should serve then as an excellent introduction to the approaches of today's therapists, leaving the reader free to pursue more in-depth reading of any systems of interest.

When a dozen or so therapists are selected for coverage from a much larger field, the reader may wonder about the basis of choice. The selection of systems chosen for the course stemmed from the recommendations of faculty, students, and therapists in the community. Each therapy seemed to have a following among practicing and future therapists and among clients. Perusal of community bookstores further indicated the popularity of the therapeutic approaches included.

The reader may also wonder what is modern about all the therapies. During the 1960s and continuing into the 70s considerable change has occurred in mental health approaches. Among these changes one finds that

Psychologists and psychiatrists are no longer devoting as much of their energies to diagnosis.

Brief therapies are replacing the extended psychoanalytic model.

Families and groups instead of individuals are more frequently the focus of treatment.

Therapies in which behavior change (symptom removal) is the goal are now considered acceptable.

Areas once considered too mystical, such as meditation and psychedelic experiences, are now viewed with more respect, as one can see in noting the serious work on Transcendental Meditation and LSD therapy.

Research designs for assessing therapies and determining what works are more prevalent. Note the extensive research on an approach as recent as Implosive Therapy.

The setting for therapy has moved from the professional office out into the community.

Theories designed to explain malfunctioning of the individual are being applied to disorganization in the community. For example, Glasser has translated the concepts of Reality Therapy for the school system.

Paraprofessionals are becoming accepted as counselors and some orientations such as behavior modification are advocating parents and teachers as therapists.

Mental health professionals in general have become increasingly aware of the multitude of factors (social, biological, and environmental, as well as personal dynamics) that influence human behavior.

The general panorama of therapies included in this volume are in accord with these changing emphases. Though Gestalt Therapy and Rational-Emotive Therapy can be traced to the 40s and 50s, the manner in which they are currently practiced makes them quite contemporary. For example, both minimize the importance of diagnosis, are brief, and utilize the group approach. Similarly, each therapy system presented highlights some of these modern trends.

Finally, we should comment on the organization of the book. As mentioned earlier, the selection of therapies to be included was on the basis of general popularity rather than content category or logical relationship, and the result was a diverse array of therapies that was very challenging to the editors from an organizational perspective. Such standard dichotomies as insight versus action, verbal versus behavioral, intellectual versus emotional, and past versus present orientation were inadequate. Trial and error, involving modification and expansion of these dichotomies, eventually led to the following format:

Therapies emphasizing cognitive and emotional processes
Therapies emphasizing activity and behavioral processes
Therapies emphasizing biological processes

It is clear that this selected organizational format is less than ideal. Almost all the therapies emphasizing cognitive and emotional processes have at least some focus on actual behavior. And changes in cognitive and emotional systems are critical in Sex Therapy, although obviously this approach is principally behaviorally directed. Finally, therapies dealing with biological events are often used in the context of methods found in the other two categories.

Therefore, the categories and placements reflect our collective biases as to the major mode of approach; we can only argue that they are reasonable, not that they are the only correct way to present modern therapies.

Virginia Binder
Arnold Binder
Bernard Rimland

I

INTRODUCTION

The word "therapies" as used in the title of this book refers to procedures that are seemingly effective in removing psychological or physical discomfort on the part of patients. Explanation of the principles and operation of each therapy forms the central twelve chapters of the book.

The Introduction that follows, on the other hand, places the explanations in a philosophical context by discussing the various features that they have in common with other conceptual frameworks. It becomes apparent that modern therapies have bonds with both religious systems and scientific theories. It is noted that psychotherapy and biochemical therapy as practiced in the Western world are not so different from the practices of so-called "primitive" peoples as many assume.

1

Cultural and Scientific Perspectives on Therapy

Arnold Binder

An infant is not in this world very long before parents begin using symbols in attempts to influence behavior. The early symbols may be "baby-talk" sounds to encourage smiling, or abrupt shouts to abort dangerous movements; and early in the interchange comes the inevitable "No!".

As life proceeds, more and more symbolic equivalents replace direct manipulation of the child — bathing the child, changing diapers, and putting the child to bed become "It's time to give you a bath," "Go to the bathroom," and "It's now your bed-time." And the use of symbols, *primarily in the form of language and gestures,* to influence behavior expands in content over the developing years, becomes mutual as motor ability permits, and eventually assumes a dominant role in all relationships. Long before adulthood, the youngster may properly be considered a product of symbolic interaction between himself and his social environment. Traditionally, a child's success has been measured by the degree of language skills he or she has developed.

It is natural, therefore, that the predominant mode of treating people with problems of living in our culture has been verbal communication. The modern era dates with the method of free association introduced by

"Cultural and Scientific Perspectives on Therapy," by Arnold Binder, Ph. D. © 1976 by Arnold Binder. This article appears in print for the first time in this volume.

Arnold Binder is the originator of the Program in Social Ecology at the University of California, Irvine. His teaching experience includes professorships (some visiting) at New York University, UCLA, University of Colorado, and Indiana University. He has written numerous papers in areas ranging from mathematical theories of statistics to clinical psychology. He is currently interested in juvenile diversion.

Freud. However, the association between communication and relief of personal distress has been with us for a vastly longer period; for example, the method of confession (Sacrament of Penance) has been in widespread use in Catholic churches since the beginning of the third century. Confession, as a type of catharsis, has been shown to be effective in the reduction of guilt and related tensions.

While verbal communication forms a part of the treatment package in non-Western cultures — most notably in the non-Western equivalents to our processes of diagnostic evaluation, suggestion, and catharsis (or confession) — the principal intervention mode is action, including the use of nonverbal symbols. In addition to the conversation involved in evaluation and confession, many non-Western treatment methods include indirect verbal communication between patient and healer, as when the healer speaks to and receives messages from supernatural sources or when the healer interprets the current implications of cultural myths. But the non-Western treatment ceremony is likely to consist more of actions such as dancing in a frenzied manner, beating on a drum, sucking "foreign objects" from the patient's body, applying painful stimuli like hot irons and knives to the body, bombarding the patient with sensory stimuli, and entering a trance state. One other frequent feature of non-Western treatment practice is the use of drugs. These range from psychedelic drugs such as peyote and psilocybin to mild medicinal herbs. Seguin (1970) reported that more than forty different plants (including several with psychedelic properties) were used by native healers of Peru alone.

One interesting development in several recently evolved Western therapies has been a decrease in the use of verbal communication and an increase in the more active techniques of the non-Western cultures. There are, for example, the supplementary tasks and games assigned in Gestalt Therapy (Chapter 5) and shouting and crying that may be components of the abreaction phase of Feeling Therapy (Chapter 6). Perhaps this reflects the broader tendency of many groups in our culture to reject our "mechanistic" society and identify with "natural" (or "primitive") ways of life. (See Gould, 1970, for an interesting analysis of this identification process and its many ramifications.) Perhaps it reflects the increasing knowledge available in the area of folklore or cultural psychiatry (see Seguin, 1970, and Kennedy, 1973). But in any event, considering recent changes in our culture, the process would seem to illustrate Torrey's (1972, p. 78) argument that "techniques of therapy are intimately related to culture. They are related to the theories of causation of illness, the personality types valued, and the goals of therapy in the culture. The last is a reflection of more general cultural values." We may be moving away from the cultural values of hard work, independence, rationality, and personal responsibility that call for such goals as insight, self-sufficiency, adjustment, and mastery by diligent effort.

Another development in Western approaches that parallels non-Western treatment methods is the increased use of drugs. And one of these drugs, LSD, is the Western (and synthetic) equivalent of the psychedelic drugs used in non-Western cultures (see Chapter 12).

THERAPY AS A TYPE OF RELIGIOUS EXPERIENCE

Owing to a variety of pressures, both personal and social, the study of religious beliefs and practices on an objective basis has predominantly involved religions other than those in the culture of the investigator. Thus, we are far more likely to find such terms as "magic," "mythology," and "superstition" in the reports of religious practices of the Baganda of East Africa or the Zuñi of New Mexico than in the descriptions of the various sects of Christianity and Judaism — even when describing phenomena that are all but identical. During certain periods of Western development, indeed, such differential perception was necessary to maintain life and limb. Only very indirect references could be made of any relationship between the "pagan" practices of the primitive and Christianity. For example, there is a note in the diary of one of the conquistadors who participated in Cortez's rape of the Aztecs to the effect that it was strange that the statues of the Aztecs were destroyed as evil images only to be replaced by another set of statues.

Although there is no physical danger in most Western communities at this time in pointing out similarities between Christian "beliefs" and primitive "mythologies," there remains considerable restraint in doing so, particularly in the mass communication media.

Similar restraint has been shown, at least until quite recently, in the area of treatment and cure, both physical and psychological. Since the institutions of Western medical and psychological practice have never reached the heights of power reached by the institutions of Western religion, there has never been a threat to life or limb to enforce that restraint. But it was not until the early 1960s that we find prominent voices (e.g., Kiev, 1964) suggesting that Western psychiatry could learn much from primitive practitioners. In 1972, we do find the psychiatrist Torrey going so far as to argue that there is no essential difference in the techniques, functions, and goals of witch doctors and psychiatrists. But it is perhaps noteworthy that on the title page of Torrey's book there is a bold disclaimer from the National Institute of Mental Health (his employer) stating that the author's opinions "do not represent the official policy" of either NIMH or the Public Health Service.

In non-Western cultures, religious and healing ceremonies are almost always ideologically intertwined, and the healer is likely to be a religious practitioner. There are a great number of generic terms for such healers, including "witch doctor," "medicine man," and "shaman." To minimize the pejorative connotations associated with the first two, "shaman" has been adopted for this chapter. The term originally was used for the healer in certain Siberian tribes, but it is widely used now for therapists whose work has religious overtones.

The shaman is most often assumed to be effective in curing illness and alleviating personal distress by his contact with supernatural powers. Attributes frequently associated with shamans and similar folk healers are charisma, forcefulness or authoritarianism, emotional instability, ability to enter altered states of consciousness, showmanship, and personal detachment.

Common in non-Western treatment methods are dramatic rituals involving trance states; manipulation, sometimes violently, of the patient's body; sensory assault involving drum beating and frenzied praying and singing; symbolic bombardment in the form of colors, shapes, and objects; and re-enactment of myths. But in some societies the shaman performs only routine and rather monotonous rituals. Supernatural forces are freely called upon or invoked in the curative process. Treatment may include a special setting or physical arrangement, such as lying on sand paintings of divinities or sleeping in a sacred temple ("incubation"), to enhance the general atmosphere of awe and anxiety.

Since treatment ideology is part of the broader religious ideology of a non-Western culture, the specific techniques of the shaman are based upon the belief system of the culture relating its members to their universe. For example, supernatural spirits in the form of mountain spirits, water beings, the coyote spirit, and others play a central role in the religion of the Chiricahua Apache. They are predominant features of everyday occurrences, and each adult Apache has a connection with a spirit source. When an Apache shaman works with a troubled patient, he urges, pleads, and may "struggle" with the familiar spirit (in songs and prayers and symbolic actions) for full restoration of the patient's functioning and comfort. The ghosts of the dead, on the other hand, are feared but not worshipped among the Chiricahua, while these ghosts are the most important element in the religious beliefs of another group, the Baganda. In fact, illness may result from the neglect of the shrine or grave of a deceased person, in the belief system of the Baganda. As one would expect, the shaman of the Baganda, but not of the Chiricahua, will attempt to effect a cure by propitiating an offended ghost and, if that fails to produce a cure, attempt to destroy the malevolent ghost by burning or drowing.

It is obviously not easy to trace the specific origins of the belief systems of cultures, but evidence indicates that many stem from the life circumstances of the people. For example, Seguin (1970) has compared the explanations of disease and distress of Peruvian Indians living in the Amazon jungle with those of people living on the coast. In the jungle, distress is assumed to come from natural forces—it results when the soul is stolen by mountains or rivers; on the coast of Peru, distress is presumably caused by people who produce harm rather than by nature. Seguin points out that in the jungle, man must fight for the preservation of life against nature, while on the environmentally benign coast, man is the major enemy.

From the detached perspective of the Western observer, one would certainly not expect treatment results without belief on the part of the patient in the curative power of the approach as specified in the explanatory system—we are not, of course, likely to accept the possibility that spirits or ghosts really intervene. Writers like Frank (1961, 1968), Kiev (1964), and Prince (1964) have particularly stressed the contributions of faith, hope, belief, and suggestibility in the effectiveness of non-Western curative approaches, as a point of departure in comparing and contrasting non-Western and Western methods. It is abundantly clear that the background of religious fervor, as enhanced by the various props used by the shaman or healer to inspire awe, is a potent force toware producing complete receptivity.

And if such factors as faith, hope, belief, and suggestibility (supplemented, perhaps, by catharsis and guilt reduction) are central to the curative process of the shaman or folk healer, one would surely expect them to enter as components in the operation of Western therapy. It is undoubtedly true, as Frank (1961) states, that the aura and intensity of religious healing cannot possibly be achieved in a psychotherapeutic, or similar, context. But the difference may not be as great as it superficially seems when consideration is given to the range of factors discussed by Shapiro (1971) as important in therapeutic effects. His orientation is the placebo effect in therapy—meaning a nonspecific effect produced by belief in the efficacy of the therapy rather than its specific content or agent. The placebo effect is most commonly associated with drugs, but the operation depends upon the psychological power of belief and faith rather than upon the agent or form of treatment. The factors of importance in producing the effect in Western therapy, according to Shapiro, include newness of approach and its intellectual, emotional, and financial status (or its fame and popularity); prestige of the therapist; therapist's interest and attitude toward the patient, the treatment, and the likely outcome of treatment; degree of patient suggestibility; and concordance between the therapeutic approach and patient's biases and attitudes as moulded by social class.

The comparability of these factors to the religious awe, the esteem of the shaman, the enthusiastic performance of the shaman, and the match between religious belief and therapeutic practice of the non-Western approach is obvious enough. But as Shapiro (1964, p. 439) states in regard to the placebo effect in Western therapy, "This concept is not popular because psychotherapy is frequently believed to be a modern treatment based on scientific principles, while the placebo effect is viewed as a superstitious response to a drug." In a fashion strikingly similar to that of the religious sphere, the words "superstitious" and "placebo" are widely reserved for therapies that are advocated by other, distant practitioners. As Shapiro (p. 439) further states, "Adamant claims that psychotherapy is not susceptible to placebo effects conform to the principle that every placebo once accepted was vigorously defended as a nonplacebo. Medical history clearly demonstrates that despite the sensitivity of many practitioners to the nonspecific or placebo effect of others, they were usually insensitive to their own."

Torrey (1972, p. 1) has carried this line of thought to the ultimate point in his position,

> Witchdoctors and psychiatrists perform essentially the same function in their respective cultures. They are both therapists; both treat patients using similar techniques; and both get similar results. Recognition of this should not downgrade psychiatrists; rather it should upgrade witchdoctors.

To Torrey, the essential features of psychological healing, common to Western psychotherapists and shamans are comparable concepts between healer and patient in regard to causation of symptoms; desirable personal qualities of the healer, such as firmness and maturity; expectation that the culturally defined treatment produces improvement; and effective technique.

THERAPY AS AN APPLIED SCIENTIFIC METHOD

The vast majority of therapeutic approaches practised in the West are based upon theories that are scientific in form. One would scarcely expect a different state of affairs, given that most protagonists of the therapies have backgrounds in medicine (psychiatry) or scientific psychology. But science and the scientific method have not been with us all that long — and their influences in psychiatry and psychology extend back not much more than the duration of this century.

In fact, several of the prescientific approaches of the West were all but indistinguishable in broad form from those of the so-called "primitive" cultures. There was not just similarity of certain techniques, but close parallels in supernatural and religious overtones. For example, Mesmer (a physician who lived mostly in eighteenth-century France) believed that the human body had a property that made it susceptible to influence by heavenly bodies, as well as by various inanimate objects on earth. Because of its similarity to magnetism in operation across empty space, he called the property "animal magnetism." He argued that illness resulted from obstruction of the free flow of animal magnetism in the body. His method of treatment consisted of seating a group of patients around a tub containing iron filings in bottles. The patients held iron rods that protruded from the tub; animal magnetism from the filings presumably flowed through the rods. He used music, lighting, and dramatic gestures like pointing an iron rod, or a finger, at an individual to make that individual the focus of attention. Music, lighting, and dramatic gestures, it should be noted, are frequently the props of the shaman (as well as of some very current therapies).

All approaches to cure, non-Western and Western, have explanatory systems to account for the process whereby certain behavior on the part of the shaman or therapist produces change in the patient. These explanatory systems range, in the Western world, from the highly elaborated psychoanalytic theory to a set of empirical relationships, as frequently found in the area of psychopharmacology. The following is an example of a non-Western explanatory system.

In the Navajo curing ceremony, the use of emetics and cathartics, sweating, and bathing is followed by placing the patient on sand paintings of deities, rubbing his body with the sand, and touching his body with sacred articles. The explanation is that illness implies evil in the body — it is necessary, therefore, to drive the evil forces out and replace them with the powers of good associated with representations of deities. And to make sure that evil spirits do not sneak in during expelling and replacing phases, fasting and strict continence are necessary.

Clearly, an explanation may be considered "reasonable" ("satisfactory") or "unreasonable" ("unsatisfactory") by the person to whom it is directed. The decision as to reasonableness-unreasonableness is a psychological judgment that depends upon the person's cultural and educational background, knowledge of alternative explanations, scientific grounding, personal philosophy of life, suggestibility, and so on. An explanation of psychotic behavior in terms of early child-rearing practices would be as unsatisfactory to a traditional Navajo as an explanation in terms of evil spirits would be to most of us. Owing to our cultural heritage, which includes knowledge of the success of the sciences in controlling and altering our environment, we tend to accept as satisfactory only explanations that are scientific in both language and form.

But what are the characteristics of a scientific explanation, and how does a scientific explanation differ from one that is not scientific?

Science studies all phenomena that are open to public inspection, and uses in its explanatory systems the language of nature (as opposed to such supernatural concepts as gods, spirits, ghosts, devils, witches, and angels). There are three aspects to a scientific theory: description derived from classification, explanation, and prediction.

At its crudest level, a scientific theory consists purely of a set of descriptions of the world of interest. Some, it should be noted, prefer not referring to a set of descriptions as a scientific theory. There are categories, classifications, statements of common properties, nomenclature, etc. that are used to systematize information acquisition. Description is not much more than a catalogue of important aspects of the domain of concern.

An advance occurs when regularities are observed over descriptive categories and statements of these regularities are formulated (these are called empirical relationships or laws). For example, we may have a patient who states that she is unable to achieve orgasm, and has never achieved orgasm. It has been found that women falling into the "inorgasmic" category are helped by the discovery of sensitive erogenous areas of the body in a process called "sensate focus." The relating of method of intervention to expected change in the patient is a statement of empirical relationship.

Although explanation does occur in a trivial sense at the descriptive level (e.g., Why does that animal have such a long neck? Because it's a giraffe.), it is only at this second level that satisfying explanation can be attained. Explanation is typically defined as accounting for particular occurrences or events by deductive reference to the generally found relationships or laws. Explanation leads to understanding in the sense of placing a given phenomenon in a broader context of interactions; the given phenomenon is deducible as a consequence in the more general state of affairs. To illustrate in the psychological realm, to explain a given type of behavior we attribute to the behaving person certain attitudes, personality characteristics, beliefs, character traits, motivations, moral standards, and the like. Then we determine what general relations are available that relate the behavior in question to these personal attributes. Why does

Helen stammer at cocktail parties? Because Helen is an extremely shy girl — and it has been established empirically that shy girls have a tendency to be anxious and stammer in demanding social situations.

The theory passes through stages of greater sophistication as higher-order generalizations are developed to encompass the empirical (or low-level) relationships. This involves the process of induction to a level that does not include any references to directly observable phenomena. Explanation using these higher-order constructs would be the classical psychoanalytic statement that paranoia is a defensive reaction against latent homosexual desire. Latent homosexual desire and the process of defensive reaction are remote indeed from observable behavior, and can be used to explain many diverse behavioral manifestations — even behavior as remote from homosexuality as extreme suspiciousness of others.

But it is difficult, and perhaps impossible, to differentiate scientific from nonscientific explanatory systems on the basis of this deductive framework. If ghosts invade the bodies of people who neglect their memorial symbols, it is simple to deduce that a given illness can only be cured by getting rid of the invading ghost. The third aspect of scientific theory — namely, prediction — provides the key to differentiation.

The same deductive process is used in prediction as in explanation, only it is applied to a future event. In explanation, one starts with an occurrence or event, and laws or regularities are sought to make the event plausible as a deducible consequence; in prediction, one starts with the laws or regularities and deduces future outcomes. It is not likely that a shaman would be able to predict future consequences accurately, except by chance, on the basis of supernatural forces. A severe storm may be explained on the basis of the wrath of the gods, but one is not likely to find the prediction that the gods are to be wrathful next Sunday, and so a severe storm should be expected at that time.

While the explanatory theories for Western therapies are scientific in form and in language use, almost all specific procedures have arisen out of clinical practice rather than from deduction using higher-order constructs. A therapist typically tries a novel technique, observes certain results in patients, then develops an explanatory system on the basis of his or her professional knowledge of relevant sciences and his or her idiosyncratic beliefs and attitudes. The particular types of patients seen by a therapist of course determine the nature of such observations; it it upon these observations that the therapist's knowledge and beliefs must operate. Thus, Freud's formulations reflect the fact that he worked primarily with Victorian, middle-class neurotics, while Roger's client-centered approach was based upon therapy with articulate college students who had principally transitory difficulties.

An explanatory system explains why patients have various types of problems and why certain interactions between client and therapist produce change (improvement). Specific predictions may be deduced within the derived system, but testing of these predictions is not usually done in a rigorous scientific style.

The behavioral therapies (see Chapters 9, 10, 11) are anchored in formal learning theories that are very general and well developed. There is considerable doubt that the efficacy of specific techniques for certain problems is directly deducible from the generalizations or constructs of these theories, but it is the case that a broad category of appropriate techniques is deducible. Thus, one can deduce immediately from operant learning theory that behavior A may be reduced in frequency by reinforcing a behavior B that precludes the occurrence of A.

Finally, it should be pointed out that Torrey (1972) has allowed only certain of the physical therapies (particularly drug and shock therapy) scientific status on the basis of accurate outcome predictions. His overly strong position is that "the techniques used by Western psychiatrists are, with few exceptions, on exactly the same scientific plane as the techniques used by witchdoctors. If one is magic then so is the other. If one is prescientific, then so is the other" (p. 8). He then provides an example from a textbook of psychiatry in which the authors "make the inevitable but fallacious assumption that Western psychiatric therapies are based on science" (p. 9). It does seem, however, that Torrey accepts a more delimiting definition of scientific theory than specified above and generally accepted by philosophers of science.

THE THERAPIES THAT FOLLOW

This book contains accounts of twelve therapeutic approaches, encompassing both the relationship between therapeutic practice and the problem pictures presented by clients, and the relationship between the interaction of those two factors and expected changes in clients. The accounts range in level of abstraction from sets of statements of empirical relationships to elaborate theories containing higher-order constructs.

There are a number of questions one might ask about both a specific explanatory system and the therapy with which it deals. For example, there are the questions: Is the explanatory system reasonable? Is the explanatory system valid? Is the therapy effective in producing change as claimed?

The reasonableness (satisfactoriness) or unreasonableness (unsatisfactoriness) of an explanatory system is a judgment made on the basis of the personal proclivities of the judge. There is substantial agreement in our culture in regard to the criteria of reasonableness in an explanation, but note the widespread acceptance of astrology and demonology. In any event, the reasonableness of each explanation must be left to the reader's judgment — that person will bring to bear his/her knowledge, biases, philosophy of life, attitudes, and tolerance of uncertainty, in making the judgment.

The question of validity depends upon the accuracy of predictions from the explanatory system. Only very simple predictions are possible from explanations that are at the level of empirical laws or only somewhat beyond that level. For these explanations in particular, but for all others too, the most salient predictions are those related to the outcomes among clients in using the prescribed methods. This of course encompasses the question of the effectiveness of the therapy. And that issue is taken up in Chapter 14 of this book. It is hardly possible, or even useful, to consider other types of prediction in the present context.

Beyond the questions directed toward specific therapies and explanations is the broad issue of the purposes of the explanatory systems in general. What are the purposes for the client, for the therapist, and for the people outside the therapeutic relationship — as, for example, the reader of this book?

First, explanation leads to understanding and to enlightment in a new domain of organized knowledge. That certainly is an end in itself, particularly for the casual reader, since understanding and knowledge are highly valued in our cultures.

Second, to the extent that an explanatory system is a valid scientific theory, it allows the therapist to select the specific approach to be used with a client on the basis of a diagnostic interview (observational evaluation) with the client. Moreover, a valid theory enables the therapist to deduce changes in approach that may become desirable as new information is acquired over the course of therapy. This may vary from a trivial change in dosage rate for a drug to a major change in direction of interpretation.

And to the extent that the explanatory system for a therapy is reasonable to a given person, it motivates the person to choose that therapy rather than an alternative when relevant personal problems arise. Clearly one chooses Megavitamin Therapy, for example, when one prefers a biochemical rather than a psychological explanation for certain severe behavioral disturbances. That is not to deny that such other variables as fashionableness of the therapy and status of the therapist enter into the picture, but rather to add reasonableness of the explanatory system to the list. It does not seem likely that a person will choose a therapy that is not reasonable, or, in other words, not in accord with his or her overall belief network. A Polar Eskimo is no more likely to choose psychoanalysis, if available, than an upper-class matron is to choose the frenzied singing and dancing of the Eskimo shaman, if available.

Finally, belief in the explanatory system may be important in mediating the placebo effect that is apparently a component of all therapies. It creates the necessary faith, hope, and expectation. It is certainly not always necessary to have belief in an explanatory system for the placebo effect. The word of a high-status practitioner, particularly if he or she is imbued with supernatural powers, may in itself produce enough belief in efficacy to produce the effect. Further, there are certain intuitive or widely held cultural associations that seem so natural that belief flows without further encouragement; a good example of this phenomenon is the widespread use of spa therapy in Europe to produce cures for almost all physical and mental ailments.

But where factors like status of practitioner and prevalent cultural belief mode are not significant, it is clear that belief in the explanation of therapeutic operation becomes important in producing necessary faith.

Perhaps the essence of this chapter can be summarized in questions directed to the status of "modern therapies" like those included in this book. Does the newness imply processes like new insights into human problems, the discovery of powerful and specific new techniques, or the elaboration of a scientifically valid theory? Or is the following admonition from Shapiro (1971, p. 442) in regard to new techniques appropriate: *"Treat as many patients with the new remedies while they still have the power to heal"*?

REFERENCES

FRANK, J.D. *Persuasion and healing.* Baltimore: Johns Hopkins University Press, 1961.

FRANK, J.D. The role of hope in psychotherapy. *International Journal of Psychiatry,* 1968, 5, 383–412.

GOULD, R.E. The marginally asocial personality: the beatnik-hippie alienation. In Arieti, S. (Ed.), *The world biennial of psychiatry and psychotherapy* (Vol. 1). New York: Basic Books, 1970.

KENNEDY, J.G. Cultural psychiatry. In Honigmann, J. J. (Ed.), *Handbook of social and cultural anthropology.* Chicago: Rand McNally, 1973.

KIEV, A. The study of folk psychiatry. In Kiev, A. (Ed.), *Magic, faith and healing*. New York: Free Press of Glencoe, Macmillan, 1964.

PRINCE, R.H. Indigenous Yoruba psychiatry. In Kiev, A. (Ed.), *Magic, faith and healing*. New York: Free Press of Glencoe, Macmillan, 1964.

SEGUIN, C.A. Folklore psychiatry. In Arieti, S. (Ed.), *The world biennial of psychiatry and psychotherapy* (Vol. 1). New York: Basic Books, 1970

SHAPIRO, A.K. Placebo effects in medicine, psychotherapy, and psychoanalysis, In Bergin, A. E. & Garfield, S. L. (Eds.), *Handbook of psychotherapy and behavior change: an empirical analysis.* New York: Wiley, 1971.

TORREY, E. F. *The mind game: witchdoctors and psychiatrists.* New York: Emerson Hall Publishers, 1972.

II

THERAPIES EMPHASIZING COGNITIVE AND EMOTIONAL PROCESSES

When many people think of therapy for emotional problems, they picture a patient lying on a couch, revealing his thoughts, memories, feelings, dreams, and fantasies; and having a learned analyst listen attentively to him to understand and interpret the motivations underlying his actions. This portrait is based on Freud's psychoanalytic techniques, which dominated the field of psychotherapy for some fifty years. Freud's approach involved the use of diagnosis to guide the direction of therapy, a thorough probing of the individual's past history, and the study of the relationship between analyst and patient to serve as a key to the way the patient interacted with important people from his past. This approach was often called the "talking cure" to distinguish it from treatment methods based on drugs or other medical techniques.

All of the therapies included in this section can be viewed in the context of the "talking cure." They all offer clients the opportunity to talk or interact with a therapist about cognitive or emotional events, and subsequently view themselves in a new light. However, there are a number of major differences among all of the modern verbal therapies and traditional psychoanalysis. One is the time perspective. Psychoanalysis probes past history, whereas the briefer modern psychotherapies have a "here-and-now" orientation. The influence of the past, if considered at all, is considered only in the context of how it affects the present. Another important difference centers around the importance of the diagnosis. Today's therapists believe in description, but not labeling. They feel that little is to be gained by assigning a client to a diagnostic category, and much of what makes him or her a unique person is lost in the labeling process. A final difference is the speed with which current therapies hope to bring about change. Modern therapies often last less than a year (some a matter of weeks or months), while the psychoanalytic patient could spend three, four, or more years in analysis.

Despite these differences, there are many who feel that the concern and caring of an attentive listener and the relationship that develops between client and therapist are the core ingredients of verbal therapies. These can be found whether the system is called psychoanalysis, Rational-Emotive Therapy, Transactional Analysis, Reality Therapy, Gestalt Therapy, or Feeling Therapy.

Rational-Emotive Therapy (RET) focuses on having the client change his way of viewing his problem. Ellis believes that a person's negative emotional reactions do not result directly from events or experiences, but instead stem from his beliefs about them. When someone has an unpleasant experience, rational beliefs will help him recognize its unpleasantness and inspire him to handle the situation better on the next occasion. Irrational beliefs, on the other hand, cause the individual to "catastrophize" the event and to give up hope. RET attacks the client's irrational beliefs and teaches and encourages rationality.

Transactional Analysis (TA) also provides the client with a framework within which to view his behavior. The client learns to recognize the Parent-Adult-Child (PAC) components of his personality and to analyze his interactions with others (called transactions) on the basis of these various PAC categories. The client is helped to understand his typical transactions and can begin to change those which make him feel "Not OK."

In Reality Therapy, Glasser expects to bring about therapeutic change through his involvement with the client. Together they examine and evaluate the client's ongoing behavior and devise a reasonable plan for change. Then Glasser seeks a commitment for action and accepts no excuses for failure to carry out the commitment.

Gestalt Therapy (GT) teaches the client the process of being aware of what he is doing and how, rather than focusing on how he should be or why he is the way he is. GT clients learn to use their own senses to explore all aspects of their being — cognitions, emotions, and actions — and find their own solutions to their problems. In GT the client does not adjust to a given situation, but learns how to use his awareness in whatever situation emerges.

Finally, in Feeling Therapy an attempt is made to transform the client from his disordered, mixed-up way of experiencing to living based on the "true" feelings he has inside himself. The true feelings are those that are completely expressed and totally in the present. Thus the client of Feeling Therapy moves from being alone, disordered, and past-oriented to being a transformed member of a feeling, therapeutic community.

Each of the therapies in this section also involves a focus on physical actions, or active homework assignments in which the individual must change his behavior. But these assignments are given after the client has been helped to change his way of viewing himself. The therapies in the next section begin with a focus on behavior change and expect cognitive and emotional change to follow. This difference in approach of these two sections reflects the controversy within social psychology regarding whether attitude change generally precedes or follows behavior change when a person adopts a new approach to life.

2

Rational-Emotive Therapy

Albert Ellis

Rational-Emotive Therapy (RET) consists of a theory of personality, a system of philosophy, and a technique of psychological treatment. Let me, very briefly, present its main aspects and then illustrate them by a case presentation.

MAJOR ASPECTS OF RATIONAL-EMOTIVE THERAPY

Rational and Irrational Behaviors

RET clearly defines appropriate feelings and rational beliefs as those aiding human survival and happiness — particularly those enabling you to accept objective reality, live amicably in a social group, relate intimately to a few members of this group, engage in productive work, and enjoy selectively chosen recreational pursuits (Ellis, 1975; Ellis and Harper, 1975; Maultsby, 1975). Irrationality consists of needlessly harming yourself.

Albert Ellis is the founder of Rational Emotive Therapy and director of the Institute for Advanced Study in Rational Psychotherapy. He is the author of numerous best-selling books, including *Reason and Emotion in Psychotherapy, A Guide to Rational Living,* and *The Art and Science of Love.*

The Importance of Values

RET stresses the importance of human values. It holds that personality largely consists of beliefs, constructs, or attitudes; that you function healthfully when you have rational or empirically based values; and that absolutistic, perfectionistic values tend to make you feel emotionally disturbed. Recent evidence by cognitive psychologists and psychotherapists shows that values importantly influence behavior, including therapeutic change (Kelly, 1955; Rokeach, 1968; Raimy, 1975).

The A-B-C Theory of Disturbance

According to RET, when you have an emotional reaction at point C (the emotional Consequence), after some Activating event or experience has occurred at point A, A does *not* cause C. The Belief system (B) that you hold about A creates C. Thus, if you feel depressed at point A after a rejection at point C, the rejection does not cause your depression. Your *Beliefs* (at point B) do.

Your first set of Beliefs has rationality because, since your basic value system includes *wanting* to stay alive, feel happy, and gain acceptance from others, you *will* find rejection unfortunate and you'd *better* feel appropriately sad about it. Your second set of Beliefs has little rationality because you only *define* rejection as "awful" (meaning *more than* unfortunate). You *can* bear it — though you'll rarely like it. And it doesn't make you a slob or a worthless individual — but at worst a person with some slobbish traits.

Your rational Beliefs and appropriate Consequences of feeling sorry and frustrated when someone rejects you, moreover, will help you work harder to get accepted in the future. But your irrational Beliefs and inappropriate Consequences of feeling depressed will encourage you to mope, to see future acceptance as hopeless, and to act badly, so that more people tend to reject you.

Since I first propounded the A-B-C theory of emotional reaction twenty years ago, literally hundreds of experiments have shown that emotion and behavior significantly depend on cognitive mediating processes. I list many of them in my other writings (Ellis, 1974).

Confronting and Attacking Irrational Beliefs

Far more actively than other cognitive systems of therapy, RET vigorously helps people to confront and attack their disturbance-creating beliefs. It clearly brings their magical (illogical and/or self-defeating) philosophies to their attention, explains how these cause emotional upset, attacks them on logico-empirical grounds, and teaches people how to change disordered thinking. This view can be extended to work with "normal" children as well as moderately "disturbed" adults. The Institute for Advanced Study in Rational Psychotherapy in New York City runs The Living School, a facility where methods of rational-emotive teaching for youngsters are developed and brought to children in other private and public schools.

Homework Assignments

From its beginnings, RET has advocated activity homework assignments or *in vivo* desensitization to help people think, feel, and behave more rationally (Ellis, 1962, 1973, 1975). Several RET-related studies have shown that this approach can produce better therapeutic results than less activity-oriented forms of desensitization (Shelton and Ackerman, 1974).

Operant Control of Thinking and Emoting

RET frequently employs Skinner's (1972) reinforcement or operant conditioning techniques for self-management purposes to help people change their overt behaviors and their thinking. Many of my clients learn to surrender their irrational Beliefs by reinforcing themselves with something they truly enjoy (e.g., eating or having sex) after they work at least ten minutes a day at disputing one of their self-defeating ideas; they can also penalize themselves (e.g., by doing house cleaning or burning a twenty-dollar bill) if they do not work at this kind of disputing. Other RET-oriented therapists, such as Goldfried and Merbaum (1973) and Meichenbaum (1974), have also done pioneering work using the principles of operant conditioning.

Group Therapy and Marathon Encounters

RET, because of its educational emphasis, stresses group therapy and marathons, using a unique cognitive-emotive-behavioral approach instead of the one-sided experiential and abreactive approach of most groups (Ellis, 1969, 1974a, 1974b). In RET groups, members do risk-taking, shame-attacking exercises to demonstrate how their irrational Beliefs ("I must do well and get everyone's approval) *make* these acts "risky" or "shameful." They also receive assertive and "anxiety-provoking" homework assignments, to help them change their inhibited thoughts and feelings.

Logico-Empiricism and Anti-Magic

RET contends that "emotional disturbance" largely consists of devout religiosity, intolerance, whining, dogmatism, and magical thinking. Clients are taught that if they follow the logical-empirical approach and forego all forms of magic and absolutism, they can eliminate most of their disturbances. This technique traces severe feelings of anxiety, depression, guilt, and hostility to the human tendency to "awfulize" and "catastrophize" —to go beyond empirical data and dogmatically hold that disadvantageous experiences absolutely *should, ought,* and must not *exist* (Ellis, 1975; Ellis & Harper, 1975).

I originally listed ten to twelve major irrational ideas that almost all humans beings tend to hold to some degree; but we can list most of them under three major forms of demandingness or *mus*turbation: (1) "I *must* act quite competently and thereby win the approval of all the people I find significant"; (2) You *must* treat me fairly, kindly, and considerately"; and (3) "Easy and pleasurable conditions *must* exist in my life." RET teaches people how to dispute and surrender these unrealistic expectations and commands, how to accept themselves and others unconditionally and undamningly, and how to put up with inevitable annoyances and frustrations.

The Semantics of Emotional Disturbance

Following some of the ideas of Korzybski (1933), RET helps people eliminate their disturbances by defining their terms, giving up overgeneralizing, and speaking and thinking more objectively. During RET sessions, I frequently stop clients and induce them to change their irrational statements to more semantically accurate statements. For example: "I'd *better* succeed," instead of "I *have to* succeed!" "I have some poor traits," instead of "I rate as a worthless person." "I made myself angry at your performances" instead of "You made me angry!" Most of my current writings on RET use a form I call *E-prime*; this makes no use of any form of the verb *to be* and thereby eliminates the "is" of identity and the "is" of predication (Ellis, 1975, 1976; Ellis and Harper, 1975).

The Theory of Human Worth

RET teaches people that although they can pragmatically tell themselves, "I have intrinsic worth because I exist," and thereby eliminate self-rating, including all forms of self-deification and self-devil-ification, they can achieve (after much serious thought) a philosophically better solution:

That is, they learn to refuse to rate themselves and their totality at all; they learn to rate or measure only their traits and performances, for the purpose of increasing their enjoyment. RET thus abolishes the pernicious aspects of the human ego while keeping the individual's sense of uniqueness, aliveness, and "ongoingness" (Ellis, 1974, 1975).

Comprehensive Approach to Personality Change

In RET, human cognition, emotion, and behavior are considered to significantly interrelate. Thus, people who want to achieve effective personality change are taught comprehensively — cognitively, emotively, and behaviorally — to attack their symptoms and the philosophies that underlie them. As uniquely cognizing creatures, they can use much rational-persuasive therapy or emotional education as the core method of their therapist-directed and self-help techniques.

Criteria for Therapeutic Change

RET acknowledges that no foolproof criteria for the occurrence of therapeutic change exists, and that of the more than forty experimental studies showing the effectivenss of RET, none remains unchallenged on methodological grounds. It suggests that counselors help people *get* better and not merely *feel* better. Thus, we can see clients with an airplane phobia as "cured" when (1) they fully believe that riding on planes may well prove undesirable and unenjoyable but hardly *awful* or *horrible*; when (2) they can think about traveling in planes without feeling anxious and without physical effects such as fast pulse or profuse sweating; when (3) they easily approach rather than avoid plane trips; and when (4) they use the anti-awfulizing, risk-taking, and behavioral methods they have learned in their RET sessions to overcome similar phobias they may inflict on themselves in the future.

CASE PRESENTATION

To help give you a real feeling for how RET works, let me show how I applied it with a 27-year-old male who presented several symptoms. This man felt shy and inhibited when trying to relate to women; he had very rapid ejaculation in intercourse, and he acted with hostility to authority figures, including his parents and his immediate supervisor at work. I first worked with him on his enormous fears of failure and his longstanding feelings of worthlessness. During our second session, we dialogued as follows (since I now write but rarely talk in E-prime, the dialogue uses regular English):

THERAPIST: You seem to be terribly afraid that you will fail at making good initial contacts with a woman and also at succeeding sexually.

CLIENT: Hell, yes! To say the least, I'm scared shitless in both these areas.

THERAPIST: Because if you fail in either area, what —?

CLIENT: If I fail, I'll be an utter slob!

THERAPIST: Prove it!

CLIENT: Isn't it obvious?

THERAPIST: Not for me! It's fairly obvious that if a woman rejects you, socially or sexually, it'll hardly be a great thing. But how will that prove that *you*, a total person, will be no good?

CLIENT: I still think it's obvious. Would this same woman reject *anyone*?

THERAPIST: No, probably not. Let's suppose that she accepts many men, but not you. Let's also suppose that she rejects you because she finds that, first, you're not terribly good at conversation and, second, you come quickly in intercourse. So she finds you doubly deficient. Now, how does that still prove that you're no good?

CLIENT: It certainly proves that I'm no good for *her*.

THERAPIST: Yes, in a way. You're no good for her conversationally and sexually. You have two rotten *traits*.

CLIENT: And she doesn't want *me*, for having those traits.

THERAPIST: Right. In the case we're assuming, she rejects *you* for having those two traits. But all we've proved is that one woman despises two of your characteristics; and that this woman therefore rejects you as a lover or a husband. Even she, mind you, might well accept you as a nonsexual friend. For you have, don't forget, many other traits — such as intelligence, artistic talent, reliability, etc.

CLIENT: But not the traits she *most* wants!

THERAPIST: Maybe. But how does this prove that *all* women, like her, would find you equally wanting? Some, actually, might like you *because* you are shy and *because* you come quickly sexually — when they don't happen to like intercourse, and therefore want to get it over rapidly!

CLIENT: Fat chance!

THERAPIST: Yes, statistically. For *most* women, presumably, will tend to reject you if you're shy or sexually inadequate, in their eyes. But a few, at least, will accept you for the very reasons that most refuse you; and many more, normally, will accept you in spite of your deficiencies, because they nonetheless become attached to you.

CLIENT: Who the devil wants *that!*

THERAPIST: Most of us do, actually, if we're sane. For, since we're all highly imperfect, we're happy that some people accept us *with* these imperfections. But let's even suppose the worst — just to show how crooked your thinking is. Let's suppose that, because of your shyness and fast ejaculation, *all* women rejected you for *all* time. Would you still be a worthless slob?

CLIENT: I wouldn't exactly be a great guy!

THERAPIST: No, you wouldn't be Jesus Christ, or Napoleon; or, certainly, Casanova! But many women, remember, wouldn't want you if you were one of them. Jesus, if he ever really existed, seems to have been pretty shy with women; and Napoleon may well have come quickly. As for Casanova, most women, at least today, wouldn't want him just *because* he was so sexy. Anyway, we're evading the question; *would* you be a total slob?

CLIENT: Well, uh, I — no, I guess not.

THERAPIST: Because?

CLIENT: Well, because I'd still have other, uh, good traits. Is that what you're getting at?

THERAPIST: Yes, partly. You'd still have other good traits. And *you*, if you were ratable at all, would equal *all* your traits, and not merely two of them, such as shyness and sexual prematurity.

I kept working, along these cognitive lines, revealing to the client his underlying philosophic assumptions, how they led to his "emotional" problems (including his anxiety, fear of failure, and semi-impotence), and how he could change them. I especially used the A-B-C's of RET to get him to attack his disturbance-creating Belief System. We started with his emotional Consequence (C), his shyness and inhibition when approaching attractive women. Then we went to his Activating experiences (A) — usually his seeing an attractive woman at a social affair and wanting to approach her. Immediately after A occurred, he felt self-conscious and inept at C.

I showed him that instead of A causing C, his Belief system at B directly created it. First, at B, he had a rational Belief (rB): "I'd like to befriend this woman, but I may fail and get rejected; and I would find that unfortunate. How annoying to experience rejection!" If he stayed rigorously with this rational Belief, he would feel, at C, *appropriately* concerned and somewhat cautious; and, if he did try to make contact with the woman and actually got rejected, he would feel sorry, regretful, and frustrated.

But the real issue, I showed the client, consisted of his irrational Belief (iB): "How *awful* if she rejected me! I *couldn't bear* it! It would prove me an utter worm!" These irrational Beliefs made little sense for several reasons:

1. A woman's rejecting the client wouldn't make things *awful* because the term "awful" (when clearly defined) means: (a) extremely disadvantageous or noxious, in terms of the individual's basic goals of surviving and getting what he wants out of life; (b) practically 100% obnoxious; (c) *more than* 100% obnoxious; and (d) something so undesirable that it *should* not, *must* not exist. Although the client could legitimately hold the first of these hypotheses, the second one can practically never prove true (for what experience has 100% obnoxiousness?), and the last two include magic and unverifiability. Nothing, clearly, can reach 101% unfortunateness; and nothing *must* not exist because someone finds it most disadvantageous that it does.

2. Although the client might never *like* rejection by a woman, he clearly can *bear* this rejection. It won't kill him. He can go on to other rejections — and acceptances. And he can live fairly happily in spite of it. Only his foolish *belief* that he can't bear it would make it "unbearable."

3. How could a woman's rejection make him a *worm* or a *worthless individual*? It might indicate wormy *behavior* on his part — or it might not (since he could get rejected if a woman liked a man with blue eyes and he had brown). But even if he showed poor, inept, or inadequate behavior with the woman, that would only consist of a *part*, and never the *whole*, of his existence and his humanness. No one could ever legitimately label him, as a *total person*, a worm. Actually, his entire personhood would remain too complex for any kind of a global rating. And he would always consist of a *process*, an ongoingness — and how can he (or anyone) validly rate an ever-changing, future-oriented process?

I kept showing the client how he illegitimately rated *himself* rather than appropriately evaluating his *traits* and *performances*. He began to see how this kind of self-rating would almost inevitably lead to feelings of worthlessness, depression, and the false conviction that he could *never* find acceptance by a woman he found attractive. These feelings and convictions, in turn, caused him to experience shyness, withdrawal, and inept behavior with women.

As the client saw the philosophic underpinnings of his inhibited behavior and his anxiety, he asked, "How can I get rid of my irrational beliefs? What can I do to change them?" Our dialogue about this question follows:

THERAPIST: For example, for ten minutes every day you can take *any* irrational or nutty belief that you have—such as the one that it's terrible for you to be rejected by a woman you find attractive—and prophylactically practice giving it up, even when you are not being rejected.

CLIENT: How?

THERAPIST: By using the logico-empirical method of seeing whether your hypothesis is consistent with your other goals and hypotheses, and by asking for factual evidence to sustain or invalidate it.

CLIENT: Can you be more specific?

THERAPIST: Yes, in my group therapy sessions, recently, I have been giving most of the members of the group Disputing assignments and also using operant conditioning—a self-management technique adapted from B. F. Skinner's theories—to help them carry out these ten-minute-a-day disputations.

CLIENT: What do you mean by operant conditioning?

THERAPIST: I'll explain in a minute. But first, the point is for you to decide exactly what hypothesis or nutty idea you want to work on for at least ten minutes a day. And, in your case, it would be the idea, again, that it's terrible for you to get rejected by a woman you find attractive. You would take this idea, and ask yourself several basic questions, in order to challenge and dispute it.

CLIENT: What kind of questions?

THERAPIST: Usually, four basic questions—though they have all kinds of variations. The first one is, "What am I telling myself?" or "What silly idea do I want to challenge?" And the answer, in your case, is, "It's terrible if a woman whom I find attractive rejects me." The second question is, "Is this, my hypothesis, true?" And the answer is—?

CLIENT: Uh, well, uh. No, it isn't.

THERAPIST: Fine. If you had said it was true, the third question would have been, "Where is the evidence for its being true?" But since you said it isn't true, the third question is, "Where is the evidence that it's not true?" Well—?

CLIENT: Well, uh, it's not true because, as we said before, it may be very *inconvenient* if an attractive woman rejects me, but it's not *more*, uh, than that. It's *only* damned inconvenient!

THERAPIST: Right. And there's other logico-empirical evidence that it isn't terrible. For one thing, because *this* woman rejects you hardly means that *all* will. For another, you obviously have survived, so far, even though you have been rejected. For still another, lots of other people in the world have been rejected by the woman they most love, and it has hardly been terrible for all of them, has it?

CLIENT: I see. There are several evidences that my being rejected isn't awful. And there is no reason, as we again noted before, why I *should* not get rejected. The world simply isn't a totally nonrejecting place!

THERAPIST: Yes. I think you're getting that well. Now, the fourth question is, "What's the worst thing that could happen to me, if an attractive woman rejects me?"

CLIENT: Very little, I guess. I, uh, was at first going to say that the worst thing that could happen to me was that I would be very depressed for a long time. But I now see that such a thing would not happen from any rejection but from my *view* of the horror, uh, of being rejected.

THERAPIST: Really, then, not so much could happen to you, if you got rejected. Is that right?

CLIENT: Yes. As a matter of fact, I would learn something about approaching an attractive female. And I might learn something valuable about myself.

THERAPIST: Right. Now, this method of asking yourself these four questions, and persisting until you get sensible answers to them, is something you can do at least ten minutes every single day, even when there is not much going on in your life and you are in no danger of being rejected. And you can combine it with operant conditioning, to increase the probability of your actually spending the ten minutes a day working at doing it.

CLIENT: Oh, I know now. That's Skinner's reinforcing technique.

THERAPIST: Yes, basically. You first discover what you really like to do and tend to enjoy — or would enjoy if you did it — every day. Like sex, eating, smoking, talking to your friends, etc. What would you say was the thing you like best, along these lines?

CLIENT: How about eating ice cream?

THERAPIST: You really eat some, or try to eat some, every day?

CLIENT: Oh, yes. I rarely eat less than a pint a day. I love it!

THERAPIST: Fine. Now, what do you intensely dislike doing, that you intend to avoid doing?

CLIENT: Uh. Cleaning my apartment. I keep putting it off. I rarely do it.

THERAPIST: O.K. Then, let's say you agree with me — really, with *yourself*—that if you work at least ten minutes a day at contradicting and disputing your nutty idea, "It's awful to be rejected by a woman I find attractive," you will then, and only then, allow yourself to have any ice cream that day. And if you fail to work at it, this idea, you will not only not have the reinforcement, the ice cream, but you will also take on the penalty of cleaning your apartment for at least an hour.

The client agreed to this kind of anti-awfulizing, combined with operant self-management, and within the next three weeks began to give up his idea that attractive women *had to* accept him. He did so well, in this respect, that he also started disputing his irrational belief that he had to last a long time in intercourse; and as he began to surrender this notion, and to stop putting himself down for coming to orgasm quickly, his fast ejaculation slowed down considerably.

I also employed a number of other cognitive, emotive, and behavioral methods with the client, in accordance with RET's comprehensive approach to treatment. Cognitively, I employed sensory imagery and rational emotive imagery. With sensory imagery, I got him to practice seeing himself in bed with a woman, getting a fine erection, and enjoyably using it in penile-vaginal copulation for five minutes or more of active intercourse. Using rational emotive imagery, as outlined by Maultsby (1975; Maultsby and Ellis, 1975), I showed him how vividly to picture himself failing to date a woman and failing, at times, to last long in intercourse; and, while imagining failure, to change his "normal" feelings of panic and depression to those of sorrow and disappointment by concomitantly changing his awfulizing about failing.

Cognitively, I also explained to the client some common myths and facts about sex and showed him how he could easily satisfy most females non-coitally, in case he did not get an erection or last long enough in intercourse; and how he could employ the sensate focus made famous by Masters and Johnson (1970) but also taught in RET sex therapy during the 1950s.

Emotively, I and other members of the client's therapy group used direct confrontation to help him face some of his basic problems and discuss them openly. We showed him, via feeling feedback from group members, his attractiveness to females; and we provided him, at times, with direct support from a few people in group, who volunteered to go with him on some of his dating homework assignments and make sure that he actually approached some attractive women.

Behaviorally, I used several active-directive homework or *in vivo* desensitizing assignments with this client. I (and his fellow group members) gave him graduated assignments to meet, talk with, try to date, and make sex-love overtures to women. Also, while working on his hostility to authority figures, I deliberately assigned him to have more contacts with his parents, whom he normally avoided, so that (1) he could experience intense feelings of hatred and rebellion toward them, (2) observe exactly what he irrationally told himself to create these feelings, and (3) work at disputing his hostility-creating beliefs.

In the course of fourteen sessions of individual and thirty-seven sessions of group RET, the client significantly improved in his presenting symptoms. He lost almost all his shyness about making contact with women and easily approached those he found personable. He normally lasted more than five minutes in active intercourse, and sometimes held off orgasm so long that he had to resort to intense sensory imagery to bring it on. He no longer felt hostile to his parents, though he didn't greatly desire to visit with them. He lost his anxiety and anger toward his supervisor at work and, by using RET educational methods with this person, the supervisor even felt considerably helped and somewhat dependent on the client.

At the close of therapy, the client reported, "I don't think I'll fall back into self-downing. I know that I shall continue to screw up, in various ways, for the rest of my life. I've come a long way during the last several months; but I still haven't been able to maintain a steady love relationship with one woman, which I really want to do. But I'm sure—well, I'm *practically* sure— that I'm just not going to put myself down any more, no matter how stupidly I behave. I am determined to accept *me*, in spite of my nutty, self-defeating behavior. At least, I'm going to try!"

SUMMARY

Rational-emotive therapy (RET) consists of a comprehensive form of treatment that heavily stresses the cognitive, philosophic, value-oriented aspects of human personality. It holds that people largely manufacture their own psychological symptoms and have the ability, with consistent work and effort at changing basic attitudes, to eliminate or minimize these symptoms and make themselves much less disturbable. It does not strive for symptom removal so much as for a worthwhile philosophic solution to people's fundamental "emotional" problems. It keeps gaining support through controlled clinical and experimental studies; and it thrives as an intrinsic and vital part of the newly developing field of cognitive-behavior therapy. Although hardly a panacea for all ills, RET provides an important part of today's psychotherapeutic methods.

REFERENCES

ADLER, A. *Understanding human nature.* New York: Greenberg, 1929.

ELLIS, A. *Reason and emotion in psychotherapy.* New York: Lyle Stuart, 1962.

ELLIS, A. *A weekend of rational encounter.* In Burton, A. (Ed.), *Encounter: the theory and practice of encounter groups.* San Francisco: Jossey-Bass, 1969

ELLIS, A. *Growth through reason: verbatim cases in rational-emotive therapy.* Hollywood: Wilshire Books, 1973.

ELLIS, A. *Humanistic psychotherapy: the rational-emotive approach.* New York: Julian Press and McGraw-Hill Paperbacks, 1974. (a)

ELLIS, A. The group as agent in facilitating change toward rational thinking and appropriate emoting. In Jacobs, A., & Spradlin, W. W. (Eds.), *The group as agent of change.* New York: Behavioral Publications 1974. (b)

ELLIS, A. *How to live with a "neurotic."* (Rev. ed.) New York: Crown Publishers, 1975.

ELLIS, A. *Sex and the single man.* (Rev. ed.) New York: Lyle Stuart, 1976.

ELLIS, A., & HARPER, R. A. *A new guide to rational living.* Englewood Cliffs, N.J.: Prentice-Hall, and Hollywood: Wilshire Books, 1975.

GOLDFRIED, M. R., & MERBAUM, M. (Eds.), *Behavior change through self-control.* New York: Holt, Rinehart and Winston, 1973.

KELLY, G. *The psychology of personal constructs.* New York: Norton, 1955.

KORZYBSKI, A. *Science and sanity.* Lancaster, Pa.: Lancaster Press, 1933.

MASTERS, W. F., & JOHNSON, V. E. *Human sexual inadequacy.* Boston: Little, Brown, 1970.

MAULTSBY, M. C. JR. *Help yourself to happiness.* Boston: Esplanade Publishers, and New York: Institute for Rational Living, 1975.

MAULTSBY, M. C., JR., & ELLIS, A. *Technique for using rational emotive imagery.* New York: Institute for Rational Living, 1975.

MEICHENBAUM, D. H. *Cognitive behavior modification.* Morristown, N.J.: General Learning Press, 1974.

RAIMY, V. *Misunderstandings of the self.* San Francisco: Jossey-Bass, 1975.

ROKEACH, M. *Beliefs, attitudes and values.* San Francisco: Jossey-Bass, 1968.

SHELTON, J. L., & ACKERMAN, J. M. *Homework in counseling and psychotherapy.* Springfield, Ill.: Charles C Thomas, 1974.

SKINNER, B. F. *Beyond freedom and dignity.* New York: Knopf, 1971.

3

Transactional Analysis: An Introduction

Thomas A. Harris

A central reason why Transactional Analysis offers a valid degree of promise for filling the gap between need for and supply of treatment for the universal problems in living that beset every person at one time or another is that it works at its best in groups. It is a teaching and learning device rather than a confessional or archeological exploration of the psychic cellars. In my private practice of psychiatry this made possible the treatment of four times as many persons as before. During the past twenty-five years in my work as a psychiatrist in working with individuals and in the administration of large institutional programs, nothing excited me so much as the authentic change in the individual's way of handling himself in the group setting using the knowledge and applications of Transactional Analysis.

One of the most significant contributions of Transactional Analysis is that it has given persons a tool they can use. Anybody can use it. People do not have to be "sick" to benefit from it. It does require the motivation for sustained application in every setting where persons have significant relationships. Transactional Analysis has given a new answer to people who want to change rather than to adjust, to people who want transformation rather than confirmation. It is realistic in that it confronts the patient with the fact that he is responsible for what happens in the future no matter

"Transactional Analysis: An Introduction," by Thomas A. Harris, M.D. is a summary of Preface and Chapters 1–5 in *I'm OK — You're OK: A Practical Guide to Transactional Analysis* by Thomas A. Harris, M.D. Copyright © 1967, 1968, 1969 by Thomas A. Harris, M.D. Reprinted by permission of Harper & Row, Publishers, and Jonathan Cape Ltd.

Thomas A. Harris, M.D., is a psychiatrist and founder of the Institute for Transactional Analysis in Sacramento. He is the author of the bestselling book, *I'm OK — You're OK.*

what has happened in the past. Moreover, it is enabling persons to change, to establish self-control and self-direction, and to discover the reality of a freedom of choice.

It is a profoundly rewarding experience to see people begin to change from their first group experience, get well, grow, and move out of the tyranny of the past. We base our even greater hope on the affirmation that what has been can be again. If the relationship between two people can be made creative, fulfilling, and free of fear, then it follows that this can work for two relationships, or three or one hundred or, we are convinced, for relationships that affect entire social groups, even nations. The problems of the world—and they are chronicled daily in headlines of violence and despair—essentially are the problems of individuals. If individuals can change, the course of the world can change. This is a hope worth sustaining.

Throughout history one impression of human nature has been consistent: that man has a multiple nature. Most often it has been expressed mythologically, philosophically, and religiously. Always it has been seen as a conflict: the conflict between good and evil, the lower nature and the higher nature, the inner and outer man. "There are times," said Somerset Maugham, "when I look over the various parts of my character with perplexity. I recognize that I am made up of several persons and that the person who at the moment has the upper hand will inevitably give place to another. But which is the real one? All of them or none?"

When Sigmund Freud appeared on the scene in the early twentieth century, the enigma was subjected to a new probe, the discipline of scientific inquiry. Freud's fundamental contribution was his theory that the warring factions existed in the "unconscious." Tentative names were given to the combatants: the Superego became thought of as the restrictive, controlling force over the Id (instinctual drives), with the Ego as a referee operating out of enlightened self-interest.

We are deeply indebted to Freud for his painstaking and pioneering efforts to establish the theoretical foundation upon which we build today. Through the years scholars and clinicians have elaborated, systematized, and added to his theories. Yet the "persons within" have remained elusive, and it seems that the hundreds of volumes which collect dust and the annotations of psychoanalytic thinkers have not provided adequate answers to the persons they have written about.

Any hypothesis must depend for its verification on observable evidence. Until recently there has been little evidence about how the brain functions in cognition, precisely how and which of the 12 billion cells within the brain store memory. How much memory is retained? Can it disappear? Is memory generalized or specific? Why are some memories more available for recall than others?

One noted explorer in this field is Dr. Wilder Penfield, a neurosurgeon from McGill University in Montreal, who in the early 1950s began to produce exciting evidence to confirm and modify theoretical concepts which had been formulated in answer to these questions. During the course of brain surgery, in treating patients suffering from focal epilepsy, Penfield (1952) conducted a series of experiments during which he stimulated the temporal cortex of the brain of the patient with a weak electric current transmitted through a galvanic probe. His observations of the responses to these stimulations were accumulated over a period of several years. In each case the patient under local anesthesia was fully conscious during the exploration of the cerebral cortex and was able to talk with Penfield. In the course of these experiments he heard some amazing things.

Perhaps the most significant discovery was that not only past events are recorded in detail but also the feelings that were associated with those events. An event and the feeling that was produced by the event are inextricably locked together in the brain so that one cannot be evoked without the other. Penfield reported: "The subject feels again the emotion which the situation originally produced in him, and he is aware of the same interpretations, true or false, which he himself gave to the experience in the first place. Thus, evoked recollection is not the exact photographic or phonographic reproduction of past scenes or events. It is reproduction of what the patient saw and heard and felt and understood." Penfield concluded that recollection evoked from the temporal cortex retains the detailed character of the original experience. When it is thus introduced in the patient's consciousness, the experience seems to be in the present, possibly because it forces itself so irresistibly upon his attention. Only when it is over can he recognize it as a vivid memory of the past.

Another conclusion made from these findings is that the brain functions as a high-fidelity recorder, putting on tape, as it were, every experience from the time of birth, possibly even before birth. (The process of information storage in the brain is undoubtedly a chemical process, involving data reduction and coding, which is not fully understood. Perhaps oversimple, the tape recorder analogy nevertheless has proved useful in explaining the memory process. The important point is that, however the recording is done, the playback is high-fidelity.)

Early in his work in the development of Transactional Analysis, Berne observed that as you watch and listen to people you can see them change before your eyes. It is a total kind of change. There are simultaneous changes in facial and body functions, which may cause the face to flush, the heart to pound, or the breathing to become rapid.

We can observe these abrupt changes in everyone: the little boy who bursts into tears when he can't make a toy work, the teenage girl whose woeful face floods with excitement when the phone finally rings, the man who grows pale and trembles when he gets the news of a business failure, the father whose face "turns to stone" when his son disagrees with him. The individual who changes in these ways is still the same person in terms of bone structure, skin, and clothes. So what changes inside him? He changes from what to what?

Changes from one state to another are apparent in manner, appearance, words, and gestures. A 34-year-old woman came to me for help with a problem of sleeplessness, constant worry over "what I am doing to my children," and increasing nervousness. In the course of the first hour she suddenly began to weep and said, "You make me feel like I'm 3 years old." Her voice and manner were that of a small child. I asked her, "What happened to make you feel like a child?" "I don't know," she responded, and then added, "I suddenly felt like a failure." I said, "Well, let's talk about children, about the family. Maybe we can discover something inside of you that produces these feelings of failure and despair." At another point in the hour her voice and manner again changed suddenly. She became critical and dogmatic: "After all, parents have rights, too. Children need to be shown their place." During one hour this mother changed to three different and distinct personalities: one of a small child dominated by feelings, one of a self-righteous parent, and one of a reasoning, logical, grown-up woman and mother of three children.

Continual observation has supported the assumption that these three states exist in all people. It is as if in each person there is the same little person that was there at age 3. There are also within him his own parents. These are recordings in the brain of actual experiences of internal and external events, the most significant of which happened during the first five years of life. There is a third state, different from these two. The first two are called Parent and Child, and the third, Adult. (See Figure 3-1.)

These states of being are not roles but psychological realities. Berne (1961) says that "Parent, Adult, and Child are not concepts like Superego, Ego, and Id . . . but phenomenological realities." The state is produced by the playback of recorded data of events in the past, involving real people, real times, real places, real decisions, and real feelings.

THE PARENT

The Parent is a huge collection of recordings in the brain of unquestioned or imposed external events perceived by a person in his early years, a period which we have designated roughly as the first five years of life. This is the period before the social birth of the individual, before he leaves home in

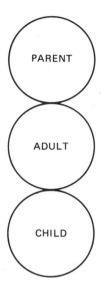

Figure 3-1 The Personality.

response to the demands of society and enters school. (See Figure 3-2.) The name Parent is most descriptive of this data inasmuch as the most significant "tapes" are those provided by the example and pronouncements of his own real parents or parent substitutes. Everything the child saw his parents do and everything he heard them say is recorded in the Parent. Everyone has a Parent in that everyone experienced external stimuli in the first five years of life. Parent is specific for every person, being the recordings of that set of early experiences unique to him.

The data in the Parent was taken in and recorded "straight" without editing. The situation of the little child, his dependency, and his inability to construct meanings with words made it impossible for him to modify, correct, or explain. Therefore, if the parents were hostile and constantly battling each other, a fight was recorded with the terror produced by seeing the two persons on whom the child depended for survival about to destroy each other. There was no way of including in this recording the fact that the father was inebriated because his business had just gone down the drain or that the mother was at her wit's end because she had just found she was pregnant again. In the Parent are recorded all the admonitions and rules and laws that the child heard from his parents and saw in their living. They range all the way from the earliest parental communi-

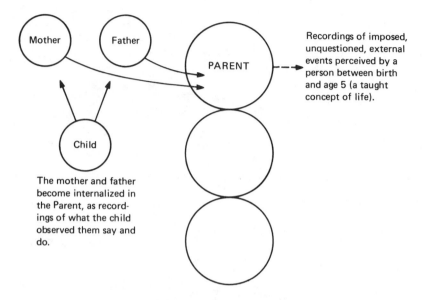

Mother

Father

PARENT

Child

Recordings of imposed, unquestioned, external events perceived by a person between birth and age 5 (a taught concept of life).

The mother and father become internalized in the Parent, as recordings of what the child observed them say and do.

Figure 3-2 The Parent.

cations, interpreted nonverbally through tone of voice, facial expression, cuddling, or noncuddling, to the more elaborate verbal rules and regulations espoused by the parents as the little person became able to understand words. In this set of recordings are the thousands of "no's" directed at the toddler, the repeated "don't's" that bombarded him, the looks of pain and horror in mother's face when his clumsiness brought shame on the family in the form of Aunt Ethel's broken antique vase.

Likewise are recorded the coos of pleasure of a happy mother and the looks of delight of a proud father. When we consider that the recorder is on all the time, we begin to comprehend the immense amount of data in the Parent. Later come the more complicated pronouncements: Remember, Son, wherever you go in the world you will always find the best people are Methodists; never tell a lie; pay your bills; you are judged by the company you keep; you are a good boy if you clean your plate; waste is the original sin; you can never trust a woman; you're damned if you do and damned if you don't; you can never trust a cop; busy hands are happy hands; don't walk under ladders; do unto others as you would have them do unto you; do others in that they don't do you in.

The significant point is that whether these rules are good or bad in the light of a reasonable ethic, they are recorded as truth from the source of all ethic, they are recorded as truth from the source of all security, the people who are "six feet tall" at a time when it is important to the two-foot-tall child that he please and obey them. It is a permanent recording. A person cannot erase it. It is available for replay throughout life.

When we realize that thousands of these simple rules of living are recorded in the brain of every person, we begin to appreciate what a comprehensive, vast store of data the Parent includes. Many of these edicts are fortified with such additional imperatives as "never" and "always" and "never forget that" and, we may assume, pre-empt certain primary neurone pathways that supply ready data for today's transactions. These rules are the origins of compulsions and quirks and eccentricities that appear in later behavior. Whether Parent data is a burden or a boon depends on how appropriate it is to the present, or whether or not it has been updated by the Adult, the function of which we shall discuss after describing the Child.

There are sources of Parent data other than the physical parents. A 3-year-old who sits before a television set many hours a day is recording what he sees. The programs he watches are a "taught" concept of life. If he watches programs of violence, I believe he records violence in his Parent. That's how it is. That is life! This conclusion is certain if his parents do not express opposition by switching the channel. If they enjoy violent programs the youngster gets a double sanction—the set and the folks—and he assumes permission to be violent provided he collects the required amount of injustices. The little person collects his own reasons to shoot up the place, just as the sheriff does; three nights of cattle rustlers, a stage holdup, and a stranger foolin' with Miss Kitty can be easily matched in the life of the little person. Much of what is experienced at the hands of older siblings or other authority figures also is recorded in the Parent. Any external situation in which the little person feels himself to be dependent to the extent that he is not free to question or to explore produces data that is stored in the Parent. (There is another type of external experience of the very small child which is not recorded in the Parent, and which we shall examine when we describe the Adult.)

THE CHILD

While external events are being recorded as that body of data we call the Parent, there is another recording being made simultaneously. This is the recording of *internal* events, the responses of the little person to what he sees and hears. (See Figure 3-3.) In this connection it is important to recall Penfield's observation that the subject feels again the emotion which the

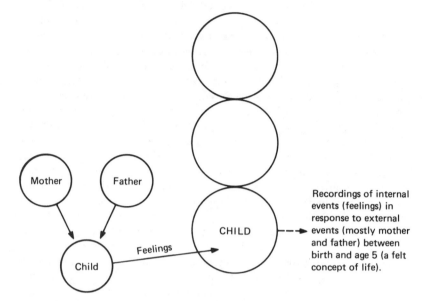

Figure 3-3   The Child.

situation originally produced in him, and he is aware of the same interpretations, true or false, which he himself gave to the experience in the
first place. Thus, evoked recollection is not the exact photographic or
phonographic reproduction of past scenes or events. It is reproduction of
what the patient *saw and heard and felt and understood* (Penfield, 1952).

It is this "seeing and hearing and feeling and understanding" body of
data which we define as the Child. Since the little person has no vocabulary
during the most critical of his early experiences, most of his reactions are
feelings. We must keep in mind his situation in these early years. He is
small, he is dependent, he is inept, he is clumsy, he has no words with
which to construct meanings. Emerson said we "must know how to estimate
a sour look." The child does not know how to do this. A sour look turned in
his direction can only produce feelings that add to his reservoir of negative
data about himself. "It's my fault. Again. Always is. Ever will be. World
without end."

During this time of helplessness there are an infinite number of total
and uncompromising demands on the child. On the one hand, he has the
urges (genetic recordings) to empty his bowels ad lib., to explore, to know,
to crush and to bang, to express feelings, and to experience all the pleasant

sensations associated with movement and discovery. On the other hand, there is the constant demand from the environment, essentially the parents, that he give up these basic satisfactions for the reward of parental approval. This approval, which can disappear as fast as it appears, is an unfathomable mystery to the child, who has not yet made any certain connection between cause and effect.

The predominant by-product of the frustrating, civilizing process is negative feelings. On the basis of these feelings the little person early concludes, "I'm not OK." We call this comprehensive self-estimate the NOT OK, or the NOT OK Child. This conclusion and the continual experiencing of the unhappy feelings which led to it and confirm it are recorded permanently in the brain and cannot be erased. This permanent recording is residue of having been a child. Any Child. Even the child of kind, loving, well-meaning parents. It is the situation of childhood and not the intention of the parents which produces the problem. It is the predominant human dilemma, the universal position of very early childhood.

When the children of "good" parents carry the NOT OK burden, one can begin to appreciate the load carried by children whose parents are guilty of gross neglect, abuse, and cruelty.

As in the case of the Parent, the Child is a state into which a person may be transferred at almost any time in his current transactions. There are many things that can happen to us today that recreate the situation of childhood and bring on the same feelings we felt then. Frequently we may find ourselves in situations where we are faced with impossible alternatives, where we find ourselves in a corner, either actually or in the way we see it. These "hook the Child," as we say, and cause a replay of the original feelings of frustration, rejection, or abandonment, and we relive a latter-day version of the small child's feelings, we say his Child has taken over. When his anger dominates his reason, we say his Child is in command.

Frequently I am asked, when do the Parent and Child stop recording? Do the Parent and Child contain only experiences in the first five years of life? I believe that by the time the child leaves the home for the first independent social experience — school — he has been exposed to nearly every possible attitude and admonition of his parents, and henceforth further parental communications are essentially a reinforcement of what has already been recorded. The fact that he now begins to "use his Parent" on others also has a reinforcing quality in line with the Aristotelian idea that what is expressed is impressed. As to further recordings in the Child, it is hard to imagine that any emotion exists that has not already been felt in its most intense form by the time the youngster is 5 years old. This is consistent with most psychoanalytic theory, and, in my own observation, is true.

If, then, we emerge from childhood with a set of experiences which are recorded in an inerasable Parent and Child, what is our hope for change? How can we get off the hook of the past?

THE ADULT

At some point in the first year of life, a remarkable thing begins to happen to the child. Until that time his life has consisted mainly of helpless or unthinking responses to the demands and stimulations of those around him. He has a Parent and a Child. What he has not had is the ability either to choose his responses or to manipulate his surroundings. He has had no self-direction, no ability to move out to meet life. He has simply taken what has come his way.

At ten months, however, he begins to experience the power of locomotion. He can manipulate objects and begins to move out, freeing himself from the prison of immobility. It is true that earlier, as at eight months, the infant may frequently cry and need help in getting out of some awkward position, if he is unable to get out of it by himself. At ten months he concentrates on inspection and exploitation of toys. According to the studies conducted by Gesell and Ilg, the ten-month-old child enjoys playing with a cup and pretends to drink. He brings objects to his mouth and chews them. He enjoys gross motor activity; sitting and playing after he has been set up, leaning far forward, and re-erecting himself. He secures a toy, kicks, goes from sitting to creeping, pulls himself up, and may lower himself. He is beginning to cruise. Social activities he enjoys are peek-a-boo and lip play, walking with both hands held, being put prone on the floor, or being placed in a rocking toy. Girls show their first signs of coyness by putting their heads to one side as they smile (Gesell & Ilg, 1943).

The ten-month-old has found he is able to do something which grows from his own awareness and original thought. This self-actualization is the beginning of the Adult. (Figure 3-4.) Adult data accumulates as a result of the child's ability to find out for himself what is different about life from the "taught concept" of life in his Parent and the "felt concept" of life in his Child. The Adult develops a "thought concept" of life based on data gathering and data processing.

The motility that gives birth to the Adult becomes reassuring in later life when a person is in distress. He goes for a walk to "clear his mind." Pacing is seen similarly as a relief from anxiety. There is a recording that movement is good, that it has a separating quality, that it helps him see more clearly what his problem is. The Adult is "principally concerned with

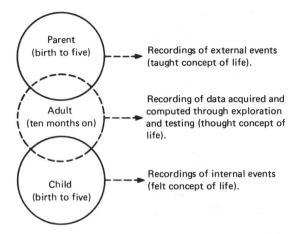

Parent
(birth to five) ----▸ Recordings of external events
(taught concept of life).

Adult
(ten months on) ----▸ Recording of data acquired and
computed through exploration
and testing (thought concept of
life).

Child
(birth to five) ----▸ Recordings of internal events
(felt concept of life).

Figure 3-4   Gradual emergence of the Adult beginning at ten months.

transforming stimuli into pieces of information and processing and filing that information on the basis of previous experience." (Berne, 1961.) It is different from the Parent, which is "judgmental in an imitative way and seeks to enforce sets of borrowed standards, and from the Child, which tends to react more abruptly on the basis of prelogical thinking and poorly differentiated or distorted perceptions." (Berne, 1961.) Through the Adult the little person can begin to tell the difference between life as it was taught and demonstrated to him (Parent), life as he felt it or wished it or fantasied it (Child), and life as he figures it out by himself (Adult).

The Adult is a data-processing computer, which grinds out decisions after computing the information from three sources; the Parent, the Child, and the data the Adult has gathered and is gathering. (Figure 3-5.) One of the important functions of the Adult is to examine the data in the Parent, to see whether or not it is true and still applicable today, and then to accept it or reject it; and to examine the Child to see whether or not the feelings there are appropriate to the present or are archaic and in response to archaic Parent data. The goal is not to do away with the Parent and Child but to be free to examine these bodies of data. The Adult, in the words of Emerson, "must not be hindered by the name of goodness, but must examine if it be goodness"; or badness, for that matter, as in the early decision, "I'm NOT OK." The Adult's function in updating the Parent and Child is diagramed in Figure 3-6.

Another of the Adult's functions is the estimating of probability. This function is slow in developing in the small child and, apparently for most

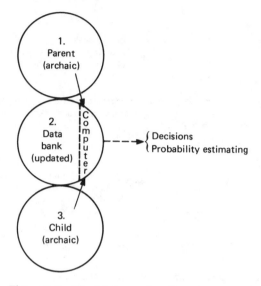

Figure 3-5 The Adult gets data from three sources.

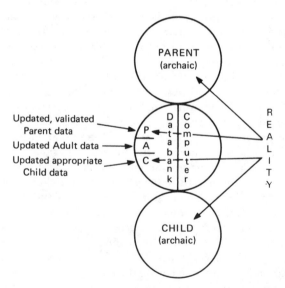

Figure 3-6 The updating function of the Adult through reality testing.

of us, has a hard time catching up throughout life. The little person is constantly confronted with unpleasant alternatives (either eat your spinach or you go without ice cream), offering little incentive for examining probabilities. Unexamined probabilities can underlie many of our transactional failures, and unexpected danger signals can cause more Adult "decay," or delay, than expected ones.

Unrealistic, irrational, non-Adult responses are seen in a condition referred to as traumatic neurosis. The danger or "bad news" signal hits the Parent and Child at the same time it hits the Adult. The Child responds in the way it originally did, with a feeling of NOT OK. This may produce all kinds of regressive phenomena. The individual may again feel himself to be a tiny, helpless, dependent child. One of the most primitive of these phenomena is thought blocking. One place this can be seen is in psychiatric hospitals that have a locked-door policy. When the door is locked on a new patient, his retreat is rapid and pronounced.

The ongoing work of the Adult consists, then, of checking out old data, validating or invalidating it, and refiling it for future use. If this business goes on smoothly and there is a relative absence of conflict between what has been taught and what is real, the computer is free for important new business, *creativity.* Creativity is born from curiosity in the Child, as is the Adult. The Child provides the "want to" and the Adult provides the "how to." The essential requirement for creativity is computer time. If the computer is cluttered with old business there is little time for new business. Once checked out, many Parent directives become automatic and thus free the computer for creativity.

THE FOUR LIFE POSITIONS

Very early in life every child concludes, "I'm not OK." He makes a conclusion about his parents, also: "You're OK." This is the first thing he figures out in his life-long attempt to make sense of himself and the world in which he lives. This position, I'M NOT OK — YOU'RE OK, is the most deterministic decision of his life. It is permanently recorded and will influence everything he does. It is the universal human dilemma — a product of the situation of very early childhood. Because it is a decision it can be changed by a new decision. But not until it is understood.

In order to support these contentions I wish to devote a few paragraphs of this brief outline of Transactional Analysis to an examination of the situations of the newborn, the young infant, and the growing child, in both the preverbal and verbal years. Many people insist they had a "happy childhood" and concluded nothing like I'M NOT OK—YOU'RE OK. I believe strongly that *every* child concluded it, "happy childhood" notwithstanding. First, I wish to examine the situation of his entry into life and point to the evidence that the events of his birth and his infant life are recorded, even though they are not remembered.

In this connection we note again Penfield's conclusions that the brain performs three functions: (1) recording, (2) recalling, and (3) reliving. Although recall from the earliest period of life is not possible, we have evidence that we can and do relive experiences in the form of returning to the feeling state of the newborn infant. Because the infant cannot use words, his reactions are limited to sensations, feelings, and perhaps vague, archaic fantasies. His feelings are expressed by crying or by various body movements that indicate either distress or comfort. His sensations and fantasies, though ineffable because of his wordlessness at the time they were recorded, do replay occasionally in dreams in later life.

Almost immediately following birth, the infant is introduced to a rescuer, another human being who picks him up, wraps him in warm coverings, supports him, and begins the comforting act of "stroking." This is the point of Psychological Birth. This is the first incoming data that life "out there" isn't all bad. It is a reconciliation, a reinstatement of closeness. It turns on his will to live. Stroking, or repetitious bodily contact, is essential to his survival. Without it he will die, if not physically, then psychologically. Physical death from a condition known as marasmus once was a frequent occurrence in foundling homes where there was a deprivation of the early stroking. There was no physical cause to explain these deaths except the absence of essential stimulation.

At what point does the child make final his decision as to the position, I'M NOT OK—YOU'RE OK? Piaget (1954) on the basis of meticulous observations of infants and small children, believes the development of causality (what follows what) begins in the early months of life and is acquired by the end of the second year. In other words, data, in the form of a jumble of impressions, begins accumulating in certain sequential patterns, to a point where a preverbal position, or conclusion, is possible. Piaget says: "In the course of the first two years of childhood the evolution of sensorimotor intelligence, and also the correlative elaboration of the universe, seem to lead to a *state of equilibrium* bordering on rational thought." I believe this state of equilibrium, evident at the end of the second year or during the third year, is the product of the child's conclusion about himself and others: *his life position.*

Once his position is decided he has something solid to work with, some basis for predictability. Piaget says that these early mental processes are not capable of "knowing or stating truths" but are limited to desiring success or practical adaptation: If I'M NOT OK and YOU'RE OK, what can I do to make you, an OK person, be good to me, a NOT OK person? The position may seem unfavorable, but it is a true impression to the child, and it is better than nothing. Thus the state of equilibrium. The Adult in the little person has achieved its first mastery in "making sense of life," in solving what Adler called "life's central problem"—the attitude toward others—and what Sullivan called the "self-attitudes which are carried forever by the individual."

Transaction Analysis constructs the following classification of the four possible life positions held with respect to oneself and others:

1. I'M NOT OK — YOU'RE OK
2. I'M NOT OK — YOU'RE NOT OK
3. I'M OK — YOU'RE NOT OK
4. I'M OK — YOU'RE OK

One of the clearest statements on the development of positions is made by Kubie: "It is possible to make one certain deduction: namely that early in life, sometimes within the earliest months and sometimes later, *a central emotional position is frequently established.* . . . The clinical fact which is already evident is that once a central emotional position is established early in life, it becomes the affective position *to which that individual will tend to return automatically for the rest of his days.* This in turn may constitute either the major safeguard or the major vulnerability of his life. In fact the establishing of a central emotional position may turn out to be one of the earliest among the universals in the evolution of the human neurotic process, since it may start even in the preverbal and largely presymbolic days of infancy . . . the individual may spend his whole life defending himself against it, again using conscious, preconscious, and unconscious devices whose aim it is to avoid this pain-filled central position." (kubie, 1958; italics mine.)

The important consideration about life positions rests in the understanding that the first three positions are in the Child and are the result of the accumulation of impressions from the significant early experiences in the life of the individual in his first five years. The fourth position, I'M OK — YOU'RE OK, can be achieved only by the Adult through the application of new data and the examination of archaic data in the Parent and Child which hampers the function of the Adult in establishing reality-based data and achieving freedom of choice and the development of new options for decision making in the present. In the language of Transactional Analysis the phrase "decontaminating the Adult" refers to this process whereby the Adult works to update and validate the data used in current and ongoing transactions in living.

ANALYZING THE TRANSACTION

One of the reasons for the criticism that the psychotherapeutic sciences are unscientific, and for much of the disagreement evident in this field, is that there has been no basic unit for study and observation. It is the same kind of difficulty as that which confronted physicists before the molecular theory and physicians before the discovery of bacteria.

Eric Berne, the originator of Transactional Analysis, has isolated and defined this basic scientific unit: "The unit of social intercourse is called a transaction. If two or more people encounter each other . . . sooner or later one of them will speak or give some other indication of acknowledging the presence of the others. This is called the *transactional stimulus*. Another person will then say or do something which is in some way related to the stimulus, and that is called the *transactional response*." (Berne, 1964.)

Transactional Analysis is the method of examining this one transaction wherein "I do something to you and you do something back" and determining which part of the multiple-natured individual is "coming on." Transactional Analysis also is the method of systematizing the information derived from analyzing these transactions in words which have the same meaning, by definition, for everyone who is using them. This language is clearly one of the most important developments of the system. Agreement on the meanings of words plus agreement on what to examine are the two keys which have unlocked the door to the "mysteries of why people do as they do." This is no small accomplishment.

Having developed a language, we come to the central technique: using that language to *analyze a transaction*. As we have noted, the transaction consists of a stimulus by one person and a response by another, which response in turn becomes a new stimulus for the other person to respond to. The purpose of the analysis is to discover which part of each person — Parent, Adult, or Child — is originating each stimulus and response.

There are many clues to help identify stimulus and response as Parent, Adult, or Child. These include not only the words used but the tone of voice, body gestures, and facial expressions. The more skillful we become in picking up these clues, the more data we acquire in achieving our goals for self-understanding by using Transactional Analysis.

In this brief introduction to Transaction Analysis I have limited the content to the most important basic aspects of this new investigative tool for understanding personality growth and development and the psychology of everyday living. Berne divided his original lectures on Transactional

Analysis into four divisions: Structural Analysis (the PAC of individuals), Transactional Analysis (the self-revealing aspect of social interaction), Game Analysis (the analysis of the most significant and meaningful transactions originating in the first position), and Script Analysis (the method of uncovering the early decisions, made unconsciously, as to how life shall be lived).

Since Berne's original introductory presentation of Transactional Analysis in 1958, the interest and involvement in the many applications of TA has spread throughout the world. A part of this development has been the increasing list of definitive writings by trained and experienced Transactional Analysts who are members of the International Transactional Analysis Association with headquarters at 1772 Vallejo Street, San Francisco, California 94123. Requests for resource material directed to that address will supply the serious student, whether professional or lay person, with a most comprehensive list of books, recordings, and various other teaching materials.

In my own experience in the teaching, training, and use of TA, I have seen an extremely gratifying number of serious, highly motivated individuals achieve remarkable degrees of change in significant areas of their life situations.

REFERENCES

BERNE, E. *Games people play*. New York: Grove Press, 1964, p. 29.

BERNE, E. *Transactional analysis in psychotherapy*. New York: Grove Press, 1961, p. 24.

GESELL, A. & ILG, F. L. *Infant and child in the culture of today*. (Rev. Ed.) New York: Harper, 1974, pp. 120–121.

KUBIE, L. S. The neurotic process as the focus of physiological and psychoanalytic research. *The Journal of Mental Science*, 1958, *104*, 435.

PENFIELD, W., Memory mechanisms. *Archives of Neurology and Psychiatry*, 1952, *67*, 178–198. With discussion by L. S. Kubie et al. Quotations from Penfield & Kubie later in this chapter are from the same source.

PIAGET, J. *The construction of reality in the child*. New York: Basic Books, 1954.

4

Reality Therapy

William Glasser

When I formulated the principles of Reality Therapy I noted that all people had both physiological and psychological needs. I stressed that the two major psychological needs were the need to love and be loved and the need to feel worthwhile to oneself and others. In order to be worthwhile, one has to maintain a satisfactory standard of behavior. People unable to satisfy those two basic psychological needs, without interfering with the needs of others, I called irresponsible, rather than "mentally ill." In *The Identity Society* I noted that most people in the Western world are no longer primarily concerned about economic survival or power—the traditional, physiologically related goals. Instead, since about 1950, we are living in a role-oriented society. People are trying to find an identity for themselves. Those unable to do so can be called failures. Failures become involved with themselves and with symptoms or irresponsible behavior that causes them and those around them to suffer. Reality Therapy is designed to help people I call irresponsible or failing people become involved and to gain and then maintain a successful identity.

In the Veterans Administration Psychiatric Hospital in West Los Angeles, where I worked as a resident at the beginning of my career, we would often get patients who were completely crazy. When such a patient arrived, I would tell the chief ward attendant, a man of considerable

"Reality Therapy," by William Glasser, M.D. © 1976 by William Glasser. This article appears in print for the first time in this volume.

William Glasser is founder of Reality Therapy and currently head of the Institute of Reality Therapy in West Los Angeles and the Educator Training Center. He is the author of several well-known books including *Reality Therapy: A New Approach to Psychiatry; Schools without Failure; The Identity Society;* and *Positive Addiction,* all published by Harper & Row.

experience and humanity but little formal training, "Mr. Bland, work with this new patient and do what you always do so that by Monday he is settled down, no longer crazy, and I can talk with him." Over the weekend he always accomplished this — he talked with the patient, almost always made friends with him and became involved with him. Mr. Bland was a superb Reality Therapist. He had warmth, kindness, strength, and the desire to help people. Based upon successful involvement, the principles of Reality Therapy evolve into an approach to life that can help a person become successful or, at least, help him understand his failure and try another direction. In discussing the principles of Reality Therapy, I will show their application by lay persons in situations of everyday life, as well as their application by professionals to people with serious failure identities.

THE PRINCIPLES OF REALITY THERAPY

Involvement

Basic to human beings is the need for involvement. For Reality Therapy to work, the therapist must become involved with the person he/she is trying to help; the therapist, therefore, must be warm, personal, and friendly. One can't break the intense self-involvement of failure by being aloof, impersonal, or emotionally distant. Warmth and understanding are important for two people to become initially involved. Whatever time it takes, someone must break through the loneliness and the self-involvement where little or none existed before. Whether you seek help for failure or for becoming more successful, you must feel that you are warmly and personally accepted by the person who is helping you, or your chance of becoming successful is small.

Involvement is the foundation of therapy. It is the basic principle on which all other principles build. As early as possible, the person being helped must begin to understand that there is more to life than being concerned with his own misery, symptoms, and problems. He must see that another human being cares for him and is willing to discuss his life and talk about anything both consider worthwhile and interesting. In this relationship any subject of mutual interest can serve as a bridge to build involvement.

One problem of the patient-therapist relationship is to establish this warmth and friendship yet limit the involvement to what is feasible in the formal therapy situation. The deliberate involvement of the professional therapist may seem to make therapy artificial, but to someone who is lonely, warm and friendly acceptance is not artificial. The therapist's problem is to provide enough involvement to help the patient develop confidence to make new, deep, lasting involvement of his own.

The helping person, whether friend, family member, or professional therapist, must never promise to give more time than he plans to give. Even a patient who desperately needs the therapist will, upon becoming involved, accept an honest statement of a specific time commitment. The therapist should point out that even though there are time limitations, the patient will still be experiencing more involvement than he or she had before. To express this successfully requires great skill, however. It is difficult to tell a starving man that he can have only a little food when he believes there is so much more. The therapist's job is to convince the patient that there is plenty of food around if he will go out and look for it; the therapist is not the only one with food. The Reality Therapist becomes enough involved with the patient in the hour or two a week they spend together to help the patient gain confidence that he can develop ties with others. An advantage of group therapy is that each patient has other persons besides the therapist with whom relationships can be formed.

Though the therapist has little time, it does not mean that he cannot have a big impact. The time with the patient is devoted exclusively to that person. Although an hour a week may not seem like a lot of personal attention, it can be. Many people, husbands and wives, parents and children, do not in their ordinary lives get more than an hour a week of warm, exclusive time with someone who has the skill and interest to be really involved. A suggestion I make to many parents having difficulty with a child is to devote an hour a week — the hour I would give to the child if he saw me — just to the child, doing what he wants to do. Although this invariably helps the child greatly, it is disheartening to see how many parents refuse to make this simple effort.

In the therapy relationship anything is open for discussion. This is a difficult concept for patients and beginning therapists to understand, but it is natural and easy for friends or family to accept. Current events, movies, books, plays, goals, and personal and family relations are all good grist for positive involvement. The patient's problems often do not enter into many of the therapy hours. Interesting nonproblem discussions are valuable in therapy because they develop the intellectual sharing that is important in Reality Therapy. They should be stimulating, with values, opinions, and beliefs brought out and some emotion experienced.

Extensive talking about a patient's problems and his feelings about them focuses upon his self-involvement and consequently gives his failure meaning. Long discussions about the patient's problems can be a common and serious error in psychotherapy. For example, a patient may come to me feeling depressed, valueless, and unwanted. The less we talk about his depression, drug taking, and suicidal gestures, and the more we discuss the options that are open to him, the better he feels.

It is tempting to listen to his complaints because they seem so urgent. Doing so may reduce his pain and make him feel better for a while as he basks in the attention he receives. If he doesn't change his behavior, however, his pain will return and he will grow disillusioned with therapy. Also, to gain continued attention, he may act more and more irresponsibly so that he has something valid to complain about. If we then listen with renewed interest, we only compound the error. Later, when other subjects are discussed, he will resist because he has been getting his failure reinforced and his pain temporarily reduced with each new complaint that is heard.

Among friends and in well-run groups, conversation on many subjects naturally occurs. The worst thing anyone can do for a depressed friend is to let him whine excessively about his troubles. Instead, good friends say, "Come on, let's get busy. Let's talk about something else. Let's forget our concerns and enjoy talking." They know that they cannot solve problems by simply listening to complaints. A therapist should never give the impression that he can change a patient's life simply because he is aware of the patient's problem. The therapist's actions do not parallel common medical practice. He can never prescribe and cure as the doctor often can. Rather, the relationship that makes good friendships should guide therapy. People who have not been in previous therapy usually do not question the Reality Therapy approach, and they do not try to dwell on their problems. Those who have had prior therapy, after being in Reality Therapy for a while, begin to understand how it differs. Then they accept it because they feel better.

Talking enjoyably about worthwhile subjects is the best way to help a person get involved. No one can gain a success identity alone. Trying to help others, if only through warm, enjoyable conversations, is the best way to help oneself. From talking, people begin doing things together, and each helps the other by means of the involvement. Self-help requires getting involved with someone else. It is only in a few cases and with special knowledge that it can be achieved alone.*

Current Behavior

No one can work to gain a successful identity or to increase personal success without being aware of his current behavior. If a person does not acknowledge his behavior or claims to be unaware of it, he won't be able to gain

---

*See *Positive Addiction* by William Glasser, M.D., Harper & Row, 1976.

or to maintain a successful identity. Accompanying the consistent warmth and involvement discussed above must be constant effort by the therapist to help the patient become aware, in detail, of his own behavior at the present time. Examining current behavior is usually done matter-of-factly, although sometimes the therapist must work slowly and subtly. Because a patient may avoid therapy when he becomes aware of what he is doing, the therapist must judge the strength of the involvement as he helps the patient become aware of his behavior patterns.

People often avoid facing their present behavior by emphasizing how they feel rather than what they are doing. Although Reality Therapy does not deny that emotions are important, successful therapists learn that unless they focus on behavior they do not help the patient.

Feelings are always important, whether the situation concerns Reality Therapy, raising children, husband-wife relationships, or in any other involvements. Nevertheless, for a relationship to be successful, how we *behave* toward others is crucial. If we behave toward them in a competent, responsible way, we will eventually, if not immediately, feel good. If a child is having a tantrum and we attempt to soothe his feelings and stop his crying by promising whatever he wants, he may learn only to respond with a tantrum when frustrated. We fail the child because he does not learn to behave in a way that will let him relieve his own frustrations.

Patients often come to my office complaining of how bad they feel. A woman who is depressed, upset, worried, and miserable is a good example. Believing she should tell me about these feelings in great detail (in fact, she wants to), she is surprised when I, a psychiatrist, a person supposed to be keenly attuned to misery, cut her rather short and say, "I believe you. You have convinced me that you are depressed, and I appreciate that you are upset. But what are you doing?"

I may not always be this blunt, but I make a statement to this effect as soon as I can. The patient commonly replies, "What do you mean?" She is telling me she believes that most of what she is "doing" is feeling bad. Wrapped up in her misery, she cannot believe that I am naive enough to think that she is doing anything other than suffering. Actually, she is doing, or not doing, much that continues to keep her in pain. Applying the second principle of Reality Therapy I must get her behavior out on the table so she can become aware of it.

Identification of oneself as a failure leads to antagonism and withdrawal, accompanied by pain. The resultant self-involvement, which is an effort to reduce the pain, ordinarily keeps the patient from moving toward others. The patient must be helped to exchange self-involvement for involvements with others, the first step toward success. To help the patient see his behavior and choose new behavior that will lead to involvement with others, we continually ask, "What are you doing? What are you doing now? What did you do yesterday? What did you do the day before yesterday? What did you do last week?"

In my therapy practice, I have often heard husbands and wives, together and separately, make a long series of complaints about the other's behavior. Each tells me how upset the other's behavior has made him feel and how destructive it is to the marriage. I ask, "I understand that you're having difficulty because of what your husband (wife) is doing and how it makes you feel, but what are *you* doing? Do you think *you* are doing anything destructive to the marriage?" These questions come as a surprise to many people. Unwilling to look at what they are doing, they hope the therapist will spend his or her time listening to their complaints.

No husband or wife can change a spouse's behavior without altering his or her own. Each must change. Some marriage counseling neglects this vital point and, in doing so, may harm rather than help. Even in a case in which one partner is all wrong, the other probably must change his/her behavior in some way to break the ice and motivate the other person to change.

When the girls from the Ventura School for Delinquent Girls went home, they often wrote me to say, "My mother has changed; she's so much nicer to me now than she used to be." They do not recognize that their *own* behavior has changed. They are no longer running around, drinking, taking drugs, staying out all night. They are going to school, perhaps holding a job, coming home, and keeping normal hours with different friends. Naturally, their behavior change has caused drastic changes in their parents' approach to them.

Friends need not behave as therapists and separate behavior from feelings. Even if one person is trying to help another, the friendship may become boring, especially if one person is complaining all the time. In friendship people must do things together. The best feelings arise from what people do together that they enjoy.

Evaluating Your Behavior

Now the patient must look at his behavior critically and judge it on the basis of whether or not it is his best choice. The Reality Therapist asks him to judge his behavior on the basis of whether he believes it is good for him and good for the people he cares about. He must also ask him whether his behavior is socially acceptable in his community. For example, if the patient is depressed or afraid to fly or has an ulcer, what he does usually has little effect on others, but if he pushes drugs in a high school, what he does significantly affects the community, and he must consider community mores in making his judgment.

This principle is often misunderstood. Some people accept and others reject Reality Therapy because they misunderstand this principle. The Reality Therapist does not act as a moralist; he never tells a patient that what he is doing is wrong and that he must change. The therapist does not *judge* the behavior; through their involvement and by bringing the actual behavior out in the open, he leads the patient to evaluate his own behavior. Sometimes there is no clear-cut choice, but the patient must still decide what to do. Occasionally, it is necessary for people to make a decision that seems to hurt someone else in order to help themselves. Although making such a choice is usually better than making no decision, it is hard to do. For example, a divorce may hurt a couple's children, at least temporarily, but sometimes, unless the patient is strong enough to make this choice, the conflict may become intolerable and hurt the children even more.

I believe that many people can evaluate their own behavior. This can be done without the help of a therapist if a person has involvement that gives him some success and can do some honest self-evaluation. Husbands and wives, teachers and ministers, employers and parents can help those near them make value judgments. Whoever helps another, however, must be careful not to make judgments himself but rather to lead toward self-judgment.

A person with a serious failure identity behaves in ways that actually reinforce his negative self-opinion. He may think, "This is the best I can do for myself; I can't change." In Reality Therapy, when we lead a peson to evaluate his behavior, we ask him to re-evaluate what he is doing, and eventually he usually sees that better choices are available. The therapist does not intimate that he or she knows better than the patient what should be done with that person's life. Once the patient makes a judgment, the therapist may, and usually does, help him plan its implementation. The judgment "I ought to change" belongs solely to the patient, however.

For example, when an alcoholic patient drinks, he has made the value judgment that he wants a drink right now, even though he may recognize that drinking is bad for him and that he may get in trouble if he drinks. Nevertheless, he makes the value judgment that the drink is worth it, or he would not drink. Later, he can complain and become involved with all the trouble and emotional turmoil caused by his choice to drink: how he lost everything he valued. The therapist is not fooled by this complaining, for it means little as long as he chooses to drink. If he stops drinking, then he may indeed complain. From his complaint, that life is tough without alcohol, he may be led to a better choice. No matter what he says or how much he moans, as long as he drinks, alcohol is his choice.

Whatever the morality or the laws of the society, we can rarely excuse our behavior because we do not agree with the laws. We must understand that we have to accept the consequences of our behavior if we defy the existing morality or existing laws. Guidance by a concerned person able to point out the realities of the society helps us recognize what we are doing. If a person wants to protest the illegality of smoking marijuana by smoking it openly, he knows his behavior is cause for arrest. It is his decision, and he should prepare himself for jail.

In my experience, most individuals who feel failure gain strength more readily by conforming to the ongoing morality and laws of society; later, when they are stronger and more successful they may wish to defy them. The job of the Reality Therapist, when discussing morality and law and the patient's role in society, is to bring out everything possible to make these factors relevant to the decision the patient must make. Then, if the patient chooses an action that is in opposition to prevailing laws or codes, he has made a rational, not an emotional, decision.

Planning Responsible Behavior

Once someone makes a value judgment, he or she must be helped to develop realistic plans for action to follow that judgment. Many people can examine their behavior and decide that it is not helping them, but they have no experience or background for planning a more successful life. They do not know how to plan for more responsible, more competent behavior.

Because planning requires knowledge of what options are available, a therapist who talks with many people about making plans gains experience not available to the average person. Because many problems revolve around family life, a therapist who is married and has children tends to be better able to help plan in this area. Encouraging the person who needs the help to make most of the plan himself is part of the therapist's skill. It is often necessary to put a patient in touch with someone else. I have sent patients to friends or associates who have more experience in particular fields to help a patient work out a detailed plan.

A plan should never be made that attempts too much; it will usually fail and reinforce the already present failure. A failing person needs success, and he needs small instances of success to gain it. A student who has never studied should not plan to study one hour a night; at the start, fifteen minutes once or twice a week is more realistic and is still a big change from the present failing behavior. The plan should be ambitious enough so that some change, small though it may be, can be seen, yet not so great that failure is likely. Little steps can be extended; it is much harder to cut back on big steps.

A sample plan for a student failing in school might be to sit in the front instead of the back of the class, to take notes, to study at a certain time, and to acquire friends who are successful in class and study with them. This four-point plan almost always works if it is carried out.

Plans are not final. If one does not work, successive plans can be made until a better one is found. Being locked into one plan is similar to being locked into self-involvement. On the other hand, jumping from plan to plan as soon as a little stress is encountered is also bad. The therapist or helping person must develop skill in assisting the patient to evaluate the plan's feasibility.

Commitment

After a reasonable plan has been made, it must be carried out. In Reality Therapy, to give a person greater motivation to fulfill his or her plan, we ask him or her for a commitment to us. The commitment may be verbal or written; it may be given to an individual or to a group. Without commitment, the feeling of, "I'll do it for you as well as for me," plans are less likely to be implemented. Some people believe that commitment means dependence, and that people should be self-motivated. But nothing is wrong with trying new behavior partly for someone else; it is very difficult to live our lives alone successfully. Successful people only seem to commit themselves on their own; they really commit themselves to everyone they are involved with. A definite commitment to one person or a few people can be instrumental in achieving success.

Characteristic of people with failure identities is their unwillingness to commit themselves, because in their loneliness they do not believe that anyone cares what they do. In addition, they fear that if they commit themselves and fail, as they expect, they expose themselves to more pain.

Commitment means involvement. It verifies that the person to whom I commit myself is involved with me; thus I will do what we have planned because we are involved. If friends make a date to go somewhere together, a commitment is implicit. If someone continually fails his commitments, he will soon cease to have any friends. His only commitment is to himself and his self-involvement.

A commitment is often more binding if it is in writing. A colleague of mine asks his patients to carry a small book with them in which they write their plan and sign a commitment to carry it out. On a weekly basis he and the patient review what the patient did to fulfill the commitment. The patient writes this evaluation in the book. Such written commitments help his patients gain the discipline to fulfill their plans. Furthermore, the notebook carries my colleague into the person's life; their involvement continues during the week because of what has been written in the book during the therapy hour. It also avoids argument about the content of the plan and about whether or not the commitment to the plan was fulfilled.

Accept No Excuses

When a person does not fulfill his commitment, a common occurrence, the value judgment that preceded the plan must be rechecked. If the value judgment is still valid, then the plan must be re-evaluated. If the plan is reasonable, the person must either recommit himself or state, "I am no longer going to commit myself to this plan." If he says this, then he is no longer responsible. If he remains committed to the plan, however, the therapist must continue to ask him to honor the commitment. The therapist cannot hold the patient to the commitment in a legal or punitive sense, nor, because of his implicit commitment never to do so, can he withdraw. The only course of action — and it is a powerful one — open to the therapist or helping person is never to excuse the person who needs help from the responsibility of the commitment.

Because no excuses are accepted in Reality Therapy, we rarely ask, "Why did you do it?" because we believe everyone involved knows the answer. An excuse is the easiest way off the hook. We cannot help anyone if we admit that there are valid excuses for not fulfilling a reasonable plan. Valid or not, to become successful, the patient must fulfill the plan.

When someone does not fulfill his commitment, his failure should not be emphasized. To say, "It's your fault, you failed, you've done wrong" is not helpful. We simply ask, "Are you still going to try to fulfill the commitment? If you say you are, then when?" We wait; time is rarely a serious obstacle. If we keep our involvement, if we keep making plans and getting commitments, eventually the patient will begin to fulfill them.

The therapist must insist that a commitment made is worth keeping. The only commitments many people who fail have made are to their own irresponsibilities, their emotions, and their involvement with themselves. The therapist cannot help unless he and the patient are both willing to re-examine the plan continually and make a mutual decision either to renew the commitment, if the plan is a good one or to give it up, if it is not. The therapist must say to the patient, "If you are not going to do it, say so, but don't say you are and then give excuses when you fail." Excuses, rationalizations, and intellectualizations can become the death knell of any successful relationship; they have no place in Reality Therapy.

To do Reality Therapy well requires the ability not to accept excuses, not to probe for fault, not to be a detective to find out Why. Many of the girls at the Ventura School for Delinquent Girls told me, "I knew you cared about me when you didn't take the excuse." Excuses provide temporary relief, but they eventually lead to more failure and a failure identity.

No Punishment

Not punishing is as important as not accepting excuses. Punishment is any treatment of another person that causes him pain, physical or mental. Eliminating punishment is very difficult for most successful people to accept, because they believe that part of their success stems from their fear of punishment. We believe that punishment breaks the involvement necessary for the patient to succeed. When he does succeed, we give praise. Unlike punishment, praise solidifies the involvement. Praise, always involving, leads to more responsible behavior. The purpose of punishment, however, is to change someone's behavior through fear, pain, or loneliness. If it were an effective means of getting people to change, we would have few failures in our society. Many incompetent and irresponsible people have been punished over and over again throughout their lives with seemingly no effect.

For many delinquents, punishment actually serves as a source of involvement. They receive attention through delinquent behavior, if only that of the police, court, probation counselor, and prison. The punishment is painful, but it is better than no attention or involvement at all. In addition, it somewhat reduces the pain of failure. A failing person rationalizes the punishment as a reason for the anger that causes him to be hostile. He considers his behavior to be revenge against those who punish him. Punishment, if immediate and severe, may deter the individual from doing the same thing again. If we immediately slap a child's hand when he touches something he should not, he may learn "Hands off!" He may also learn to be more crafty; punishment may only motivate him to be a more careful criminal.

Mild punishment is sometimes effective when it serves to remind people that better options are open than their present choice. People who are successful and who have various options available may be deterred by punishment. Thus, if punishment has any value, it is for successful people, but they usually do not need punishment or the example of it to continue behaving successfully.

Reasonably agreed-upon consequences of irresponsible behavior are not punishment. For example, a parent who makes a plan with a daughter to allow her privileges if she accepts certain responsibilities is no longer bound to the plan if the daughter fails in her accepted responsibilities. If the parent says, "You can use the family car on Saturdays providing you wash it once a week," and the daughter does not wash the car, then the parents can and should refuse the use of the car. The parent is holding to the agreement. The child will learn nothing if the parent does not have the discipline to fulfill his part of the plan. It would, however, be excessive and punitive for the parent to say, "Since you failed to wash the car, you can't use it for six Saturdays." Even if the daughter, under pressure, had agreed to this condition, it would be a bad plan because it would invite resentment over a major loss for a mild transgression. Certainly, if she did not wash the car that week, she should be deprived of it for that Saturday, but as soon as she washes it, she fulfills her part of the bargain and can have the car again. This arrangement is not punitive; it is a reasonable and acceptable plan. The child may be upset over losing the car if she fails to wash it, but she can understand why her parent stands firm, and she knows her parent still cares about her.

The parent who lets a son or daughter use the car anytime while casually asking him/her to keep it clean, and then suddenly says, "Well, you don't wash it enough, so you can't have it anymore for a while," is punitive and irrational. The child, with no preparation for this capricious behavior, reacts by being less involved, by loving, respecting, and listening to the parent less.

Problems can be solved without punishment. Punishment was devised by people with power. In a survival society, powerful people use punishment to keep control. In the identity society, however, internal control is needed instead of external control.

Because punishment reduces involvement and causes failures to identify more securely with their failure, we must stop using it. We must eliminate punishment as a major weapon of government and institutions, families and marriages, social organizations and individual relationships. Giving praise for a job well done instead of rejection for a job below expectations will motivate people toward success.

THE SUCCESS OF REALITY THERAPY

The test of any practice, therapy, or a series of therapeutic concepts designed to help people succeed is whether or not it works. After more than ten years of using the principles of Reality Therapy and teaching them to others, I contend that they do work and that their application can be taught to competent people who wish to use them. These principles are clear, they are explained without jargon, and they are applicable to any failure, whether it is long-lasting and deeply seated or short-term and lightly rooted.

We considered the use of Reality Therapy with delinquents at the Ventura School for Girls successful. Of 370 girls who left the program at a recent count, only 43 had returned. This figure can be compared with return rates of up to 90 percent at similar institutions. We felt we succeeded with about 80 percent of the girls. Similarly, the use of Reality Therapy with chronic psychotic patients at the Veterans Administration Neuropsychiatric Hospital in West Los Angeles has revolutionized a ward of 210 patients. Before Reality Therapy, the average discharge rate was two patients a year. Since an intensive Reality Therapy program has been instituted, there is almost yearly turnover of the patient population. My office practice documents the usefulness of Reality Therapy on an out-patient basis.

Because of the consistent ineffectiveness of our current institutions I believe failures such as people on probation or parole, chronic psychiatric patients, drug addicts, alcoholics, those on welfare, or the chronically unemployed could be helped through community involvement centers. Such centers would be based on the principles of Reality Therapy, be located in each community, and be staffed by involved volunteers as well as professionals.

An even more exciting use of the principles of Reality Therapy is in the school.system. If the ideas of Reality Therapy can be implemented in schools, it should be possible to prevent many people from growing up perceiving themselves as failures. Thus there will be fewer clients in institutions and in therapists' offices.

The principles of Reality Therapy may be used by parents with children, teachers with students, ministers with parishioners, and employers with employees. One of the best ways to gain a successful identity is to use these principles in everyday life; as you try to live a better and happier life yourself, you will help those around you.

REFERENCES

GLASSER, W. *Reality Therapy: a new approach to psychiatry.* New York: Harper & Row, 1965.

GLASSER, W. *Schools without failures.* New York: Harper & Row, 1969.

GLASSER, W. *The identity society.* New York: Harper & Row, 1972.

GLASSER, W. *Positive addiction.* New York: Harper & Row, 1976.

5

Gestalt Therapy: Clinical Phenomenology

Gary M. Yontef

Gestalt Therapy (GT) is an outgrowth of psychoanalysis (Freud, Reich, Horney, Rank, etc.) and heavily influenced by existentialism (Buber, Tillich, Sartre). However, it owes a major part of its conceptual framework to Gestalt psychology, which was phenomenological and experimental and believed that traditional explanations of our perceptions in terms of sensory elements and their combinations were not enough—that the whole is different than the sum of its parts.

The word *Gestalt* (plural: Gestalten) refers to the shape, configuration, or whole, the structural entity. Nature is orderly; it is organized into meaningful wholes. Out of these wholes, figures emerge in relation to a ground, and this relationship of figure and ground is *meaning*. Thus, in terms of GT, a good Gestalt is clear and the figure/ground relation responsive to and energized by the changing pattern of a person's immediate needs. A good Gestalt is neither too rigid and unyielding nor too quickly changing and tenous.

Behavior and experience are more than a summation of separate parts. A person's behavior and experience form unities or organized wholes; each whole is organized around an emerging foreground or figure that is spon-

"Gestalt Therapy: Clinical Phenomenology," by Gary M. Yontef, Ph. D. © 1976 by Gary M. Yontef. This article appears in print for the first time in this volume. The author expresses his appreciation to Jeffrey Hutter, Ph.D., Robert Martin, D.S.W., Robert Resnick, Ph.D., and Lolita Sapriel, M.S.W., for their aid in the preparation of this chapter.

Gary Yontef is president and chairman of the Training Committee of the Gestalt Therapy Institute of Los Angeles. Formerly on the Psychology Department faculty at UCLA, he is a clinical psychologist and clinical social worker in private practice with Gestalt Associates in Santa Monica. He is the author of *A Review of the Practice of Gestalt Therapy*.

taneously energized and given a positive or negative weight by the person's dominant need. When a need is met, the Gestalt it organized becomes complete and no longer commands organismic energy. When this Gestalt formation and destruction is blocked or rigidified, when needs are not recognized and expressed, unmet needs form incomplete Gestalten pressing for attention and interfering with the formation of new Gestalten.

> I look up from my writings, noticing I am thirsty, ard I think about getting a drink of water; going into the kitchen, I pour a full glass of water, drain it, and return to my desk. I notice it is sunny and cool in the room where I am writing; the cats are playing with each other and there is traffic passing by outside. All of these were as true a few minutes ago as they are now, but I did not notice them then. I ignored them, reaching out first to the deficit of moisture in my body and then to the water faucet, and my manipulative system organized around the water. There are many possibilities in my environment, but I organized around my thirst, in preference to the other possibilities. I was not stimulated randomly and passively by the field; rather my senses organized around my thirst. (Latner, 1973, pp. 17–18.)

Through this Gestalt process human beings regulate themselves in orderly and meaningful ways. This self-regulation depends on two inter-related processes: sensory awareness and the use of aggression (n.b.: in GT, aggression is a force, life energy, without positive or negative moral overtones).

To survive, the person must exchange energy with the environment (e.g., breathe, eat, touch) and yet maintain himself as an entity somewhat separated from it. The organismically self-regulating person picks and chooses for himself what part of each thing he encounters to take in and what to reject. He takes in what is nourishing to him and rejects what is toxic to him, using his awareness to discriminate and his aggression to destroy (de-structure) the foreign stimuli. The nourishing parts are integrated into the self (assimilation), and the unusuable are rejected. Taking in any particle whole without this assimilation process is *introjection*. For example, an infant who swallows a piece of corn without de-structuring it—i.e., without chewing it—has a foreign object within his gastrointestinal tract. It shows up, unchanged, in his feces and he derives no nourishment. So too beliefs, rules, self-images, role definitions, etc., are frequently swallowed whole (introjected), and later form the basis of "character"—i.e., rigid and repetitive behavior that is unresponsive to present need. Inducing patients to accept any extrinsic goal without *Awareness* and assimilation inhibits growth.

WHAT IS AWARENESS

Awareness is a form of experiencing. It is the process of being in vigilant contact with the most important event in the individual/environment field with full sensorimotor, emotional, cognitive, and energetic support. A continuing and uninterrupted continuum of *Awareness* leads to an Aha!, an immediate grasp of the obvious unity of disparate elements in the field. *Awareness* is always accompanied by Gestalt formation. New, meaningful wholes are created by *Aware* contact. Thus *Awareness* is in itself an integration of a problem.

Since understanding GT depends on understanding the GT concept of *Awareness*, I suggest a careful and thoughtful second reading of the previous paragraph and the corollaries below. Each corollary refers particularly to awareness in the context of the whole person in his human life space. While all living creatures have some awareness, some means of experiencing and orienting to the world, people have a special capacity for surviving with partial awareness. For example, a neurotic may think about his current situation without sensing or knowing his feelings, or he may express emotions physically without cognitive knowing. Both of these forms of human awareness are incomplete and not the *Awareness* we seek in GT.

Corollary One: Awareness is effective only when grounded in and energized by the dominant present need of the organism. Without this the organism (person or animal) is aware, but not of where the nourishment or toxicity is most acute *for him.* And without the energy, excitement, emotionality of the organism being invested in the emerging figure, the figure has no meaning, power, or impact. Example: A man is on a date and worrying about a forthcoming interview. He is not *Aware* of what he needs from his date and thus reduces the excitement and meaningfulness of his contact with her.

Corollary Two: Awareness is not complete without directly knowing the reality of the situation and how one is in the situation. To the extent that the situation, external or internal, is denied, awareness is distorted. The person who acknowledges verbally his situation but does not really SEE it, KNOW it, REACT to it, is not *Aware* and is not in full contact. The person who "sort of" knows his behavior, but does not really KNOW in a feeling, physical way *what* he does, *how* he does it, that he has alternatives and CHOOSES to be as he is, is not *Aware*. *Awareness* is accompanied by

Owning — i.e., the process of knowing one's control over, choice of, responsibility for one's own behavior and feelings (lit. response-ability, ability to respond, to be the primary agent in determining one's own behavior). Without this the person may be vigilant to his own experience and life space, but not to what power he has and what he does not have. So, functionally full *Awareness* is equal to responsibility — i.e., when I am fully *Aware* I am at that instant response-able, and I cannot be responsible without being Aware.

To say "I am" with the belief that it was not chosen is self-deception or bad faith (Sartre). *Awareness* must include self-acceptance, real self-acknowledgment. To be "aware" and to reject oneself is to say both "I am" and that "I who am aware am different." This is not a direct knowing of oneself, but a way of not really knowing. And neither is *Awareness* merely knowing that one is dissatisfied with a problem without knowing directly, intimately, and clearly what is being done to create and perpetuate the situation.

Corollary Three: Awareness is always here and now and always changing, evolving, and transcending itself. Awareness is sensory, not magical: it exists. Everything that exists does so here and now. The past exists NOW as memory, regret, body tension, etc. The future does not exist except NOW, as fantasy, hopes, etc. In GT we stress *Awareness* in the sense of knowing what I am DOING, NOW, in the situation that IS, and not confusing this IS with what was, could be, should be. We take our bearing from *Awareness* of what is, by energizing the figure of attention according to our present interest and lively concern.

The act of *Awareness* is always here and now, although the content of *Awareness* may be distant. To KNOW that "now I am remembering" is very different from slipping into remembering without *Awareness. Awareness* is experiencing and knowing what I am doing now (and how).

The now changes each moment. *Awareness* is a new coming together and excludes an unchanging way of seeing the world. *Awareness* cannot be static, but is a process of orienting that is renewed at each new moment. The "awareness" that is static is an abstract representation of the flowing *Awareness* that is felt. We trust the evolving *Awareness* more than any pre-set, abstract idea.

GESTALT PHENOMENOLOGY AND THE PARADOXICAL THEORY OF CHANGE

Phenomenology is a search for understanding based on what is obvious or revealed by the situation rather than the interpretation of the observer.

Phenomenologists refer to this as "given." Phenomenology works by entering into the situation experientially and allowing sensory *Awareness* to discover what is obvious/given. This necessitates discipline, especially sensing what is present, what IS, excluding no data in advance.

The phenomenological attitude is recognizing and putting aside preconceptions about what is relevant. A phenomenological description integrates both observed behavior and experiential, personal reports. Phenomenological exploration aims for an increasingly clear and detailed description of the IS, and de-emphasizes what would be, could be, was, might be.

People often fail to *see* what is right in front of them, and do not realize it. They imagine, argue, get lost in reverie. The difference between this filtered perception and an immediate, full-bodied grasp of the current situation can best be appreciated by those who have struggled for an esoteric answer and found instead the joy of a simple and obvious Aha!

Beginning therapy patients often cannot say what they mean and mean what they say because they are not *Aware*. They have lost the sense of who they are and who it is that must live their life. They have lost the sense of: this is what *I* am thinking, feeling, doing. They ask for a cure or an explanation before *they* observe, describe, and try to know *what* it is they are doing and *how*. Thus they try to explain, to justify something whose exact existence is unclear to them. They miss the obvious.

These patients maintain this lack of clarity by two related processes: thinking without integrating the sensory and affective AND using their aggression more against themselves than for contact and assimilation. Their behavioral Gestalten are formed more by these two rigid character habits than by the needs of the present (see The Neurotic section, below).

What is needed is experimentation in trying new modes of experience and new uses of psychobiological energy. The patient needs to see, to do, to cope and learn. The therapy hour provides situations that are safe enough to warrant experimentation and challenging enough to be realistic. In GT we call this the "safe emergency." If the therapist is too helpful, the patient does not have to do anything and if the therapist emphasizes verbal content (e.g., why–because), the patient can think without experimenting or feeling. If the patient only repeats in therapy the processes he already uses — e.g., obsessing (anticipating, analyzing, asking why) and being passive and uncreative ("tell me what to do") — the probability is that the patient will make little improvement.

GT is based on patients learning to use their own senses to explore for themselves, learn and find their own solutions to their problems. We teach the patient the process of being *Aware* of what he is doing and how he is doing it rather than talk about the content of how he should be or why he is as he is. We give the patient a tool; in a sense we teach him to cook rather than feed him a meal.

Traditional psychotherapy is content-oriented in that the actual emphasis during the therapy hours is on the content of what is talked about. GT is process-oriented in that the emphasis is on *Awareness* of how the patient is going about the search for understanding. We do more than talk about; we "work." Work refers to phenomenological experimentation, including guided *Awareness* exercises and experiments. The exercises are not merely to make patients aware of something, but to become *Aware* of how to be *Aware,* and as a corollary to that, to be *Aware* of how they avoid being *Aware.*

In traditional verbal therapy and behavior therapy there is an extrinsic goal: the patient is not okay as he is. Often this is agreed to by both the patient and the therapist. In these therapies the therapist is a change agent and the patient gets to some ideal state (content goal) by trying to be what he is not. In GT, change is thought to occur first by clearly knowing and accepting the given: who you are and how you are. The therapist in GT does not change the patient. The goal for both is learning and using this *Awareness* process.

The GT theory of change states:

> *that change occurs when one becomes what he is, not when he tries to become what he is not.* Change does not take place through a coercive attempt by the individual or by another person to change him, but it does take place if one takes the time and effort to be what he is — to be fully invested in his current positions. By rejecting the role of change agent, we make meaningful and orderly change possible.

The Gestalt therapist rejects the role of "changer," for his strategy is to encourage, even insist, that the patient *be* where and what he *is.* He believes change does not take place by "trying," coercion, or persuasion, or by insight, interpretation, or any other such means. Rather, change can occur when the patient abandons, at least for the moment, what he would like to become and attempts to be what he is. The premise is that one must stand in one place in order to have firm footing to move and that it is difficult or impossible to move without that footing.

The person seeking change by coming to therapy is in conflict with at least two warring intrapsychic factions. He is constantly moving between what he "should be" and what he thinks he "is," never fully identifying with either. The Gestalt therapist asks the person to invest himself fully in his roles, one at a time. Whichever role he begins with, the patient soon shifts to another. The Gestalt therapist asks simply that he be what he is at the moment.

The patient comes to the therapist because he wishes to be changed. Many therapies accept this as a legitimate objective and set out through various means to try to change him, establishing what Perls calls the "top-dog/ under-dog" dichotomy. A therapist who seeks to help a patient has left the egalitarian position and become the knowing expert, with the patient playing the helpless person, yet his goal is that he and the patient should become equals. The Gestalt therapist believes that the top-dog/under-dog dichotomy already exists within the patient, with one part trying to change the other, and that the therapist must avoid becoming locked into one of these roles. He tries to avoid this trap by encouraging the patient to accept both of them, one at a time, as his own.*

If the patient abandons trying to be what he is not, even for a moment, he can experience what he is. This gives him the support to begin growth through *Awareness* and choice. *Awareness* develops through contact and experimentation based on wanting to know what one needs, a willingness to stay with the confusion, conflict, and doubt that accompanies the search for the given, and a willingness to take the responsibility for finding or creating new solutions. "Man transcends himself only via his true nature, not through ambition and artificial goals." (Perls, 1973, p. 49.)

HUMANISM AND TECHNOLOGY

GT's phenomenological work is done through a relationship based on the existential model of Martin Buber's I and Thou; Here and Now. In GT we are both humanistic and technological. This involves *both people, therapist and patient, working together* to experiment in order to increase the patient's ability to experience on his own. The work may focus on a task—e.g., sorting out a problem of the patient's—or maybe on the re-lationship itself. The work, structured or unfocused, unifies sensing, feeling, and thinking into a continuum of *Awareness* in the Now.

We allow each person to regulate himself without substituting an ex-trinsic goal of ours for their mode of self-regulation. We observe when the patient interrupts and rejects himself, lacks faith in himself, and wants us to take over. But we trust in the orderliness and meaningfulness of the patient's behavior and his ability to cope with life. We do not use verbal or reconditioning methods to manipulate the patient into living an ideal.

However, therapists can do more than refuse the "change me" contract. We have a whole phenomenological technology to use. We can suggest a way in which the patient can take the risk of doing something new that might lead him to new experience. Our goal is *Awareness* of the structure/

*A. Beisser, "The paradoxical theory of change." In J. Fagon & I. L. Shepherd (Eds.), *Gestalt Therapy Now*. Palo Alto, Cal.: Science and Behavior Books, 1970.

function of any dysfunctional behavior and we use our phenomenological technology in the service of that goal.

Every therapeutic intervention in GT is based on seeing and feeling. Sometimes we simply share what we see (feedback) or what we feel in reaction (disclosure). Sometimes our seeing and feeling give rise to a vision of something the patient can do to be *Aware* more clearly. We value that technological creation as much as disclosing and giving feedback. Such techniques arise out of an I-Thou dialogue, sometimes technological intervention is required. Example: A patient talks without looking at the therapist. The dialogue has been interrupted in that the patient talks, but to no one in particular. A real dialogue now would require a vigorous response by the therapist. Possibilities: (1) "You aren't looking at me"; (2) "I feel left out"; (3) "I suggest an experiment: Stop talking and just look at me and see what happens."

So GT combines verbal work with tasks given the patient. This is very powerful, as the new Masters and Johnson-derived therapies have recently indicated. These tasks are as varied as the creativity and imagination of the therapist and the patient.

This includes work on sensing the outside world, enjoying one's body, polarity dialogues (aloud or in writing), expressive modalities (dreams, art, movement, poetry), ad infinitum. These methods, however, are sometimes confused with gimmicks used for turn-on, catharsis, or short-cuts to cure. In GT these tasks are all used to continue exploring the therapist-patient relationship and the patient's problem solving and growth through *Awareness*.

Often patients have a preconceived notion that therapy is just talking and that change comes automatically. They react to a request to try an experiment with confusion, reluctance, fright. As the work begins to produce new knowledge, real change, patients react in different ways: sometimes they really perceive the glorious possibilities and hunger for more — and sometimes they are frightened by a method that produces a clarity about what they are doing, their need for change, and most of all by the prospect of really changing.

Note that while this approach looks for the obvious, the surface, it is far from superficial. In traditional therapy the real structure of the patient's life could be understood only by going linearly to the distant place (e.g., the past) where the determinants were though to be located. But according to Gestalt theory, all forces that have an effect are present and cannot have an effect when removed in space or time. *Awareness* training gets to the actual structure/function of the here and now forces regulating the patient's existence. This becomes more obvious as the processes of *Aware-*

ness are grasped by the patient, and other fundamental forces that are present and have been previously avoided are better understood.

THE NEUROTIC

The neurotic does not let himself be *Aware* of, accept, and allow his true needs to organize his behavior. Instead of allowing his excitement to go fully and creatively into each need, he interrupts himself: he uses part of his energy against himself, and part to control the therapist's half of the dialogue. The neurotic has a rigid character; his self-support is reduced, and he usually believes he cannot grow out of his repetitive and unsatisfying pattern of behavior. He tries to fuse with the therapist, to draw on his strength instead of allowing his own to develop. His sense of his own boundaries is weak, for he rejects *Awareness* of aspects of himself (e.g., projection) and accepts alien things as if they were himself (e.g., introjection). Thus the neurotic loses *Awareness* of the IS.

This self-rejection and unawareness reduces the self-support readily available to the neurotic. He comes to believe that he cannot be self-regulating and self-supporting, and therefore must manipulate others to tell him how to be, or else he forces himself to live by the rigid rules he swallowed without assimilating. Thus the neurotic controls himself and others as things or allows himself to be so controlled.

So the neurotic makes the therapeutic situation into a repeat of an old one: someone tells him how to be, and he resists or acquiesces. If the therapist believes he knows best what is good for the patient, the problem intensifies. Even if the patient changes, he does so without learning how to regulate himself. This does not foster *Awareness* of the structure of the patient's behavior by the patient so he can use his strength to support himself.

Although many patients come to therapy to be changed, they do not want to make real changes themselves — they want the therapist to do it for them. They resist growth and invest energy in the failure of the therapist. This last motivation is almost always out of the immediate *Awareness* of beginning patients.

The problem, thus, is not that the patient manipulates his environment, but that he manipulates others to help him stay a cripple more comfortably. He does not rely on self-support in a giving/taking, contact/withdrawal relationship with his environment. The therapist must give close, exclusive, nondemanding attention to the patient and at the same time frustrate the subtle neurotic manipulations and force him thereby to "direct all his manipulatory skill towards the satisfaction of his real needs" (Perls, 1973, p. 108; see also Resnick, 1975).

> . . . if the therapist withholds himself . . . he deprives the field of its main instrument, his intuition and sensitivity to the patient's on-going processes. He must, then, learn to work with sympathy and at the same time with frustration. These two elements may appear to be incompatible, but the therapist's art is to fuse them into an effective tool. He must be cruel in order to be kind. He must have a relational awareness of the total situation, he must have contact with the total field—both his own needs and his reactions to the patient's manipulations and the patient's needs and reactions to the therapist. And he must feel free to express them. (Perls, 1973, p. 105.)

EVALUATION AND MATURITY

GT is successful when a patient is able to regulate himself with a process of Gestalt formation and destruction that clearly and spontaneously forms his behavior and *Awareness* into wholes that are organized and energized by his dominant need. Such a person will "be *Aware*"—i.e., have the characteristics of *Awareness* discussed above. He will be in contact with the most important event in his life space, have excitement that flows into his behavior, be responsible and self-regulating, be able to risk new exploration, etc.

Thus we define maturity as a continual process rather than arriving at an ideal end-state. The mature person engages in this process; he is engaged in the process of *Creative Adjustment*. *Creative Adjustment* is a relationship between person and environment in which the person (1) responsibly contacts, acknowledges, and copes with his life space, and (2) takes responsibility for creating conditions conducive to his own well-being. Individual behavior is mature only in the context of coping with the environment. And coping or adjusting without being responsible for creating conditions conducive to the satisfaction of one's most basic needs and values also fails to meet this definition. Working, loving, asserting, yielding, etc. are mature only insofar as they are part of *Creative Adjustment*.

Maturity, then, is not a static ideal but rather is the process of engaging with *Awareness* in a creatively adjusting process of self-regulation in the real world. In GT we work for the *Awareness* that is a necessary support for *Creative Adjustment*.

Success in GT is measured in terms of how clearly the patient can experience and judge for himself rather than relying on any extrinsic measure of adjustment. We expect the patient to learn how to experience for himself the extent to which any process, including GT, satisfies or frustrates his important needs. This means he must know what he needs/wants/prefers and be responsible for his own values, judgments, and choices.

This maturity and *Awareness validly and reliably confirm the success* of GT only when they are clearly and obviously manifest to the patient and the therapist. Success is measured by both externally visible behavior and internal experiencing. The patient must feel differently: he must feel increased clarity, excitement, well-being, exploration, etc. There should be an obvious congruence between the patient's experience and the therapist's observation of overt behavior. Every internal *Awareness* should be accompanied by an external manifestation — e.g., the patient's feeling of greater aliveness should show in observable, physiological changes. Failure of this clear evidence of success to therapist or patient indicates a need for further clarification.

COMPARISON OF MODELS OF PSYCHOTHERAPY

The foundation for traditional talk therapies is still largely psychoanalytic. Neither behavior nor the experience of the patient is trusted, because both are believed to be determined by inferred, unobservable, hidden "real" causes — i.e., unconscious motivation. What the patient is left with is an unconsciousness that is unavailable and a consciousness that is powerless and unreliable. (Acceptance of the distant causes of one's present behavior is often referred to as "insight.") The concept of the unconscious is replaced in GT by the shifting figure/ground of *Awareness* concept, in which certain processes are not contacted because of a disturbance in the figure/ground formation or because the person is in contact with other phenomena (see Perls, 1973, p. 54). But the data is available and the patient can be directly and immediately taught to attend to it. *Awareness* in GT is seen as the powerful and creative integrator that can encompass what was previously unaware.

In traditional psychotherapy, the belief in the unconscious motivation of behavior leaves the patient dependent on the therapist's interpretations rather than his own explorations in *Awareness.* The therapist knows, and the patient either gets well by learning what the therapist already knows or he is "supported" by the therapist until the therapist believes the patient has enough ego strength to hear what the therapist knows.

What the therapist "knows" are interpretations, speculations of past events that are postulated to cause (justify?) present behavior. This linear causality model reduces the importance of the here-and-now forces that support the behavior and are available for exploration by the patient. In this type of therapy, only through transference is the here and now entered, and then only to interpret the patient's distortions.

All of this elevates the position of the therapist at the expense of the patient; it nullifies the patient's means of orientation: his own sense of what he sees and how he feels about it. The patient is thus not responsible for himself and cannot know himself, but rather has a disease or disability that the therapist will cure or eliminate. Even those who ostensibly reject the medical model often have this same attitude in practice. This is the very attitude that the I–Thou model of Gestalt Therapy reacts against.

There is a split between these talking therapies and the more active models, such as behavior modification. This "third force" claims to be a new alternative. Unfortunately, many of the "new" psychotherapies are merely updates of the talking cure or the reconditioning cure. Many of them are merely traditional talk therapies with a different language (new content) and a slight methodological shift (e.g., more active).

In these "new" talk therapies the therapists still act as change agents, believing they know better than the patient how he should be. They see the patient's task as learning what they already know rather than learning a process. Thus many are weak both humanistically and technologically, and many certainly do not integrate the two. They also lack the phenomenological view of *Awareness,* trusting their own analysis more. They lack a theory of causality to replace the outdated linear causality model. They lack a theory of assimilation adequate to explain an ego that has an existence apart from a sum of id impulses and external reinforcement.

The more active third-force therapies are also not phenomenological. Encounter groups that use gimmicks to produce a desired emotional expression or turn-on, body therapies designed to produce the ideal body, therapies designed to produce primal screams — all have in common with behaviorism two factors that differentiate them from GT (and any phenomenology): (1) they emphasize the external behavior *and* de-emphasize the *world as seen by the patient;* (2) they aim for control of that behavior at the expense of the kind of *Awareness* training that results in organismic self-regulation. If the goal is emotional expressiveness, then the group pushes the patient to emote rather than teaching him to be *Aware* of and accept his impulses to express and not express his emotions. The behaviorists do this reconditioning from a scientific standpoint, with an emphasis on clear terminology, specified techniques, learning theory, objective data, etc. Encounter group leaders often do their reconditioning without as adequate a support base.

In GT we reject any split between talk and behavior; we use *all* the data: that of the patient's consciousness and that which we observe. We integrate behavioral and experiential psychology into one system of psychotherapy by our full concern with the phenomenon of awareness and by using a new and more cogent definition of *Awareness.* The elements of this new definition are included in many definitions of awareness, but most other therapies do not insist on including them all in a unified concept.

By working with here-and-now Awareness and without shoulds by the therapist, the GT patient can begin learning immediately. This immediate change is exciting and frightening. But though *Awareness* and growth can start immediately, growing is a process and not an instantaneous end-state of doing just the right thing. In GT, therapists do not try to be the patient's reconditioner or all-knowing parent/guru; they share in the process of growing.

Growth occurs through *Awareness* arising out of a loving I–Thou relationship in which the patient's independence, worthiness, and sensing ability is respected. This is very similar to Rogers' theory, but with some pointed differences. Rogers started with a client-centered approach, leaving out the person of the therapist, and later advocated a completely mutual relation between therapist and patient. In GT the relationship is not completely mutual but rather is focused on the patient's learning. And in GT, the therapist is totally involved: including negative feelings, feedback of sensory and body language, creativity (creating ways of increasing *Awareness*), technological responses that guide *Awareness* work, and a willingness to allow the patient to feel his own frustration.

SUMMARY

GT involves a whole different framework; it is not just another talk therapy, another behavior therapy, or another encounter therapy. It is a new framework within which therapists have to create their own style of working. GT is more an attitude than a set of techniques. Any technique facilitating *Awareness* can be used within the system — if the GT attitude is adapted by the therapist, therapist-trainee, or patient to each circumstance, using their sensory/experiential tools within the GT framework. Unfortunately, many have confused the GT attitude with a specific therapist's techniques.

In Gestalt Therapy two aspects are always present that other systems frequently treat as contradictory or separate: (1) the immediate personal needs of the participants in the I — Thou, Here — Now dialogue, and (2) the

technical requirements of the *Awareness* work. Each therapeutic intervention has both aspects: Each is both a technical event with implications for
Awareness work (phenomenology) and a human one, expressing the
therapist's *and* the patient's needs. The humanistic dialogue and *Awareness*
"techniques" are integrated in GT. One does not have to choose between
technical expertise and human concern.

GT is very powerful and can therefore be abused. This places a great
demand on the Gestalt therapist. When he works, he must be mature
enough to be spontaneously more interested in the patient's *Awareness* than
in other needs. This means that careful training is needed so that the therapist can learn to recognize how his or her personal responses affect the
Awareness and growth needs of the patient. Gestalt therapists must learn
to use their human/technical potential to clarify the obvious through
experiencing and experimenting. They must value the immediate raw data
of perceptions both of themselves and their patients in the situation as
experienced, and stay in the continuum of *Awareness*, however confusing
or painful, until self-regulation is restored. Each element is seen as meeting
a need and is therefore allowed to become foreground; it must be com-
municated and dealt with until the need is met and the element becomes
background. This type of self-regulation replaces rigid, artificial regula-
tion. Fresh Awareness, mutual contact/exploration, and self-regulation
are more exciting and powerful for increasing growth than analyzing,
conditioning, and "talking-about" therapies.

Allowing patients to discover and explore is particularly suited to our
modern society with its constant and rapidly changing social order. Rather
than trying to be healthy by adjusting to a situation, in GT one learns how
to use one's *Awareness* in whatever situation emerges. This requires learning the structure of how we can direct our own learning and change.

REFERENCES

BEISSER, A. The paradoxical theory of change. In Fagan, J., & Shepherd, I. L.
(Eds.), *Gestalt therapy now.* Palo Alto, Cal.: Science and Behavior Books, 1970.

LATNER, J. *The gestalt therapy book.* New York: Julian Press, 1973.

PERLS, F. *Ego, hunger and aggression.* New York: Vintage Books, 1969.

PERLS, F. *The gestalt approach.* Palo Alto, Cal.: Science and Behavior Books,
1973.

PERLS, F., HEFFERLINE, R., & GOODMAN, P. *Gestalt therapy.* New York: Dell
Books, 1951.

POLSTER, E., & POLSTER, M. *GT integrated.* New York: Brunner/Mazel, 1973.

RESNICK, R. Chicken soup is poison. In Stephenson, F. D. (Ed.), *GT primer.* Springfield, Ill.: Charles Thomas, 1975.

STEPHENSON, F. D. (Ed.), *GT primer.* Springfield, Ill.: Charles Thomas, 1975.

YONTEF, G. A review of the practice of GT. In Stephenson, F. D. (Ed.), *GT primer.* Springfield, Ill.: Charles Thomas, 1975.

6

Feeling Therapy: Transformation in Psychotherapy

Werner Karle, Lee Woldenberg, Joseph Hart

In a book that surveys new therapies, an obvious question is, "Why one more psychotherapy?" The temptation is to answer "Here is what the others missed — here is the cure." We don't claim that. We do know that Feeling Therapy works for us and most of our patients. It works because Feeling Therapy is not just a new theory, but a way of life.

We live by taking care of ourselves and each other; we do the same with our patients. In our view, therapy is not an activity to be done and gotten over. Therapy represents the healing contact between human beings. It makes no sense that we would ever want to stop that contact.

So in answer to the question, "Why another therapy," our answer is "*We* needed it." This answer is intentionally personal. The question is one that we feel any founder or founders of a therapy should ask themselves. Freud was not creating a therapy when he began psychoanalysis; he was involved in a dynamic process with which he could function. We can only surmise what his answer would be to, "Why psychoanalysis?" He might have said, "Because people have a secret insanity that should be shared." And we would then have asked, "And what is yours?" And that would have been the beginning for Freud.

"Feeling Therapy: Transformation in Psychotherapy," by Werner Karle, Ph.D., Lee Woldenberg, M.D., Joseph Hart, Ph.D. © 1976 by Werner Karle, Lee Woldenberg, Joseph Hart. This article appears in print for the first time in this volume.

Werner Karle, Lee Woldenberg, and Joseph Hart are three members of the therapeutic community known as the Center for Feeling Therapy in Los Angeles, founded in 1971. Joseph Hart, with two other colleagues at the Center, Richard Corriere and Jerry Binder, has written *Going Sane: An Introduction to Feeling Therapy.* The authors also belong to the Center Foundation, which sponsors research and special projects concerning Feeling Therapy. Their publications include papers on the psychophysiological correlates of psychotherapy.

AND WHAT IS YOURS?

It is the first question we were willing to ask, and answer for ourselves six years ago when Feeling Therapy was begun by nine psychotherapists from many backgrounds. We felt the need to commit image suicide, to drop some of the roles and images that kept us apart as human beings. We could not create a process for healing without being fully human ourselves.

At the time we started, we knew two things for sure: we needed help from each other; and we could help each other. We needed to get closer to each other than in the superficial relationships we had had in our therapeutic experiences in the past. We were tired of living two lives — one life on the outside, of successful and responsible clinicians and researchers, husbands, skiers, or gardeners; the other on the inside, afraid to express thoughts and feelings that we were certain were insane. We needed to begin to show who we really were. We didn't know that this admission would result in change, or that it would create a new therapy. We only knew we were willing to admit what we needed.

What we needed was a therapy sufficiently diverse and with enough contributors so that no one person's insanity could overwhelm or retard its developments. It had to be specific enough to help us express the simplest feeling. And finally, there had to be community support so that the terrifying reality of change could be carried out in our everyday life.

What developed was the gradual formation of the therapeutic community, a group of people all facing change in their lives, and supporting it in others. And as we felt more, our community changed in order to sustain our feelings. We also came to realize that we had discovered something special — some element that allowed this continuous spiral of growth to take place on both the individual and the community levels. We call this special element "transformation."

FEELING THERAPY IS TRANSFORMATIONAL

What happens in Feeling Therapy is very simple — we help people to feel and live from their feelings.* We call this a transformative therapy not be-

---

*When we talk about feelings, we are not just referring to private and secret thoughts, emotional outbursts, physical sensations, or "dangerous things that must be controlled." These are some common misconceptions of what feelings are. By "feelings" we mean *integral* feelings — sensations, meanings, and expressions that are matched so that what the person feels on the inside is equal in intensity to what he shows on the outside. Integral feelings are transformative when their expression is both complete (carried through to the end) and ordered (not being influenced by past inpulses — the patient is totally in the present). See *Going Sane* for more detailed definitions.

cause it is such a big thing, but because it is so basic. Feeling is not special and extraordinary; it is everyday and ordinary. Transformation is metamorphosis; a person who transforms his life emerges from a cocoon of non- and partial feeling.

We apply the word "transformation" only when a person shifts from a mixed-up way of living in the world to another, based on the way he feels inside himself. When he begins to completely express integral feelings to the people around him, he is transforming his life. Transformation is not synonymous with change. People can change by imitation, by acceding to outside pressure, by pretending, by accident. But to live within, truthfully and fully, is another matter.

Why Transformation?

Because everyone is reasonably insane. Like Sigmund Freud and John Doe, we have all learned to live a life that is not what we are really feeling inside. And the sad reality of this kind of pretended sanity, of reasonable behavior, is that we forget that we ever had intense feelings inside us.

There is a continuum from holding-in to expressing, from defensiveness to openness, from being numb to being feeling people. Transformation is not a wonderful destination. It is the way we travel. It is how we go sane.

The counterpart that makes transformation necessary is disordering. Disordering is the way we moved from sanity to insanity—the way, as children, emotional order slowly became a mismatch of sensation, meanings, and expressions.

THE DISORDER THEORY OF PSYCHOPATHOLOGY

Disordering occurs whenever and wherever a child is raised by "reasonably" disordered adults. The "how" of disordering is simple: a child experiences an unremitting barrage of inappropriate responses to his feeling expressions.

The following example from the book *Going Sane* demonstrates how everyday disordering occurs:

> A little girl and her father were in a restaurant standing near the cash register. She saw some peppermint candy sticks in glass jars and this conversation took place:
>
> GIRL: I want some candy.
>
> DAD: (no response)
>
> GIRL: What is it? What is it? (points at candy)

DAD: (no response)

GIRL: Daddy, what *is* that? What *is* that? (pulling at his sleeve)

DAD: You've had enough sweets today. (He pulls away.)

GIRL: But what is it? (pointing to some red and white candy)

DAD: Oh, it's licorice.

GIRL: What's licorice?

DAD: Where's your mother? Did she go to the ladies' room again?

GIRL: I want one.

DAD: Oh, all right, but it's bad for your teeth.

The authors then go on to describe the disordering of expression and feeling in this scene.

> This brief exchange shows how little reality the child receives. First, [the father] doesn't respond at all to his daughter's direct expression of "I want." She repeats herself more emphatically, but ignored again, she is forced into indirect expression, a question about her want—"What's that?" When she touches her dad, he moves away, denying her direct efforts at contact. Next, he gives her a pronouncement—"You've had enough sweets today;" then he gives her an answer that is obviously not true—"It's licorice." Here, the little girl again resorts to indirect expression, and is answered by an irrelevant question about her mother. Finally, he teaches her that she can get from him if she persists, but he has forced her to learn by persisting in indirect expression. He doesn't give her the real contact she needs; he gives *in*—but he doesn't *give*.

This little story and its explanation give a clear step-by-step description of how this little girl's natural responding process is being disordered. It is typical of scenes that will be repeated for her for the rest of her life. The father is passing on his own inability to respond, make contact, and express a feeling. There is no trauma in this scene, only an unremitting insanity. This is the way insanity is passed on from generation to generation.

Our view of disordering differs from the Freudian concept of trauma. The relation between trauma and disorder is acknowledged, but trauma is not the staple diet of childhood. It is not the extraordinary, but rather the ordinary, which drives the hardiest child into emotional disorder. Traumatic events are infrequent and extraordinary, while disordering activity is ongoing and usual.

The Effects of Disordering

Disordering is learning to live with less expression of complete feeling. It is the way most people live but seldom recognize—it is the normal insanity of everyday life. In a statement describing his typical day, a prospective patient reveals the quiet passivity with which he accepts his loneliness and lack of human contact and his depressive outlook.

> Usually I get up around noon — usually groggy and depressed. If I see my roommate, I get even more depressed. Most of the day I spend worrying about getting a job, wondering what I'm going to do for money. Then I'll get out a book by a chess master and play a game with myself. As the day goes on, I get less depressed and by the time night comes, I'm feeling OK enough to go out and grab a hot dog or a burger. Then I spend the rest of the night in the Oasis, drinking beer with my friends and listening to the jukebox. If they pick up on some girls and I'm left alone, I'll drink until I'm wiped out and finally go home and go to sleep.

Lest there be any mistaking that this is the lifestyle of only one blue-collar worker, the following statement about her daily life is offered from a highly paid professional psychiatric social worker:

> I usually sleep lightly and don't want to get up in the morning. After I get up I stay pretty groggy until around noon. After I get to work, I start on the first cigarette of almost two full packs, and have the first of maybe a dozen cups of coffee. At work, I maintain a professional distance, preferring to eat lunch alone, and seeing as little of the clients as I can possibly get away with. I try to get home as soon as I can and generally watch TV. I think a lot about having a boyfriend.

A look at this woman's typical day reveals the disorder in her life: she never really goes to sleep when she is sleeping and has difficulty being awake when it's time to be awake. She uses drugs to awaken her and calm her. She exists in the reasonably insane role of appearing to the public as a responsible professional concerned with the mental health of others while covertly disliking her job and exhibiting little care for her own mental health; her social life is media culture while she dreams of finding a man.

Here is a person who is not completely feeling herself, and is afraid to share that level of nonfeeling with those around her. She is disordered, incomplete. There are no real reasons for holding in feelings, but there is a general prevalent social attitude that says that she cannot live exactly as she is. Yet, no matter what social and logical reasons are given against living fully, for her to live life with anything less than complete feelings is to live in a disordered way. In order to exist, she has to disorder her only bond to complete living — her body.

THE FEELING THERAPIST

A human being cannot suddenly give up all the images, roles, and symbols of his existence, for he would have to face the unknown with extreme fear. He needs someone who can take him into and through his disordered-ness to the reality of his impulses, thoughts, and expressions. He needs to make contact with another human being. The first contact is with a Feeling Therapist.

What the Feeling Therapist does in a session is described as "ordering." He tracks feelings, focuses feelings, counters resistance to developing a feeling, facilitates the full expression of a feeling, and at the end of a session, guides the patient into talking about the insights he derives from his feeling experiences. He counters all the habits and trances that the patient has followed in his years of disordering.

The Cycle of Feeling

In the therapy session the feelings are focused and experienced to a degree that a patient goes through what we call a cycle of complete feeling. It falls into five distinct but overlapping phases.

In the initial or contact phase, which we call *integration,* the therapist helps the patient express himself so that feelings surface in the present. When this is successful, the defenses surface along with the feelings; these are defenses that had antecedents in the disordering of the past. This mix of past defenses and present expression is felt and expressed by the patient, resulting in an experiencing of the defenses as defenses, rather than reality. This is *counteraction.*

In the third phase, *abreaction,* the antecedent of the defense is felt unmixed and separate from the patient's present life. The patient is re-opened to feeling expression despite regressive defenses. The sensations, meanings, and expressions become matched in the past.

Once the patient is fully expressing the pain of past disordering, he is helped to express in the present, feeling the new difference between his past and his present, unmixing them and making contact in a new way. This is a *movement* forward, called *proaction.* Finally, the patient *re-integrates* this *new* level of feeling into his life.

The following is an example of the cycle of Feeling Therapy. Here the patient, in working with his friend and therapist, moves from his current incomplete feelings to their roots in his disordered interaction with his father, and then recognizes his true feelings of helplessness and need for love.

Integration (acnowledgment of partial disordered feeling)

PATIENT: I feel like I want to choke someone. I'm feeling bad and I feel like I'm having a crazy thought.

Counteraction (process of feeling and expressing the defenses which keep a feeling incomplete)

PATIENT: I want to kill and hurt people.

Abreaction (feeling the source of defenses and expressing past feelings that were blocked)

PATIENT: I felt very helpless. I felt very sad when I would remember my dad choking me. I wanted to ask him to take care of me and not choke me.

Proaction (movement back toward feeling in the present)

PATIENT: I don't want to choke. I want to touch.

Reintegration (living from the new level of feeling awareness and expressing)

PATIENT: As I began to replace the crazy thoughts and violent wanting with just showing what I wanted, I felt both more closeness and more fearfulness than I had ever known as an adult . . . . It seemed absurd to accept less than what I now know I could get and feel with people.

This cycle of feeling may take place in one session, or slowly over several. It is both complete and powerful, but by itself, it has no intrinsic value. The cycle, for the time it takes place, is transformational. But if the movement is not sustained throughout the patient's life, the tension that results from old patterns of holding in will recur. The movement must not stop.

Structure of the Therapy

During the first stage of therapy the patient devotes himself fulltime to therapy — even giving up all outside activities for the first month. Within this intensive therapy program he has individual sessions, group contacts, and is assigned therapy-related activities. After about three months the therapy is primarily done through group work with the patient moving toward becoming a co-therapist. Because no two patients are alike, each progresses at his own rate, spending varying amounts of time individually, in groups, and in activities. The structure of the therapy is designed for the transformation of each unique patient.

CO-THERAPY

Over the past years we have made some startling discoveries. We began with the premise that as human beings we needed help. As complete feeling individuals, we both needed help ourselves and could help our patients. What was true for us was true for them also. Patients were able to do what we had done — they could begin, after a while, to help each other. Help was as natural as freely expressing what they saw, and was based on total *responsibility* to one another.

This was more than fortuitous, it was necessary. Giving or receiving help is not an arcane activity that can only be supported by years of academic pursuit, or clinical experience taking place outside the heart of the therapist. On its simplest terms, there is no difference between giving and receiving help, for it is basically a simple human response that defines it.

It was finally necessary for patients to give up the protective and limiting dependent image of the patient, just as it was originally necessary for us to give up our image, when we began, of therapists.

Any therapy in which the patients do not participate as therapists, and in which the therapists do not continue to get help for themselves, can only be a facsimile of a real therapy. To us therapy is not a job. Therapy deals with the sanity and insanity of each person. It aims not to prevent eruptions of insanity into everyday life. Real therapy is the transformation from nonfeeling into feeling.

What followed from these discoveries was the co-therapy program, in which patients were encouraged, supported, trained, and allowed to begin to help each other. The quality of the help they exchanged deepened as their feelings deepened. As their feeling integration increased, they were more and more receptive to the support for living a feeling life that they were getting from their friends.

What has flowed from this structured program of deep involvement by the therapist and the patients is a therapeutic community. For the therapist, the days of the solo practitioner, dispensing help from the lonely confines of an office (while suffering one of the highest suicide rates of any occupation), are over. For the patient, the dependent, helpless self-image can slowly be disintegrated. What remains are people sharing the life within them.

Therapy must be more than a theory or technique, and more than a personal theory no matter how caringly applied. It must engender the personal and social contacts missing in the community, and as this new community grows, what is created are the possibilities for a person to feel himself and live from his own feelings. This is a proper goal for any complete psychotherapy.

GOALS FOR COMPLETE RESEARCH

We began our therapy by asking ourselves very personal questions and answering them. As social scientists, we ask of ourselves, "Why study dreams?" or "Why study sleep?" "What is our bias?" "What do we need?" It is time for researchers to begin their study with a search of themselves, for answering personal questions first can lead to something more complete than the assembly of more unrelated and conflicting data.

We had to be sure that transformation was more than an optimistic possibility; it was, rather, a pleasurable reality. Transformation occurred in our clinical observations, so we began to look for research evidence to support these changes. We have found major shifts in dream content and processes (Corriere, 1974), physiological sleep patterns (Karle, 1975), and waking physiology (Karle, Gold, Maple, Corriere, & Hart, 1975; Woldenberg, Karle, Gold, Corriere, & Hart, 1975).

Transformation in waking behavior has also been supported through standard psychological tests (P.O.I. and E.P.I. — see Gold, 1975), newly developed experience and expression inventories (Gold, 1975), and projective assessment instruments (Binder, 1975).

These discoveries led us to begin to understand that human beings are the same in everything they do. The level of completeness of their feeling expression is reflected in their waking and sleeping and dream life outside the therapeutic confines. We discovered another parallelism, one that is obvious, but is continually overlooked — that when scientists are clinicians and clinicians are scientists, we have a completeness that improves both the research, which remains human, and the therapy, which remains practical.

A TIME FOR CHANGE

We are not advocating that anyone become either a patient or a therapist of Feeling Therapy. We are concerned with living complete feeling lives and sharing that completeness with our patients. We have presented our ideas to shock the conventional wisdom, to force you to recognize how completely or incompletely you live your life, as a patient, therapist, or interested scientist.

In Jane Goodall's book *In the Shadow of Man* she describes a scene in which a chimpanzee, accompanied by a chimp friend, is fighting a baboon. The fighting chimp goes forward, but returns to contact his companion briefly every time he becomes afraid. He then returns to the battle. Contact does not make the fight with the baboon safe. Nor does contact between people make the fight against insanity any less terrifying. But it does make it possible.

REFERENCES

BINDER, J. A process projective assessive instrument and its psychotherapeutic application. (Doctoral dissertation, University of California, Irvine, 1975) (University Microfilms).

CORRIERE, R. The transformation of dreams. (Doctoral dissertation, University of California, Irvine, 1974) (University Microfilms No. 75-11, 032).

GOLD, S. An experience and expression inventory. (Doctoral dissertation, University of California, Irvine, 1975) (University Microfilms).

HART, J., CORRIERE, R., & BINDER, J. *Going sane: an introduction to feeling therapy.* New York: Jason Aaronson, 1975.

KARLE, W. A new orientation for sleep research: the alteration of sleep patterns in psychotherapy. (Doctoral dissertation, University of California, Irvine, 1975) (University Microfilms).

KARLE, W., GOLD, S., MAPLE, C., CORRIERE, R., & HART, J. Maintenance of psychophysiological changes in feeling therapy. Part I: physiological changes. *Social Sciences Working Papers,* 1975, *71,* 1–22.

WOLDENBERG, L. S., KARLE, W., GOLD, S., CORRIERE, R., & HART, J. Psychophysiological changes in abreactive-cathartic therapy. Study II: feeling therapy. *Social Sciences Working Papers,* 1975, *71,* 1–23.

III

THERAPIES EMPHASIZING
ACTIVITY
AND BEHAVIORAL PROCESSES

The systems of therapy presented in this section have as their aim the changing of some specific behavior. Often it is the client's presenting complaint that is the target for change. Ten to fifteen years ago the suggestion that the therapist would focus on the client's identified complaint was considered dangerously naive. This strong position stemmed from viewing emotional, psychological, or behavioral problems in the same way medical symptoms are viewed; that is, the medical (or emotional or psychological) symptom is considered merely a surface manifestation rather than the "real" illness. This manner of conceptualizing emotional problems is known as the medical model. It stresses that there must be some underlying cause (either psychodynamic or biochemical) for psychological problems just as a headache or cough may be indicative of a far worse disease. In medicine a physician would never prescribe treatment for a persistent headache or cough without requiring a thorough physical examination to determine the reason for the symptom. Analogously, the therapist would never focus on eliminating the presenting complaint without a thorough and extensive attempt to determine the root of the problem. It was assumed that elimination of the presenting problem without the intense analysis of the underlying cause (generally through lengthy psychoanalysis) would result in the substitution of some other symptom.

This medical model was the prevalent way of viewing psychiatric problems for fifty years. One historical factor of importance in leading to its firm foothold in psychiatric and psychological treatment was the emphasis by early psychiatrists on the treatment of hysterics, who indeed did show patterns of symptom substitution. Recently, however, the medical analogy has been challenged by therapists from a number of different orientations largely because of its emphasis on diagnosis and the past. And the psychologists called behaviorists who emphasize current behavior rather than past history have found that the belief in symptom substitution is usually unfounded. Numerous clients whose presenting complaints were treated have shown no symptom substitution.

Because the theoretical basis for the medical model in the psychiatric/ psychological literature has been predominantly psychoanalytic, early challenges of the assumptions of the medical model were equated with challenges to psychoanalytic theory. More recently, however, a new dichotomy has arisen. While biochemical theories of human behavior have been prevalent ever since the earliest successes in physiology, the startling recent advances in biology have produced renewed emphasis upon biochemical constructs to account for specific behavior (or specific symptoms). The two sides of this dichotomy are represented by the behavioral (or symptomatic) approaches stressed in this section of the book and the biological focus of the next section.

A second feature common to the therapies included in this section is their emphasis on the importance of research evaluation. The techniques incorporated in the approaches are chosen because they seem to work. All of the therapies have considerably more documentation of effectiveness than do those in the previous section. Of course, as the last chapter of this book emphasizes, this difference in documentation reflects not only the relative interest of the therapists, but the ease of measuring change. The relief of the presenting problem is more objectively observable than change in self-understanding, which is often the goal of therapies emphasizing cognitive and emotional processes, as we have seen in the previous chapters.

Finally, the therapies in this section are considered behavioral therapies because they focus on the behavior and actions of the client rather than his cognitive, emotional, or biological processes. For some, the term "behavior therapy" means restriction to treatment based upon a learning theory foundation. Using such a strict definition, only those in the last three chapters of this section qualify. Those treatment procedures have been derived, directly or indirectly, from learning theory and the early practitioners were often experimental psychologists. It has occasionally been argued by basic learning theorists that behavior therapists are far less than rigorous in their deductive path from theory to application. However, it is probably fair to say that behavior therapists derive general trends from learning theory.

Of the therapies included in this section, Bloomfield presents the Transcendental Meditation program as a procedure for obtaining emotional and physical tranquility. Transcendental Meditation may be used alone or in conjunction with other therapies. The breadth of positive effects attributable to Transcendental Meditation is thoroughly docum-mented.

The Sexual Therapy of Masters and Johnson is described by their colleague, Runciman. He points out the many widespread misconceptions regarding sexual functioning and presents the straightforward modification system used for alleviating many sexual difficulties.

Both Systematic Desensitization and Implosive Therapy expect to reduce the client's fear by having him visualize the situations that are frightening. But the two approaches, though both based on facets of learn-ing theory, differ in that Systematic Desensitization has the client minimize anxiety during the imagery while the Implosive therapist maintains the client's anxiety at an intense level. Despite their contrasting approaches, both therapies seem to be effective in reducing the fears of a large number of clients.

Operant approaches in behavior modification attempt to change the client's behavior directly through a change in the rewards and punishment (reinforcement) available to the individual. The change in reinforcement patterns can be introduced by a therapist, a family member or friend, or can be initiated by the client himself.

The last approach described in this section is Assertion Training. Assertion Training teaches people, through a variety of techniques, to be neither too passive nor overly aggressive. The proper balancing of as-sertiveness accomplishes the joint goals of defense of personal rights without infringing on the rights of others.

7

Applications of the Transcendental Meditation Program to Psychiatry

Harold H. Bloomfield

Robert Smith is a 21-year-old college student who, during a meeting with his college advisor, reveals that he is intermittently suffering from mild insomnia, tension headaches, fatigue, and test anxiety. His advisor, recognizing the early symptoms of excess stress, recommends the Transcendental Meditation program and refers Robert to the International Meditation Society to learn more about it.

Sound unusual or even a bit strange? Not really, for more and more physicians, psychotherapists, and counselors are now suggesting that their patients, clients, and students learn the Transcendental Meditation (TM) technique. And with good reason, for this simple mental technique has been scientifically documented not only to relieve the symptoms of stress but also to enrich interpersonal relationships, increase happiness, and improve academic and job performance.

Until this decade most Westerners were skeptical of the claims that the practice of meditation can bring increased energy, clarity of thinking, emotional stability, health, and decreased drug abuse. However, beginning with an article in *Science* (Wallace, 1970) on the "Physiological Effects of Transcendental Meditation," a convincing body of physiological, psychological, and sociological data has been published showing that the

"Applications of the Transcendental Meditation Program to Psychiatry," by Harold H. Bloomfield, M.D. © 1976 by Harold H. Bloomfield. This article appears in print for the first time in this volume.

Harold H. Bloomfield is Director of Psychiatry at the Institute of Psychophysiological Medicine in San Diego, California and co-author of the best seller, *TM: Discovering Inner Energy and Overcoming Stress.*

regular practice of the TM technique does indeed result in profoundly beneficial changes.

The TM program utilizes a unique mantra-type relaxation technique that is particularly suited to active people who want the benefits of meditation without adopting a new lifestyle.* The technique is quite simple and teachers of the TM technique say it can be learned by anyone. The program is not a religion or a philosophy and requires no lengthy course of study, intellectual capactiy, or any special powers of concentration. The TM technique is taught by instructors in every major U.S. city at Centers associated with the International Meditation Society, a nonprofit educational organization.

Maharishi Mahesh Yogi, the exponent of the TM program in its modern form, first introduced it to the United States in 1959, and since then over 500,000 people have begun the practice. Its rapid spread can be traced to its ease and immediate effects; it can be learned in a few hours and is practiced for two fifteen- or twenty-minute periods a day. During meditation one simply sits in a comfortable position with the eyes closed. Reportedly, beneficial mental and physical effects are experienced almost immediately.

THE PSYCHOPHYSIOLOGY OF THE TRANSCENDENTAL MEDITATION TECHNIQUE

The recent spread of the TM program has made it possible for large numbers of subjects to be studied in well-controlled laboratory settings. Wallace et al. (1970 a, b, 1971, 1972) demonstrated that oxygen consumption, an excellent measure of metabolic activity, dropped about 16 percent during the TM technique (see Figure 7-1). This reduction occurs within the first few minutes and is almost twice that seen during deep sleep. Despite this rapid decrease, the TM technique does not produce any respiratory abnormalities. During the practice, the amount of carbon dioxide exhaled drops in proportion to the amount of oxygen consumed and the respiratory quotient remains the same. After the meditation period, oxygen consumption returns to its normal resting level, indicating a return to a metabolic level suitable for initiating activity. Other findings are also suggestive of the considerable degree of relaxation achieved during the TM technique, including a marked decrease in blood lactate levels (Wallace, Benson & Wilson, 1971; Wallace & Benson, 1972), and an increase in the intensity of the brain's alpha activity (Wallace & Benson, 1972).

---

*A mantra is a sound suited to each person's temperament that is the focus for meditation. The sound is to be practiced in solitude and is not be be shared with others.

Levels of Rest

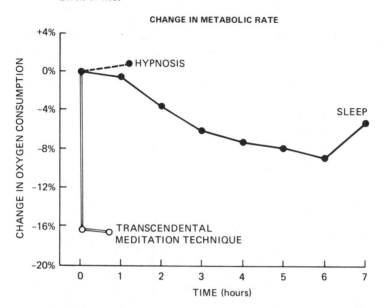

Figure 7-1   Changes in metabolic rate of sleep, hypnosis, and the Transcendental Meditation technique. From "The Physiology of Meditation," by Robert Keith Wallace and Herbert Benson, *Scientific American,* 1972, *226* (2), 84–90. Copyright © 1972 by Scientific American, Inc. All rights reserved.

The subjective experience of meditators is that despite being profoundly relaxed, they are alert and responsive to external stimuli. This unique pattern of restful alertness led Wallace to postulate that the TM technique state is a fourth major state of consciousness physiologically distinct from sleep, dreaming, and wakefulness. Corroborating data has been reported by Banquet (1973), who discovered that brain-wave synchrony during TM is uniquely different from the three ordinary states of consciousness. When he compared the known brain waves of waking, dreaming, and sleep with the patterns that characterize phases of the TM technique, there was a strong suggestion that the process of the TM technique gives rise to a fourth major state of consciousness.

Practitioners of the TM technique commonly report over a period of months an overall rise in alertness, energy, perceptual acuity, and efficiency, with a decrease in anxiety. Dr. David Orme-Johnson (1973) reported in the *Journal of Psychosomatic Medicine* that Transcendental Meditators have fewer spontaneous galvanic skin responses (GSR) than nonmeditating controls, indicating greater stability of the autonomic nervous system (see

Figure 7–2). The autonomic quiescence that the TM technique fosters continues to be maintained after meditation, even during activity. Autonomic stability, as shown by the meditator's low level of spontaneous GSR, is highly correlated with greater resistance to environmental stress, psychosomatic disease, and behavioral instability, as well as with greater efficiency in the activity of the nervous system, thereby freeing more energy for clearer perception, stronger thought, and more purposeful activity.

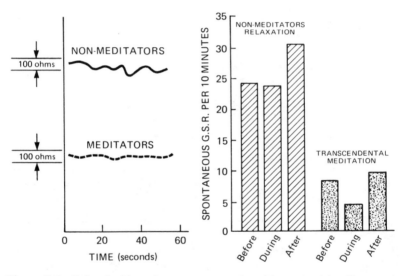

Figure 7-2 Galvanic skin resistance responses in subjects practicing Transcendental Meditation technique and controls. From D. W. Orme-Johnson, "Automatic Stability and Transcendental Meditation," *Psychosomatic Medicine,* 1973, *35* (4), 341. Used by permission of American Elsevier Publishing Co.

Many recent studies focus on the greater psychological health of persons who practice the TM technique. Seeman, Nidich, and Banta (1972) reported in the *Journal of Counseling Psychology* a study comparing the responses of fifteen undergraduate meditators with a control group. They used a well-known measure of self-actualization, the Personality Orientation Inventory, which measures the characteristics of healthy, loving, creative, fully functioning people as described in the writings of the late Abraham Maslow. They found that a meditator's sense of inner-directedness increases, as do the ability to express feelings in a spontaneous action, the acceptance of aggression, and the capacity for intimate contact (see Figure 7–3). Meditators seem to have better "psychic gyroscopes" and are more open to their own and to others' deep experiences and feelings.

Development of Personality

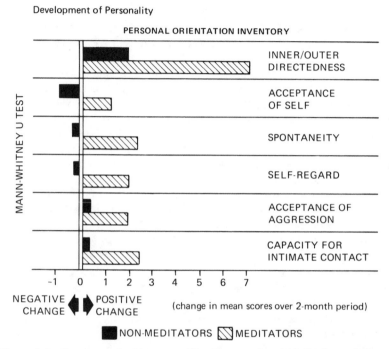

Figure 7-3 Responses of subjects practicing Transcendental Meditation technique and controls of personality testing. From W. Seeman, S. Nidich, and T. Banta, "The Influence of Transcendental Meditation on a Measure of Self-Actualization," *Journal of Counseling Psychology,* 1972, *19* (3), 184. Copyright 1972 by the American Psychological Association. Reprinted by permission.

Ferguson and Gowan (in press) conducted a study using the Spielberger State-Trait Anxiety Inventory and the Cattell Anxiety Scale. Both tests showed a significant decrease of anxiety in those practising the TM technique. Even though the short-term meditators showed the highest level of anxiety before beginning the TM technique, their anxiety level was reduced to below that of the nonmeditators after six and one-half weeks of regular practice. The anxiety level was lowest in the long-term (43 months) meditators. Further measures on the Northbridge Development Scale showed that the subjects practicing the TM technique had significantly reduced levels of depression and neuroticism, and had a significant increase in self-actualization compared with a group of nonmeditators. All measures indicated that psychological health increases with length of time in the Transcendental Meditation program.

THE TRANSCENDENTAL MEDITATION PROGRAM AS AN ADJUNCT TO PSYCHIATRIC TREATMENT

The practice of the TM technique apparently brings increased well-being on physical, psychological, and interpersonal levels. For example, Shafii reports that 92 percent of 126 meditators surveyed felt more relaxed after beginning the TM technique, and 75 percent reported improvement in their ability to concentrate and a decrease in tension, anxiety, and nervousness (Shafii, 1973). Can the TM technique also be helpful to those individuals who are so seriously disturbed that they require psychiatric care? The evidence is mounting that the TM technique can contribute significantly to the treatment of the mentally ill (Bloomfield, Cain, Jaffe, & Kory, 1975; Boudreau, 1973; Carrington & Ephron, 1975; Glueck & Stroebel, 1975; Shafii, 1973), and Dr. L. J. West (1974), professor and chairman of the UCLA Department of Psychiatry, has suggested that the TM program may be the best of the nonprofessional psychotherapies.

An increasing number of psychiatrists and psychologists have begun utilizing the TM program as an adjunct to psychotherapy. As a postdoctoral fellow in social and community psychiatry at the Yale University School of Medicine and now as director of psychiatry at the Institute of Psychophysiological Medicine, I have had over 150 of my patients start the TM program. The results have been most encouraging. It appears that a wide range of psychiatric patients can be helped by the TM program. It is easy to learn and involves no change in lifestyle, other than fitting in a twenty-minute meditation period morning and evening. A few patients refuse to learn the TM technique because of unwillingness to help themselves, disbelief in meditation, fears of introspection, or a fear of being taken over by hostile forces.

Most of my patients have been pleased with the TM program, however, and continue the practice regularly. Meditating patients improve at an uncommonly fast rate. They need fewer therapy hours, and the sessions become more meaningful and useful. With several patients this improvement has been dramatic; some have been relieved of symptoms that were not affected by previous therapy. As judged by previous experience, progress occurs at about twice the usual rate, and sometimes even faster.

'l3 l85

If a patient is not moving at a satisfactory pace, often he has been found to have stopped meditating. When he begins again, progress continues. The TM program can frequently become the principal therapy. Fewer and shorter therapy sessions are needed. The primary focus of such sessions is understanding the normalization process and the growth that is taking place. The role of the psychotherapist becomes that of a wise teacher who provides knowledge and support while the TM technique does the healing.

Anxiety is the common denominator of almost all mental disorders. Neurosis is characterized by excessive anxiety which arises when there is no manifest danger, or continues long after danger has passed, and interferes with the individual's pursuit of a normal life. Chronic anxiety may precede major depressive episodes. The anxiety that portends schizophrenic reactions is extreme and incessant, leading to marked disturbances of sleep, cognition, and social functioning. Hypochondriasis is often a response to anxiety as well. Alcoholism and drug abuse are destructive habits that attempt to relieve anxiety. Since anxiety is so basic to mental illness, and since the TM technique has been shown to relieve anxiety, there has been increasing interest within the psychiatric community as to whether it might be useful in treating severe psychic distress.

Below are a series of case studies, chiefly derived from my practice, which illustrate how the TM program can lead to improvement across a wide range of diagnostic categories. Following each case there will be some discussion of the mechanism of change which the TM program appears to catalyze.

Anxiety Neurosis

Joan was a 25-year-old graduate student who came with the chief complaint of "anxiety attacks, I'm afraid I'm going crazy." She had been suffering from anxiety attacks since about age 17, and these had increased in severity over the last six months. These were characterized by feelings of tenseness, apprehension, hyperventilation, irritability, chest pain, heart palpitations, dizziness, trembling, faintness, and easy tiring. Joan would frequently experience intense fear of impending doom or of going insane without any apparent external cause. Numerous medical work-ups for various bodily complaints had proven unremarkable.

Joan reported that as a result of "the constant pressure, pressure, pressure" she felt chronically tense and spent a good deal of time crying. She had tried tranquilizers and relaxation exercises, which offered minimal relief. As the pressure of school increased, Joan could not even get out of bed some days and felt chronically fatigued. She has now been meditating for over a year. Since her instruction she reports gradually feeling better than she ever felt before, and feels that she has received more relaxation and energy than from two previous years of therapy, pills, and exercises. She reports that now she "knows what deep relaxation is all about."

Joan no longer has chronic insomnia, gets up every morning, and looks forward to the day's activities. She still reports some tension during a particularly busy day or before a paper is due, but she feels better able to cope with such things. She states:

> The TM program has opened up new horizons in my life. Prior to beginning the TM technique I felt like I was on a treadmill. The strain was becoming unbearable, and I was on the verge of a nervous breakdown. Since meditating I gradually learned to be more at ease, with myself and with the situations in my life. It's not so much that my life situation has changed, but my view of these situations. I attribute a lot of these changes to the deep calm that I've obtained from meditation.

Joan's improvement is shown in Figure 7-4, which summarizes her MMPI scores at the time of her initial presentation and after one year of practising the TM technique. The high scores on hysteria and hypochondria indicate that Joan was quite neurotic before the TM program. Chronic anxiety probably contributed to her high depression score as well. The decrease of the hysteria, depression, and hypochondria scales into the normal range parallel Joan's clinical improvement. She no longer complained of bodily aches or attacks of fear, and felt much more autonomous and stable.

Anxiety neurosis, such as Joan suffered, is a chronic disorder that affects a significant portion of the United States population. It has been estimated that between 10 and 30 percent of the patients of most general practitioners and internists have ailments stemming from anxiety neurosis. The TM technique serves as an anti-anxiety agent by changing the response of the individual to environmental circumstances and by allowing a more adaptive response to twentieth-century living conditions. During the TM technique, oxygen consumption sharply decreases, heart rate and cardiac output decrease, muscles relax, blood lactate diminishes, skin resistance increases markedly, the brain achieves greater synchrony, and the meditator experiences a refreshing state of restful alertness. The comprehensive and integrated hypometabolic state produced by the TM technique appears to be the opposite of a maladaptive anxiety attack. A number of studies have demonstrated that the longer one practices the TM technique the greater the reduction in measurable anxiety (Ferguson & Gowan, in press; Seeman, Nidich & Banta, 1972). More importantly, preliminary scientific

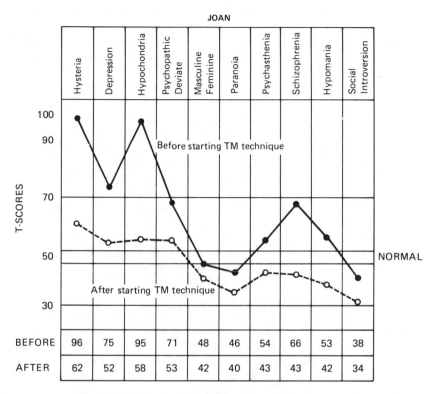

Figure 7-4 Minnesota Multiphasic Personality Inventory.

evidence (Orme-Johnson, 1973) and the personal experience of meditators indicates that the regular practice of the TM technique leads to a permanent state of resistance and resilience to environmental threats and pressures through the achievement of greater autonomic stability. The result is an altered style of functioning of the nervous system where energy is no longer consumed by inappropriate anxiety and worry but instead is utilized for greater personal satisfaction and more dynamic activity. The result is an altered style of functioning of the nervous system where energy is no longer consumed by inappropriate anxiety and worry but instead is utilized for greater personal satisfaction and more dynamic activity. The

In current practice, psychotherapy is the principal treatment for anxiety neurosis, either alone or combined with tranquilizers. But therapy usually requires long years of professional attention and produces results that are at best inconsistent. Psychotherapy is effective for only certain individuals, and only a select few in our society can afford the luxury of long-term psychiatric treatment. We suggest that the practice of the TM technique offers an alternative, not necessarily to replace the interpersonal encounter that is the core of psychotherapy, but as a significant means of reducing tension, broadening awareness and making life more meaningful and pleasurable, and thereby fulfilling the goals of all forms of therapy. Furthermore, since psychotherapy also aims at removing limitations upon the mind's full range of capabilities, the psychotherapeutic process can benefit from any technique that strengthens the individual.

Traditional psychotherapy focuses on aiding the individual to come to grips with the psychological sources of conflict. However, gaining knowledge of the source of the stress is not as important as finding ways to eliminate stress and go beyond it. Indeed, knowledge of the sources of psychic stress may be demoralizing. As many people have found after years of fruitless search, excessive analysis of previous negative experiences can lead to a loss of self-esteem rather than to its enhancement. The key to successful therapy lies instead in creating psychological and physiological conditions that optimize the natural tendency of the nervous system to stabilize itself. TM technique appears to offer a systematic method of achieving this goal in a relatively short period of time.

Of course, not all patients want to learn the TM technique, and not every patient who learns it gains immediate benefit. Psychotherapists Carrington and Ephron point out that some patient-meditators may have difficulty practising the TM technique correctly because their habitual defense patterns appear during meditation as efforts to resist thoughts. Understanding and approval from the therapist can help a patient relax during the practice of the TM technique, especially during the first few months. Also, sometimes patients refuse to continue practicing the TM technique because they feel themselves changing too quickly. For example, a patient of ours wanted to stop meditating because the pleasure she derived from the TM technique made her feel guilty! In this case, supportive reinforcement from the therapist and frequent checking by a teacher of the TM program enabled the patient to continue meditating comfortably. Frequent checking, as well as support from the therapist, is also very important for the occasional patient who complains about the intrusion of severely disturbing thoughts. Checking helps the patient learn not to resist this intrusion, but rather to continue to meditate easily until disturbing thoughts lose their frightening emotional intensity. Regular checking is included in all TM technique instruction programs for rehabilitation settings. These specially designed programs in combination with psychiatric support can have a powerful therapeutic effect.

The TM program has many advantages over minor tranquilizers in the treatment of anxiety neurosis. Such drugs as Valium and Librium are all too frequently prescribed in the treatment of daily stresses and strain. Drugs may help the patient to feel less anxious but may also make him feel listless and groggy, and may even become addicting. The TM technique has no such adverse side effects and can promote what pills cannot, natural psychological growth. Instead of becoming dependent on a chemical agent, the TM program fosters self-reliance and greater autonomy. Tranquilizers do not get at the underlying causes of anxiety. In contrast, the long-term practice of the TM technique appears to release even deep-rooted stresses. The net result is not just a cumulative decline in anxiety, but greater stability, adaptability, integration, and growth.

Obsessive Compulsive Neurosis

George was 28 and single and had suffered from obsessive compulsive symptoms since early adolescence. He became tense when around people, especially in public places. He had to perform various rituals such as straightening his clothes several times and mentally doing multiplication tables over and over again. Nonsensical thoughts constantly intruded into his mind, confusing him or arresting his attention. George had a very authoritarian personality, was hypercritical, and suffered from poor interpersonal relationships. He has been meditating for fourteen months, and reports a marked decrease in his anxiety. He feels "more alert and more alive." Whereas before he felt as though his mind "couldn't be turned off," he now has periods when, for the first time in his life, he is not thinking frantically and strenuously. George reports learning "what it means to just be," and accepts life in a more relaxed and less controlling fashion. He has been progressively less troubled by obsessional thoughts. He now is able to "let the thoughts go." In public places and with others he is less tense, and he feels a greater identification with others than ever before. He has learned that he is "not the only one trying to make a go of it in life," and feels much closer to people. He states:

> I am very happy to be a meditator. It allows me to gain control over my mind rather than my mind gaining control over me as it has in the past. I also like the fact that it is such an effortless technique. Before I felt that everything in life that I got could only be obtained by trying very hard, and that's why I frequently felt hassled and strained. It's wonderful to find a technique where, by not trying, good things happen.

The TM technique's potency as an anti-anxiety agent also leads to a reduction in obsessive-compulsive symptoms. Obsessive-compulsive behavior is an extreme case of being locked in boundaries. The regular experience of unboundedness through the TM technique reduces rigidity and gives the practitioner a greater sense of personal freedom. Obsessions are a disorder of thinking; by increasing the orderliness of the mind the TM technique spontaneously eliminates this weakness. In his twice-daily meditations, the individual leans just to "take it as it comes," in a pleasurable way, neither anticipating nor resisting change. Gradually he loses his need to manipulate and control himself and others. As a result, the authoritarian individual becomes more open and more at ease in his relationships. Life becomes more effortless, more natural.

Depression

Mary was a 26-year-old married white female who was first seen when she was presented in the emergency room, after having taken an overdose of aspirin in a suicidal gesture. The patient stated that she had been dealing with feelings of depression for her entire life and that things had been getting progressively more severe in the last few months. Family and school pressures had become "unbearable." Mary made her suicide attempt because she "didn't want to fight it any more . . . life is too full of pain and cruelty." There was no significant history of sleep disorder or vegetative symptoms. Mary stated that she found it very hard to relax because when she relaxed she became quite depressed: "I haven't been at peace with myself as long as I can remember." This patient had been in intensive psychotherapy on two previous occasions with little or no benefit and had made a number of other suicide attempts.

Mary was admitted to our psychiatric unit for four days of crisis intervention, after which she was followed as an out-patient. The patient was informed about the TM program while in the hospital and began the course of instruction on her last day on the unit. Over the next six months Mary not only recovered but, in her words, "felt better than I have ever felt; the TM program has given me a new lease on life." Mary felt much more effective as a teacher and was handling her students with less stress and strain. Her husband began the TM program as well after seeing the beneficial changes in Mary. Family life qualitatively improved, even relations with the in-laws. Whereas before Mary had felt inadequate and experienced little or no pleasure in sexual relations, now she felt "like a real woman . . . much closer to my husband." Mary states that she likes the TM technique because it "is something I can do for myself. It calms me down and yet gives me more energy."

Figure 7–5 summarizes Mary's improvement as measured by the MMPI. When she was initially tested on our psychiatric unit she appeared to be an angry, sullen person who blamed others for her difficulties. Mary's interpersonal relationships were impaired; she was argumentative, tactless, and

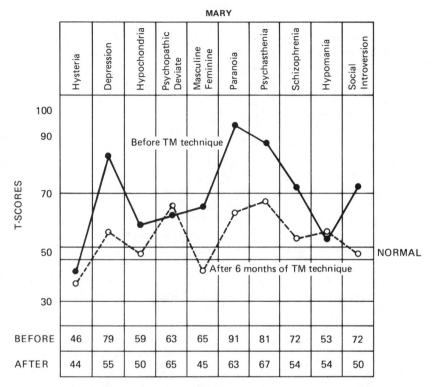

Figure 7-5 Minnesota Multiphasic Personality Inventory.

unpleasant. She showed marked depression, irritability, suspiciousness, and judgment defects, and we were concerned about the possibility of a psychotic or pre-psychotic condition. Despite her obvious distress, this patient was considered likely to show a minimal response to psychotherapy and to have a poor prognosis. Therefore, the improvement Mary demonstrated after just six months of practising the TM technique was unexpected and gratifying.

The way in which the TM technique alleviates a depression such as Mary's can be seen from a number of vantage points. The deep rest of the TM technique not only allows for the release of daily stresses and strain but also permits the gradual resolution of older and deeper psychic conflicts. It releases pent-up anger and resentment and counteracts the chronic anxiety that frequently precedes major depressive episodes. As stress and fatigue are eliminated, the body feels more energized and the mind experiences more baseline pleasure. The individual is better able to enjoy autonomous pleasures and no longer remains so dependent on others for a sense of happiness. Studies have demonstrated that the longer one has been meditating the less depression is reported.

Unlike medication and psychotherapy, the TM technique is exclusively under the control of the patient. If he or she feels better, it will not be due to a pill or the relationship with a therapist, but to a natural process triggered by his/her own efforts. Hospitals and various forms of psychiatric treatment have been criticized for not reinforcing a patient's autonomy, but instead reinforcing negative aspects of the self through exclusive concentration on the pathological. The struggle against total dependency that is characteristic of so many emotionally disturbed individuals can be meaningfully resolved by the liberating effects of the self-administered practice of the TM technique. Like psychotherapy, the TM technique encourages the resolution of emotional conflicts and allows for previously unacceptable aspects of the self to become integrated into the personality. The creative intelligence that is liberated not only increases the sense of well-being but also contributes to improved interpersonal relationships and better job performance, as was seen in Mary's case; this serves to eliminate depression and raise self-esteem.

Reports of dramatic personal change as a result of the TM program among psychiatric patients who were unresponsive to individual psychotherapy are becoming common. In some individuals the TM program can apparently effect a rapid and profound psychological transformation. The spontaneous feeling of opening up to oneself, to others, and to one's environment, allows an immediate surge of energy and progress. One may feel that one has suddenly come in contact with life.

Despite the general tendency for people to seek positive reasons for justifying whatever they happen to be doing, there are several reasons for confidence in these personal testimonials. First, the claims are often based upon specific objective changes, such as better relationships, higher grades, more efficient performance, or decreased drug use. Second, the accounts converge on several common areas of increased well-being, which are consistent with the physiological changes produced by the TM technique. Third, we don't see these kinds of consistent and cumulative changes in patients who take up some other practice instead of the TM program. It is true that anything new and promising can have a placebo effect, but the wide range of benefits that result from the TM program persist and cannot be accounted for by simple enthusiasm.

Drug Abuse

Many of our patients have ceased or reduced their use of illicit as well as licit drugs with the aid of the Transcendental Meditation program. Patients who have a long history of severe drug dependency still require a very broad eclectic approach to therapy, but the TM program appears to make a vital difference. TM technique instruction and follow-through requires a specially designed program, with frequent checking and advanced meetings.* Such programs appear to be well worth adopting and researching in prevention programs as well as in treatment settings. Because considerable evidence suggests that the TM program improves self-regard, decreases anxiety, and improves self-reliance, several researchers had hypothesized what drug surveys are now confirming—that the TM program reduces drug abuse (Benson & Wallace, 1971; Shafii, 1974).

A study of nearly two thousand meditators, which was reported in the Hearings Before the Select Committee on Crime of the House of Representatives in 1971 (Benson & Wallace, 1971), showed a drastic reduction in the use of marijuana, narcotics, and other illicit drugs as well as in cigarette smoking and alcohol intake. In a controlled study published in the *American Journal of Psychiatry*, Shafii (1974) demonstrated that the longer respondents had practised the TM technique, the sharper was the decline in their marijuana use. In another survey Shafii reported a reduction in cigarette smoking in subjects who had been meditating thirteen months or more. Seventy-one percent of the group who had practised the TM program for more than two years decreased smoking cigarettes significantly, and 57 percent totally stopped smoking. The control group figures for cigarette usage did not change. In an apparent attempt to cope with the symptoms of stress, our society has developed one of the most characteristic neuroses of our age, the reliance on drugs of all kinds. Drug abuse extends throughout all levels of society. Drugs to relieve tension have become common and even socially acceptable. Americans consume billions of tranquilizers, amphetamines, and barbiturates, in addition to hundreds of billions of cigarettes and millions of gallons of alcohol. The tremendous and growing demand for all these drugs may be the clearest indicator of how deeply stress affects our society.

To what needs is the use of drugs addressed? The tired and depressed person may take an amphetamine; the insomniac may turn to barbiturates;

*The Institute of Social Rehabilitation of Maharishi International University now has such special programs designed for incorporation into ongoing mental health and rehabilitation settings.

a bored young person may experiment with psychedelics; a tense individual may slowly become addicted to alcohol or tranquilizers. In each of these cases, the use of drugs expresses an underlying need to counterbalance an uncomfortable condition, a need to restore homeostasis. Despite all the specific effects for which people take drugs, the major purpose of drug abuse is the restoration of physiological equilibrium and a feeling of well-being. Because the TM technique restores equilibrium by reducing stress and maximizing the enjoyment of life, it may well offer a safe and plausible alternative to all forms of drug abuse.

Hosptial Psychiatry

Clinicians are finding the TM program to be a valuable adjunct to psychotherapy in treating a wide range of emotional disorders. Bloomfield, Cain, Jaffe, and Kory (1975), Boudreau (1973), Carrington and Ephron (1975), Glueck and Stroebel (1975), and Shafii (1973) have reported on its value in the treatment of anxiety neurosis, obsessive compulsive symptoms, chronic low-grade depression, identity crisis, psychosomatic illness, drug abuse, and even psychotic disturbances in carefully implemented programs.

The most extensive research project using the TM program as an adjunct to psychiatric treatment was conducted at the Institute of Living Hospital, under the direction of researcher and psychoanalyst Dr. Bernard C. Glueck (1975). In this study 187 in-patients learned the TM program; control groups were taught alpha biofeedback conditioning and Jacobson's progressive relaxation to provide comparative data. Careful records were kept of their physiological changes; their progress in therapy; their behavior in the hospital community; their feelings about the treatment; and what happened after they left the hospital. Several teachers of the TM program were utilized on the project staff.

Dr. Glueck reported that over 85 percent of the patients were able to learn the TM practice easily and meditated regularly. The study's physioogical findings were consistent with the earlier research on the deep state of restful alertness achieved by meditators, including the same observation of brain-wave synchrony and coherence reported by Banquet (1973). The results using alpha wave biofeedback and Jacobson's progressive relaxation were quite disappointing in comparison to the TM technique. A surprising finding was a relatively uniform positive response for the meditating patients across a wide range of diagnostic categories. Significant benefits were established for all parameters studied — physiological measurements, MMPI profiles, psychophysiological diaries, computerized nursing notes, dosage of medication, and reports from the treating psychiatrist.

Dr. Glueck feels that the TM technique accelerates progress in psychotherapy:

> In working in psychotherapy with the meditating patients, the ideational content that comes up in meditation can be intensely hostile and aggressive, but there is little or no affect — that is, the ideation is there, but the intensity of the emotions that usually accompany it is reduced. This is different from what we usually see in psychotherapy. The meditating patients are able to to discuss, in therapy, the ideation that came up in meditation much more easily. Both the patients and the therapists are pleased at the facilitation of psychotherapy this has provided. Some patients have covered material in two to three months that would ordinarily have taken six months to a year. Meditation appears to have a positive speed-up effect on psychotherapy. This may turn out to be one of the most significant aspects of the use of meditation in psychiatrically ill individuals.*

A decrease in the need for medication in the meditating patient group was also noted. Middle-aged patients with complaints of chronic insomnia report improvement in their sleep patterns within the first two or three weeks of meditation. This improvement in their sleep tends to continue until night sedation is no longer necessary, even in previously severe insomnia. After about three weeks of meditation the need for all types of psychotropic medication begins to decrease.

From the experiences at the Institute of Living, it would appear that reservations about using the TM program as a therapeutic adjunct for a seriously disturbed patient population are unfounded when a properly designed program and careful supervision are employed. As observed in the laboratory, Glueck points out that the TM program produces a maximum effect more rapidly and effectively than any other technique of relaxation. Adding the TM program can reduce the need for excessive sedation with tranquilizers, normalize the sleeping pattern, improve communication, accelerate the process of psychotherapy, and decrease the debilitating anxiety that is at the core of so many psychiatric syndromes.

THE TM PROGRAM AND PSYCHOTHERAPY

The interface between the TM program and psychotherapy offers great promise. Clinical experience and scientific research indicate that the TM technique offers relief from stored-up anxiety and conflict very

---

*B. C. Glueck, *A Psychodynamic and Neurophysiologic Assessment of Transcendental Meditation.* Address presented at the International Symposium on the Science of Creative Intelligence, Fiuggi Fonte, Italy, April 1972.

systematically, without the need to have these sensations verbalized. There is no need to receive interpretations from a therapist; in this way the TM program offers a short-cut to therapy. Whereas psychotherapy may help the individual gain intellectual insight into the sources of his stress, all too frequently the old fears persist on a visceral level, and the patient remains discouraged. Traditional psychotherapy too often keeps the patient preoccupied with the dark side of human nature, the cauldron of aggressive and primitive impulses. Psychoanalysis often delves into such themes as Oedipal wishes to kill one's father and sleep with one's mother, stinginess or compulsiveness as derivatives of toilet training practices, and asthmatic wheezes as the unconscious cry for mother's breast.

Maharishi Mahesh Yogi feels that such delving into past miseries is an ineffective means of relieving psychic suffering:

> It should not be a function of psychology to remind a man that his past was miserable, or that his surroundings and circumstances were unfavorable, or that his associations were depressing and discouraging, or that there was lack of love and harmony with those near to him. To remind anyone of such things will only result in lowering his consciousness . . . It should be considered criminal to tell anyone that his individual life is based on the inefficient and degenerate influence of his past environment. The psychological influence of such depressing information is demoralizing, and the inner core of the heart becomes twisted by it.*

Toward the end of his life Freud himself recognized the limitations of psychotherapy; he found that the very act of verbalizing unpleasant thoughts brought resistance to their interpretation. As a therapeutic tool, psychoanalytically oriented psychotherapy has not lived up to the expectations of its proponents. As psychoanalyst Dr. Glueck laments:

> One of the underlying propositions of all psychotherapeutic activity has been, for some 75 years, that if we can help the individual to get rid of the memory of early painful experiences we can help him to perform in a more appropriate fashion in his present life. Unfortunately, and I say this with a good deal of chagrin, the initial promise that was perceived in the discoveries of Freud and people working with him of help for so many people has not been borne out to the extent that we would have liked. Certainly we've had some very successful responses to this kind of intervention. But in general, and this is looking back on 30 years of experience now in the field, my feeling has been that I can't do enough, continuously enough, with psychotherapy for most individuals to really undo the damage that has been done. It appears to me that, and this is one of the major reasons for my interest in the

*Maharishi Mahesh Yogi, *The Science of Being and the Art of Living* (Stuttgart, Germany: Spiritual Regeneration Movement Publications, 1966), p. 264.

technique of Transcendental Meditation, through this avenue the individual now may be taught to do for himself, in a remarkably brief space of time, the same kinds of things we've been trying to help him to do in our traditional psychotherapeutic approaches in the past.

Talking with a therapist exclusively about problems may be futile or even counterproductive. Better that a patient move beyond concern with previous problems to enjoy growth in the present through the uplifting experience of pure awareness. Rather than "digging into the mud of a miserable past," one's vision should be enlarged to "the genius and the brightness of man's inner creative intelligence." The TM program spontaneously enlarges the vision to a fuller appreciation of the positive, creative, and spiritual possibilities of life.

Psychoanalysis has expanded our understanding of unconscious motivation, but as a therapeutic technique it has many failings, and as a study of the mind, it is incomplete. Through the practice of the TM technique, one learns that the territory of the mind is far more extensive than Freud realized. Indeed, the therapeutic effects of psychoanalysis have not received scientific validation. More scientific evidence of positive benefits from the TM program has been reported in the five years since Wallace's article in *Science* (1970) than in seventy-five years of psychoanalysis.

Our criticism of traditional psychotherapy should not be construed as an overall negative evaluation of psychotherapy. Psychotherapy as such does not refer to any specific way of interacting with a patient. It includes any activity between patient and therapist that aids the patient's psychological functioning. For severely disturbed patients, empathetic understanding and such supportive measures as teaching him what he needs to know about his illness, assisting him with his life plans, and advising him about work can be essential. Major psychiatric syndromes certainly require expert professional assistance, and supportive services will continue to be necessary in times of severe emotional crisis. We are hopeful that mental health professionals will study the interface between the TM program and psychotherapy and conduct research on how these approaches together can effectively contribute to the relief of suffering and the promotion of psychological growth.

Besides the growing number of reports that suggest that the TM program makes an excellent adjunct to individual psychotherapy, it should also be considered along with group and family therapy. The TM program has the same goal as all forms of psychotherapy — the release of stress and maximization of psychological growth and integration. Beginning group therapy with a group meditation often makes the session more spontaneous and meaningful, improves communication and interpersonal relationships, and contributes to a growing sense of universality.

It therefore seems logical to incorporate the TM program into the psychotherapeutic armamentarium and to research its many potential applications.

MENTAL HEALTH

The TM program can also be helpful for the vast number of individuals in our society who are ordinarily not thought of as psychiatric patients, but who are suffering needlessly by failing to actualize themselves. Alvin Toffler has popularized the term "future shock" to describe the disastrous effect of the accelerating pace of the modern world on human life. The increasing rate of change and transience is producing shattering stress and disorientation in individuals, many of whom are being pushed beyond their ability to cope. Too much change too fast weakens the physiology and causes deterioration of emotional and mental well-being. No amount of material comfort is sufficient to reverse this damage. The physiological effect of accelerating technological expansion may be a primary cause of the lack of "satisfaction" in our society. By allowing the individual to regain his vital center of energy, satisfaction, and stability, the TM program becomes the necessary antidote to future shock. As the well-known psychotherapist Fritz Perls explains:

> If you are centered in yourself, then you don't adjust anymore . . . then you assimilate, you understand, you are related to whatever happens . . . Without a center . . . there is no place from which to work . . . Achieving a center, being grounded in oneself, is about the highest state a human can achieve.*

A centered individual can fully enjoy life. He is free from the continual need to adjust and modify himself to meet demands of his activity. Instead, he experiences an inner foundation from which he can fully assimilate, understand, and work with the world. This platform of inner stability provides a basis for consistent successful action and growing fulfillment.

It is ironic that in Western psychology and psychiatry we have been talking so much about achieving a center, and yet the methods we've employed have been looking for it somewhere out there—in encounter groups, T-groups, and psychotherapy (which is after all an interpersonal process, though it may be aimed at the individual). It seems obvious, when we stop to think about it, that if we are searching for our center, then it

*F. S. Perls, *Gestalt Therapy Verbatim* (Lafayette, Cal.: Real People Press, 1969), pp. 30, 37.

must lie somewhere within us, in the very depths of our existence. So if we want to experience this center the first thing we have to do is close our eyes, turn inward, and then take advantage of a time-proven technique for re-centering, coming home to our Self.

This technique, of course, is the TM progam — the description of which can be found in the oldest records of human experience, the vedas. The TM technique does not, however, have any connection with the present fashionable cultivation of Eastern philosophy or culture. In fact, the correct practice of the TM technique does not depend on any cultural orientation, but only upon the inherent abilities of the nervous system. Furthermore, the deep state of rest achieved through the TM technique is so natural and valuable to personal development and well-being that references to it appear in a wide variety of cultural traditions. However, as can be seen from the currently available scientific evidence, no technique of meditation is as effective as the TM program in producing deep rest and neurophysiological integration.

The potential of the human mind constitutes a frontier which science has just barely explored. Brain researchers have identified the enormous capacity of the human nervous system, while psychologists have recognized our limited use of our mental potential as early as the beginning of the twentieth century. It can be argued that our failure to meet the demands of progress result from our inability to utilize our full physical, emotional, and mental potential and that the solution to the myriad problems of our society lies in the widespread application of the TM program psycho-physiologically to strengthen the individual and unfold his/her untapped potential.

Traditional psychiatric skills will of course continue to be very important in the diagnosis and treatment of the severe mental illnesses — particularly schizophrenia, manic-depressive psychosis, unipolar depressive illness, and organic dementias. Certainly mental health professionals will have carefully to assess, manage, and supervise the incorporation of the TM program into our psychotherapeutic repertoire. The enthusiasm expressed in this paper — though justified — must not become a substitute for good clinical judgment, psychiatric expertise, patience, and the full appreciation of all of the other psychiatric skills and tools which have already proven their effectiveness. But in adding the TM Program to current psychiatric practice in carefully conceived, researched, and well-supervised programs, we may well find that it lives up to its potential of becoming a principal form of psychic healing, especially for those who might be called "average middle-class neurotics." This term describes far too many of us in contemporary society — individuals who are not mentally ill, but who, despite material affluence, are unfulfilled. Perhaps the greatest promise of the TM program is the prospect of helping these millions of dissatisfied people to grow on their own in happiness and achievement without the need for professional assistance. For the TM program has been passed down through the ages and has been revived in its purity by Maharishi Mahesh Yogi as much more than just a means of relieving insomnia, hypertension, worries, and anxieties. It is the high technology of gaining enlightenment, the ultimate state of fulfillment in life.

REFERENCES*

BANQUET, J. P. Spectral analysis of the EEG in meditation. *Electroencephalography and Clinical Neurophysiology*, 1973, *35*, 143-151.

BENSON, H., & WALLACE, R. K. *Decreased drug abuse with transcendental meditation: a study of 1862 subjects presented in congressional record.* (Hearings before the Select Committee on Crime, House of Representatives, 92nd Congress, First Session, June 2, 3, 4, and 23, 1971. Serial #92-1). U.S. Government Printing Office, Washington, D.C., 1971.

BENSON, H., & WALLACE, R. K. Decreased blood pressure in hypertensive subjects who practiced meditation. *Circulation*, 1972, *XLV, XLVI*, Suppl. II.

BLOOMFIELD, H., CAIN, M., JAFFE, D., & KORY, R. *TM: discovering inner energy and overcoming stress.* New York: Delacorte Press, 1975.

BOUDREAU, L. Transcendental meditation and yoga as reciprocal inhibitors. *Journal of Behavioral Therapy & Experimental Psychiatry*, 1973, *3*, 97-98.

CARRINGTON, P., & EPHRON, H.S. Meditation as an adjunct to psychotherapy. In Arieti, S. (Ed.), *New dimensions in psychiatry: a world view.* New York: Wiley & Sons, 1975.

FERGUSON, P., & GOWAN, C. G. Psychological findings on transcendental meditation. *Journal of Humanistic Psychology*, (in press).

GELLHORN, E., & KIELY, W. F. Mystical states of consciousness: neurophysiological and clinical aspects. *Journal of Nervous and Mental Disease*, 1972, *154* (6), 399-405.

GLUECK, R. C. & STROEBEL, C. F. Biofeedback and meditation in the treatment of psychiatric illnesses. In Masserman, J. H. (Ed.), *Current psychiatric therapies* (Vol. 15). New York: Grune & Stratton, 1975.

HONSBERGER, R., & WILSON, A. F. The effects of transcendental meditation upon bronchial asthma. *Clinical Research*, 1973, *21*, 278.

KANELLAKOS, D. P., & LUKAS, J. S. *The psychobiology of transcendental meditation: literature survey.* Reading, Pa.: W. A. Benjamin Co., 1974.

ORME-JOHNSON, D. W. Autonomic stability and Transcendental Meditation. *Psychosomatic Medicine*, 1973, *35* (4), 341-349.

*A much more detailed bibliography can be obtained on the Transcendental Meditation program from the Bloomfield et al. reference herein.

ORME-JOHNSON, D. W., & FARROW, J. T. (Eds.), *Scientific research on the transcendental meditation program: collected papers* (Vol. 1). New York: M.I.U. Press, 1975.

SEEMAN, W., NIDICH, S., & BANTA, T. H. Influence of transcendental meditation on a measure of self-actualization. *Journal of Counseling Psychology*, 1972, *19* (3), 184–187.

SHAFII, M. Adaptive and therapeutic aspects of meditation. *International Journal of Psychoanalytic Psychotherapy*, 1973, *2* (3), 364–382.

SHAFII, M. Meditation and marijuana. *American Journal of Psychiatry*, 1974, *131* (1), 60–63.

WALLACE, R. K. Physiological effects of transcendental meditation. *Science*, 1970, *167*, 1751–1754.

WALLACE, R. K. Physiological effects of transcendental meditation: a proposed fourth state of consciousness. (Doctoral dissertation, University of California, Los Angeles, 1970).

WALLACE, R. K., BENSON, H., & WILSON, A. F. A wakeful hypometabolic physiologic state. *American Journal of Physiology*, 1971, *221* (3), 795–799.

WALLACE, R. K., & BENSON, H. The physiology of meditation. *Scientific American*, 1972, *226* (2), 84–90.

WENGER, M. A., CLEMENS, T. L., & CULLENS, T. D. Autonomic functions in patients with gastrointestinal and dermatological disorders. *Psychosomatic Medicine*, 1962, *24*, 267–273.

WEST, L. J. Transcendental meditation and other non-professional psychotherapies. In Freedman, A. M., & Kaplan, H. I. (Eds.), *Comprehensive textbook of psychiatry* (2nd ed.). Baltimore: Williams & Wilkins, 1974.

8

The Sexual Therapy
of Masters and Johnson

Alexander Runciman

Before the publication of Masters and Johnson's books *Human Sexual Response* (1966) and *Human Sexual Inadequacy* (1970), therapy for sexual dysfunction was basically the same as for any other psychological dysfunction: it dealt with the early childhood conditioning and with repressed emotional trauma. The research reported in *Human Sexual Inadequacy* provided a factual basis for a form of sex therapy that was far different, and far more successful, than the psychiatric model in which the therapist sat back and asked, " . . . and how did that make you feel?" Good popularly written summaries of the Masters and Johnson books may be found in Brecher & Brecher (1966) and in Belliveau & Richter (1970).

When I first joined Masters and Johnson as a co-therapist in 1967 I spent many hours listening to tape recordings of their pioneering sex therapy sessions, and then teamed with Virginia Johnson to work with a series of dysfunctional couples. In order to become a co-therapist at the Reproductive Biology Research Foundation I had to revise my vocabulary and thinking to eliminate harsh and misleading terms such as "frigidity." I also had to expand my perception of human sexual interaction to include the details of what happens physiologically, as well as psychologically. In fact, I came to the conclusion that misinformation about the physical aspects of sex was at the root of many psychological impairments. Therefore,

"The Sexual Therapy of Masters and Johnson," by Alexander Runciman, Ph. D. © 1976 by Alexander Runciman. This article appears in print for the first time in this volume.

Alexander Runciman is a marriage counselor in private practice and Associate Professor of Sociology, San Fernando Valley State University. He was the first social psychologist to join the team of Masters and Johnson, authors of *Human Sexual Inadequacy*.

I now consider it essential for anyone with an interest in the field to start with the basic physiology of the human sexual response, for the purpose of dispelling myths, as well as to obtain useful information.

In our culture, most people grow up believing that there is a fundamental difference in the way men and women function sexually. It is obvious that there are some physical differences between males and females, but the Masters and Johnson research has demonstrated that the male-female similarities are at least as significant as the differences. They found, for example, that there is a human sexual response cycle that is basically the same for both men and women. Although individual differences and circumstances may affect or even block portions of the cycle, the four phases are consistently observable in all fully functioning males and females.

SEXUAL RESPONSE CYCLE

1. *The excitement phase* occurs as a result of whatever is sexually exciting to an individual. If the stimulation is terminated, or no longer enjoyed, the response cycle ceases without going on to

2. *The plateau phase* a state of intense sexual tension which can be prolonged or even interrupted, but which usually is released by

3. *Orgasm*, the involuntary climactic spasms which are the result of sexual tensions reaching a peak; orgasm is followed by

4. *The resolution phase*, during which the sexual tensions lessen and the body returns to its normal unstimulated state.

In both males and females, this sexual response cycle involves increased muscle tension (myotonia) and blood vessel engorgement (vasocongestion), particularly in the genital organs. Furthermore, these basic physiological responses follow the same pattern, regardless of the source of stimulation or the nature of the sexual contact. There are a few imaginative females who are able to fantasize all the way to orgasm, going through all four phases of the response cycle without a sex partner.

The manifestation of this basic response cycle takes different forms in the male and female because of the obvious genital differences. (See Masters & Johnson, 1966, for a careful explication of the differences.)

PROBLEMS OF MALE SEXUAL FUNCTIONING

Impotence, the inability of a male to achieve erection or to maintain it long enough for full coitus, is a matter of great significance in general happiness as well as specifically sexual fulfillment. Many males who suffer impotence for the first time have reactions that range all the way from mild anxiety to such severe depression that they are practically unable to function. It is unfortunate that more American women aren't aware of the importance of most men's attachment to their sexual functioning. Too many times I have heard a wife say right in front of her husband, "So, he can't always get it up; that's no big deal. We have a good marriage — I don't see what the problem is." Many women simply do not realize that when a man has been able to have erections easily and then suddenly cannot, this is often felt as failure and may be very traumatic.

There are two types of impotence: primary and secondary. Primary impotence exists when a man has *never* had an erection sufficient for penetration. In secondary impotence there has been success at intercourse at least one time previously, but erection is not now possible.

There are some physiological reasons for impotence such as diabetic conditions, low-grade anemia, intake of certain drugs, or brain or spinal cord damage, but these represent only about 2 to 3 percent of cases of impotence. It is usually easy to rule out a physiological cause. When a man who is complaining of impotence says that he often awakes in the morning with an erection, or discloses, "I'm making it with my secretary, but I can't get it up with my wife," then there is no need to look for physiological causes. If erections take place under any circumstances, his plumbing is obviously in order. This is selective impotence, which simply means he can function in one situation but not in another, and the cause is clearly psychological.

One factor leading to impotence is the pattern of the husband-wife relationship. Clearly, we often choose our partners for reasons we are not aware of, rather than obvious ones, such as: "He's handsome and a good provider"; "He comes from a nice family"; "He swept me off my feet"; or "She's beautiful and refined"; "She'll make a good mother." We may, instead, find partners who complement our psychological needs. For instance, when a very passive male marries a very aggressive woman, they may have satisfying sexual functioning for a number of years, but if he tires of having her always run the show, he may withdraw. And as *he* withdraws, his penis withdraws, perhaps never to function again with that particular woman, unless their basic passive-aggressive relationship changes. A very aggressive male and a dependent type of female may marry and get along just fine for years — until one day the husband has a need for help and support. His wife probably hasn't the strength or inclination to provide it; and that can be the beginning of an impotence problem.

A therapist must also be alert to such problems as three-way interactions in a marital situation. Many middle-aged couples become involved in such difficulties. For example, there may be a teaming-up of the mother with her teenage son against the father that triggers the father's impotence. Other alliances may cause sexual dysfunctions in the mother.

The "middle-years crisis" can also be a factor in impotence. In our culture, the middle-aged man is often expected to be all things to all people: a good wage earner, highly productive in his work, a great father and husband, a super everything. There is only one problem: he doesn't have the same energy level he had twenty years earlier, yet more than ever is expected of him. And because ours is a youth-oriented culture, the pressure for performance on the job becomes greater as a man gets older; he feels threatened by younger employees, despite the advantage of his experience.

For the male, top-notch performance is demanded in every quarter, so that even one "failure" tends to make him overly fearful of subsequent failures. A typical example is the man who goes to a party with his wife and begins drinking too much. His wife fusses at him all evening, to which he responds, "I know what I'm doing; leave me alone." In the car going home there is dead silence. His wife slams the bedroom door. He takes another drink but hopes that everything will straighten out if they engage in sex. (The combination of an upset within the family unit and too much alcohol is frequent.) When he tries to have intercourse he can't get an erection. The following day there is more silence. He is irritable, but he tells himself he is not worried; tonight he will make love to his wife and everything will be all right. But he postpones attempting sex again out of his underlying fear that everything will *not* be all right; eventually, he is consumed with the thought. Finally, under a great deal of internal pressure, he tries again, and does fail. Now he is in the middle of the "fear of failure" syndrome.

When a man starts the sequence of failure, he begins to avoid making further attempts because it is so agonizing to fail. It becomes easier just to avoid all attempts at intercourse, and that may lead to permanent dysfunction. The best guarantee of continued and satisfying sexual functioning is regularity of intercourse with an interested and involved partner. But because many men cannot abide any failure to perform up to their ideal expectation of themselves, it is difficult for them to risk continuing to attempt sexual activity, the very thing that may help them.

Premature ejaculation is occasionally associated with failures of erection, but it is a serious problem in its own right. Clinical definitions of a premature ejaculator have generally specified durations after vaginal entry — for example, a man is a premature ejaculator if he cannot control ejaculation for at least one minute after entry. Masters and Johnson (1970), however, defined a premature ejaculator as a man who is unable to delay ejaculation long enough for his partner to have orgasm 50 percent of the time. They defined premature ejaculation in terms of the mutual process because of their consistent emphasis upon the relationship aspects of sexual behavior and findings like those of Kinsey et al. (1948) to the effect that three of four men reach orgasm within two minutes of insertion. The definition of Masters and Johnson is not fully adequate either because of the great range of orgasmic responsiveness in women; in the extreme, it specifies every man as a premature ejaculator who has a nonorgasmic partner.

Many premature ejaculators have a history of intercourse in situations in which they have had to be concerned about discovery. If they have had their first experiences in the back seat of a car, they may have feared being caught, or if they have had frequent encounters with prostitutes, they may have developed the habit of getting it over with as quickly as possible. The result is that sex becomes a frustrating experience, and they tend to avoid situations in which they will be expected to relax and enjoy sexual activity for an extended period of time.

Premature ejaculation has serious consequences for both men and women when it continues over a long period of time. It is a condition that can become progressively worse. Men who rationalize that premature ejaculation is a result of circumcision or noncircumcision or some other condition about which they can do nothing are only fooling themselves and denying themselves and their partner satisfying sexual functioning.

PROBLEMS OF FEMALE SEXUAL FUNCTIONING

It is amazing that so many women enjoy sex fully and are able to achieve orgasm, considering the severe degree of negative conditioning that has historically been part of female training in our culture. Frequently, a nonorgasmic female's sexual history reveals how little she has been told and how cold was the family's sexual atmosphere. A general taboo against sex has often created a situation of anxiety rather than pleasure in sexual fantasy.

The *Playboy* survey in the early 1970s (Hunt, 1974) reported that 15 percent of wives never achieve orgasm. The fact that this percentage is well below the 28 percent figure reported by the Kinsey survey (Kinsey et al., 1953) conducted about twenty years earlier indicates that sexual education for women (and men) is improving.

Disturbances in female sexual functioning include coldness, unresponsiveness, and inability to achieve orgasm or ability to do so only rarely. Before the Masters and Johnson studies, "frigidity" was almost always used to name this type of dysfunction. As a result of their efforts to take account of the woman's perspective, however, the emphasis is now on the resulting failure to achieve orgasm (that is, to go beyond the plateau phase), regardless of the circumstances preceding the failure. And that seems a good direction.

As implied in the opening paragraphs of this section, the basis of nonorgasmic response is, almost without exception, psychological. (Indeed, the vast majority of sexual dysfunctions *in both sexes* result from psychological rather than organic factors.)

In the course of taking the histories of many nonorgasmic females, I have occasionally found that there has been a rape or seduction with actual insertion of the penis at an early age. Research (MacDonald, 1971) has shown, in fact, that in at least 40 percent of cases of rape, the violator is a relative, friend, acquaintance, or employer of the victim. Since this kind of adult-child sex activity is taboo in our society, it is a very traumatic experience and is often blocked from consciousness.

Another experience common in the past of nonorgasmic women is that of observing the mother resisting the father's sexual advances, either subtly or by direct physical resistance. The message transmitted is that sex is distasteful, which may indeed supplement direct verbal expression to that effect.

The literature is full of examples of the effect upon children of sleeping with parents of the opposite sex and having sexual feelings aroused. These feelings are usually suppressed along with all sexual feelings, because of the associated guilt.

Harsh toilet training is another factor that can contribute to difficulty in female sexual functioning. Some mothers are so insistent about regularity that they force enemas on their children. The insertion process can be painful, it is not surprising when a girl grows up associating this pain with insertion of the penis into the vaginal barrel.

Lurid tales of child bearing can also have a harmful effect. A mother may say, "Oh, what I went through to have you! I hope *you* don't have to go through that!" If a child hears that kind of talk often enough she will finally reason that intercourse leads to painful childbirth. Consequently she may resist having intercourse, or her sexual relations will be so filled with fear that she won't come close to having an orgasm.

In some cases a nonorgasmic female has had a history of one or more premarital pregnancies that ended in emotionally painful ways — abortion, or giving up the child. Other factors that may contribute to female sexual dysfunction are preoccupation and fatigue. A woman who is thinking, during intercourse, about what to give the kids for lunch the next day or worrying about the grocery money hasn't much chance of enjoying a fulfilling sexual experience. Some women have simply never developed the ability to center their awareness on their own body and their own pleasure. There is a famous joke about a woman who noticed aloud during lovemaking that her husband had painted the ceiling—such an observation could hardly have brought sexual pleasure to either partner!

One difficulty for nonorgasmic women is the still-pervasive myth that they are somehow abnormal if they do not have what is termed a "vaginal orgasm." There is still a great deal of controversy about this, even though it has been shown that the triggering for the female orgasm is identical whether the stimulation is directly on the clitoris or elsewhere. Psychoanalytic theory is at least partly responsible for perpetuating the fable that the only "right" kind of orgasm is stimulated by penile thrusting. And a woman who doesn't respond to that may believe there is something wrong with her. If a woman wants to have her orgasms triggered by vaginal penetration, she can usually learn how to achieve this, and also learn to have orgasms any other way she may want to. However, it is important for both men and women to realize that a satisfying orgasm can take place by various methods of stimulation.

Another factor, one that applies to male as well as female sexual inadequacy, is severity of religious training. Masters and Johnson (1970) have convincingly shown how harsh religious orthodoxy may lead to sexual dysfunction.

Finally, it should be noted that it is possible for women to be nonorgasmic selectively. Some, for example, can have orgasm with masturbation but not with intercourse, or with a man met at a cocktail party but not with the husband. This is called "situational orgasmic dysfunction."

THERAPY PROCEDURE

The basis of the success of the Masters and Johnson sexual therapy is that a man and wife are treated as a unit. A sexual problem is never just *his* problem or *her* problem; it is a shared problem. It now seems ridiculous that in years past therapy for sexual dysfunction in a marital unit was often provided for only one of the partners. This approach was seldom successful. For example, if a man goes through analysis for a long period to try to solve his impotence problem and his wife is not included in the treatment, he obviously keeps returning to the same marital situation that contributed to or even caused the impotence in the first place.

The second principle is that there be a male-female therapy team. This is for the purpose of having someone of the same sex with whom both the husband and the wife can identify. They need to feel that there is someone there who can understand their unique feelings as a man or a woman.

The first step in therapy is usually for the male therapist to take a thorough medical and sex history of the husband and for the female therapist to do likewise with the wife. On the second appointment this process is reversed—the woman therapist takes the husband's history and the male therapist takes the wife's. This provides a means of checking to make sure that nothing has been left out, and of identifying attitudes that may be expressed differently depending upon whether the therapist is a male or a female. This may be important in determining unrecognized or unspoken attitudes. For example, if a wife is able to talk freely with the woman therapist, and becomes nervous, inhibited, and tense relating to the male therapist, this tells a great deal about her degree of comfort or anxiety with persons of her own or the opposite sex.

A medical examination is a standard requirement before sexual therapy. It is important to determine drug usage habits, because drugs are possible causes of sexual dysfunction, especially tranquilizers and other compounds that affect the central nervous system.

After the sex histories and the medical examinations are completed, there is what is called a roundtable. During this session, the male and female therapists discuss with the couple their initial opinions of the marital interaction. This does not deal with sexual function, but primarily concerns how the husband and wife are seen to affect each other by their attitudes and actions in the overall marriage situation. This information is used as the basis for the specific program of therapy appropriate for each particular couple.

At the roundtable, the parties have the option of disagreeing with the therapists' observations. There is no obligation for them to continue—in fact, the therapy cannot be beneficial if they don't agree that changes are needed in the marital relationship itself. If there is no major disagreement, the roundtable is directed toward achieving a common goal that will be shared by both the marital couple and the therapists.

Following the roundtable, the couple begins the program called "sensate focus," the first stage in the therapy program. This is used with every couple, no matter what the presenting problem. Sensate focus simply consists of learning to touch one another and to communicate what feels good or what doesn't feel good. During this stage the couple is told specifically to avoid intercourse and touching of genital regions, or the breasts of the female, is prohibited. The purpose is to allow the husband and wife to discover the numerous sensitive and sensual parts of their bodies other than genitals and breasts, and to begin to communicate with each other about the parts of the body that may be easier to talk about than the genital areas. The person who is doing the touching receives instructions from his partner (up, down, left, higher, faster, stronger, lighter, etc.).

For a male with an impotence problem, the pressure of performance is removed — he is simply learning what feels good and how to communicate this. At the beginning stage of sensate focus such a male may actually become erect because he has been specifically told that he must not attempt penetration.

Some people go through the first stage quite rapidly, while others seem to bog down. Some are so anxious to succeed that they try to hurry through each step in the process, thus losing a great deal of reinforcement. Also, they may discover new problems in their interaction which are difficult for them to admit they have. Therefore, the therapists need to carefully evaluate when a couple is ready to proceed to the next stage.

The second stage, after the couple has learned how successfully to communicate what pleasures them, consists of mutual stimulation of the genitals, but again without any attempt to engage in intercourse. The wife and husband are specifically told not to strive for orgasms but to learn and to tell each other what feels good in regard to genital stimulation.

The nondemand position is used for genital stimulation of the female so that the man has free access to her breasts and genital area, and so neither partner will feel under any pressure to have this contact lead them into intercourse. The man rests comfortably in a sitting position with his partner leaning her back comfortably against his chest. In this position the woman can direct her partner's touch by moving his hands how and where she wants them, and by instructing him verbally. She has complete control and is under no pressure to reciprocate. In this manner she can learn to experience the good sensations in her body.

This is a learning experience for the male, too. Many men move directly to the clitoris, which they stimulate vigorously without realizing that other kinds of touch are usually necessary before the clitoris engorges and is ready for stimulation.

After a couple has completed these two stages, the therapy can take various directions, depending upon the presenting problem.

In the case of impotence there is a series of procedures used in which the female learns to stimulate the penis in specific ways as instructed by the therapist. When her partner does get an erection, it is she who makes the insertion. The woman learns what to do and when to initiate insertion and movement. In this way the pressure to perform that leads to impotence is reversed — i.e., the woman assumes some of the responsibility. This release from performance pressure enables him to relax and enjoy, and incidentally "perform" successfully.

Figure 8-1 The nondemand position for female stimulation.

For premature ejaculation, the "squeeze technique," which requires communication and cooperation between the partners, has been found to be very effective. After a man achieves an erection there comes a point called "ejaculatory inevitability," which is knowledge that he is about to "come." Ejaculation takes place only seconds after he has felt that sensation; he has no control over this. With the squeeze technique, the man must let his partner know when he wants her to squeeze, just before the moment of ejaculatory inevitability. The woman places the index finger of her hand on the glans just above the coronal ridge of his penis; the middle finger is placed just below the coronal ridge, and the thumb is placed on the frenulum. In this position she squeezes the penis hard for about three to four seconds or longer until the male feels that his urge to ejaculate has subsided. There is no discomfort or pain associated with squeezing as long as the penis is erect. This process can be repeated as many times as desired. Couples usually have to use the squeeze technique for several weeks before the male's tendency toward premature ejaculation is reversed. The procedure is done first without penetration.

When the technique has been mastered without penetration, then the woman assumes the superior position and the couple practises its use with penetration. When her mate tells her, she raises herself off the penis and squeezes, then she inserts the penis again. In this way a man can have a total of fifteen or twenty minutes of vaginal containment and thrusting, with his mate squeezing as often as necessary.

This technique has been used since ancient times, but has not been generally known or used in modern America except by prostitutes. Some of these women were used as original research subjects by Masters and Johnson.

If the presenting problem is nonorgasmic response in the female, there is a step-by-step process the couple is instructed to follow. It is important for the female to take the superior mounting position. The reason for this is that most women have been pinned underneath their partners for so many years, and have never really learned to know what their body wants to do. With the penis fully erected and the vaginal area well-lubricated, the woman inserts the penis under instructions to remain still and experience the pleasurable feel of vaginal dilation without orgasmic demand.

The process continues over days of repetition through phases of mild female thrusting, mild male thrusting under female verbal control, mutual thrusting with a period of separation for general caressing, and attempts to break the pattern of unilaterally initiated and demanding pelvic thrusting.

Toward the end of therapy, the lateral coital position is generally recommended for all couples, regardless of the presenting problem. In this the man lies on his back with his wife supine over him at a 30-degree angle with her left leg outside his right leg, her right thigh upon his left thigh and right leg between his two, his head and her face resting on pillows. The major part of her weight is on her left knee. This position provides maximum freedom for experimentation and offers the best chance of ejaculatory control. Masters and Johnson report that couples subsequently choose the position 75 percent of the time they have intercourse.

The central theme in the Masters and Johnson therapy program is the necessity for continued communication between the partners. While physical instruction and practice are important elements, greater stress is placed upon the relationship between the partners and re-education of the ways of satisfying sexual functioning. These elements of the therapeutic process are in evidence from the start of history taking and roundtable, but they come into focus when some improvement has been shown as a result of the physical practice, when the couple has overcome certain negative feelings and becomes amenable to this focus.

Perhaps the key to success of this type of therapy is that the therapists consciously take the role of authority figures. When patients' sex histories

Figure 8-2   Lateral coital position.

indicate ignorance, misinformation, and negative conditioning — and
everyone who comes for therapy falls into this category to a degree — the
therapists make a point of identifying these sources of difficulty and then
explaining that the patients do not need to let these things from the past

continue to be negative influences forevermore. For example, the wife may be asked to become an active member of the sex team, taking the initiative to do many things which she has felt to be taboo, such as touching herself, stroking the penis, or letting her body feel the pleasure of being caressed. By following these direct, yet permissive instructions from the therapist authority figures, a woman can recondition herself in the here and now, and break through her inhibitions.

And, as necessary, attitudes and mutual behavior are explored in such areas as religious and early childhood conditioning, drinking habits, general inadequacy and dependence, use of sex as a weapon or as a tool for ulterior purposes, and unrealistic sex fears.

THE RESULTS OF TREATMENT

In their treatment of impotence, Masters and Johnson (1970) report a success rate of 59.4 percent for the primary type and 73.8 percent for the secondary type. Premature ejaculation is the easiest of the male dysfunctions to treat. Treatment has resulted in a 97.8 percent success rate; indeed, Masters and Johnson argue that this problem could be eliminated in a decade of widespread use of their technique.

Of 342 nonorgasmic women, Masters and Johnson reported a success rate of 80.7 percent. In some of the failures the marital relationship was considered hopelessly destructive.

High success rates were reported, too, for two sexual inadequacies not covered in this chapter: ejaculatory incompetence (the inability to ejaculate while the penis is in the woman's vagina) — 82.4 percent, and vaginismus (a condition in which any sexual approach produces a powerful and often painful contraction of the muscles surrounding the vaginal barrel) — 100 percent.

REFERENCES

BELLIVEAU, F., & RICHTER, L. *Understanding human sexual inadequacy.* New York: Bantam Books, 1970

BRECHER, R. & E. (Eds.), *An analysis of human sexual response.* Boston: Little, Brown and Co., 1966.

HUNT, M. *Sexual behavior in the 1970's.* Chicago: Playboy Press, 1974.

KINSEY, A. C., POMEROY, W. B., & MARTIN, C. E. *Sexual behavior in the human male.* Philadelphia: Saunders Co., 1948.

KINSEY, A. C., POMEROY, W. B., MARTIN, C. E., & GEBHARD, P. H. *Sexual behavior in the human female.* Philadelphia: Saunders Co., 1953.

MACDONALD, J. M. *Rape: offenders and their victims.* Springfield, Ill.: Charles C. Thomas, 1971.

MASTERS, W. H. & JOHNSON, V. E. *Human sexual response.* Boston: Little, Brown and Co., 1966.

MASTERS, W. H. & JOHNSON, V. E. *Human sexual inadequacy.* Boston: Little, Brown and Co., 1970.

9

Implosive Therapy: An Alternative To Systematic Desensitization

Lowell H. Storms

Before I discuss Implosive Therapy in depth, I will consider three other major approaches to desensitization. All use the technique of gradual or not-so-gradual exposure to fear stimuli — *repetitively*. This is an important point: there must be repetition. There is no doubt that certain of these desensitization techniques are extremely effective in reducing neurotic fears. It is my position that Implosive Therapy in particular is of value to people suffering from fear and anxiety. (For our purposes here, we shall equate fear and anxiety. Anxiety is less clearly attached to a specific stimulus, but both fear and anxiety may originate in an association of painful events with some other stimuli.)

The current categorization of the types of desensitization includes (1) *in vivo* ("in life") or contact desensitization; (2) systematic desensitization, also called deconditioning or reciprocal inhibition; (3) assertiveness training, an approach that involves modeling and behavior rehearsal; and (4) Implosive Therapy, also referred to as flooding.

"Implosive Therapy: An Alternative to Systematic Desensitization," by Lowell H. Storms, Ph. D. © 1976 by Lowell H. Storms. This article appears in print for the first time in this volume.

Lowell Storms is Professor of Psychiatry at the University of California, San Diego School of Medicine and Clinical Psychologist at the San Diego Veterans Administration Hospital. He teaches behavior therapy, psychological assessment, and abnormal psychology to residents and interns and also supervises individual and group psychotherapy. He also carries on a variety of clinical activities and conducts research on schizophrenia, behavior therapy, and assessment.

Contact or In Vivo Desensitization

Mary Cover Jones (1924a, 1924b) is a pioneer of desensitization approaches and a founder of behavior therapy. In a well-known study of fear she helped a 3-year-old child, Peter, to lose his fear of furry things. This fear had generalized out of a specific fear of rabbits. Jones treated the child by gradually exposing him to the feared stimulus; she brought a rabbit closer and closer to him while he was playing until he could tolerate the animal quite close to him, and finally could pet and hold it. Eventually he completely lost his fears of furry things.

In situations in which fears have been displaced from other, general fearfulness or conflict situations, it is often possible to use this gradual contact technique in helping people overcome fears. For a person who is afraid of heights, or elevators, for example, the therapist can slowly acclimate the patient to the fear stimulus. He (or she) might gradually take the patient up a few steps at a time, later encouraging that person to go alone. Then the therapist might accompany the patient to a higher elevation — some outside stairs or a fire escape, for example. In this way a toleration of greater and greater heights is achieved.

Sexual fears are treated by people like Masters and Johnson using contact desensitization methods (see the previous chapter). A man with an impotence problem, for example, is often instructed just to lie with his wife, caressing and stroking with explicit directions *not* to engage in sex. Gradually, the man becomes comfortable in the various stages of sexual intimacy, and after his fears have been eased, he is finally encouraged to engage in intercourse. This method has had high success in sexual therapy.

Systematic Desensitization

Systematic desensitization, also called reciprocal inhibition or deconditioning, was popularized by Joseph Wolpe (1958). This technique involves pairing relaxation with imaginal representations of feared stimuli. That is, a person is told to visualize or imagine feared situations. This differs from in vivo desensitization, which involves direct and real exposure to fear-inspiring stimuli. The patient is first trained in relaxation. Then an imagined hierarchy is developed. If a person is afraid of ambulances and hospitals, for example, his hierarchy might include seeing an ambulance in the distance, seeing it come around the corner, hearing it come around the corner with the siren on, then imagining riding in the ambulance going fast with a patient in the back, then being the patient, and so on. Each scene in the hierarchy, beginning with the least frightening, is described while the patient is relaxed; it is presented repeatedly for increasing lengths of time until no more anxiety is reported.

There are many recent studies indicating the effectiveness of systematic desensitization. In fact a study by Paul (1966, 1968) is widely cited as a model for therapy evaluation. Variations of systematic desensitization have also been studied. P. J. Lang (1970), for example, has developed an interesting technique in which he uses a "device for automated desensitization," or DAD. DAD is a computer tied to tape recorders. This computer gives the instructions to the patient; it describes a scene, gives relaxation instructions, then re-describes the scene and advances to another scene when the patient reports no fear.

Wolpe believes that responses other than relaxation can be *substituted* for fear. In his work on assertiveness training, he has shown that assertive responses are incompatible with fear. There is evidence that sexual responses, too, can be substituted.

Assertiveness Training

Wolpe's (1969) technique of assertiveness training sometimes simply involves exhorting a person to go out and stand up to his wife or boss or friend (if the outcome is likely to be positive) or tell somebody what he wants. But there are also ways of teaching assertiveness that involve behavioral rehearsal. In these situations, the patient *pretends* he is asserting himself in various situations (see Chapter 11). This technique involves desensitization because very unassertive people are often frightened of doing anything that might offend other people. They may even fear asking for things which they have a legitimate right to. Desensitization in assertion training is a way of encouraging such a person gradually to do the things he is afraid of doing.

Assertion techniques probably involve some suggestion or effects of expectations induced by instructions. In one study by Leitenberg, Agras, Barlow, & Oliveau (1969), desensitization worked better *with* suggestions that the therapy would work than *without* these suggestions. But even techniques that are much slower, like conventional psychotherapy, also involve a lot of suggestion (see Chapter 1) so suggestion is clearly not the only reason for success.

The relationship with the therapist may play a part in desensitization approaches, but it probably works most importantly as a motivating force. A well-developed relationship is clearly not essential. Lang, Melamed, & Hart (1970) demonstrated that desensitization using the DAD device led to effective reduction of fears. For a client using DAD, there is some initial contact with the therapist. The patient is given some suggestions about effectiveness, but when he sits down with a computer and a tape recorder, he begins the major part of his therapy — with a machine. An article by Kahn and Baker (1968) reports a study in which people were given instructions and kits, then told to go home and follow the instructions to reduce their fears. There was some suggestion involved but very little contact with the therapist. For these cooperative subjects the do-it-yourself method worked as well as standard systematic desensitization. Often the phenomenon of relief of some anxiety occurs when a person has found a definite course of action he can take. This is true of any kind of therapeutic approach. However, research indicates that the effects of desensitization are stronger and more lasting than this initial relief. People can seek help with the expectation of finding it and be disappointed. A definite course of action alone probably won't alleviate distress.

IMPLOSIVE THERAPY

Implosive Therapy is a technique for overcoming fears that involves an apparent paradox. It reduces fears by arousing as much fear as possible. My first acquaintance with implosive therapy occurred when I was asked to read the manuscript of a book called *Modes and Morals of Psychotherapy* by Perry London (1964). In the book, London contrasted the action therapies (behavior therapies) with insight therapies. One of the action therapies he talked about was the Implosive Therapy of T. G. Stampfl, none of whose work had been reported in the literature at that time. Later I heard an audiotape of Stampfl doing Implosive Therapy with a patient. The patient was groaning and sobbing as Stampfl described a snake going into her mouth, biting her tongue, slithering down her throat, and eating out her insides. I was impressed and a little horrified. My initial reactions were, "Why scare a patient half to death? Why should this work?"

Later, in 1966, a series of articles started appearing showing the effectiveness of Implosive Therapy. These impressed me enough so that I decided to try it when an appropriate case appeared.

Implosive Therapy is also known as flooding, especially among English writers (Marks, Boulougouris, & Marset, 1971, for example), and is related to *response prevention*. In 1970, M. Baum did a series of studies and a theoretical review article on response prevention as a means of overcoming avoidance behavior. Briefly, response prevention can be described by the following example. Suppose you put a rat in a cage with a divider so that he can jump over to another side of the box. If you shock him on one side, he will learn to jump over to escape the shock, and if you give him a signal indicating when the shock is going to come, he will learn to jump over whenever the signal comes on and therefore always avoid the shock. Even if you turn off the shock but keep using the warning signal, he will just keep jumping over. To get him to stop this jumping, this avoidance response, once the shock has been discontinued, you have to keep him in the box. Put up a wall. Don't let him get out when the signal sounds. He will just sit there and be scared for a long period of time, but he will learn not to avoid. Baum has found that the rat must be kept in the box for at least five minutes. Better results are obtained if the animal is forced to stay even longer.

In a related 1956 study by Bersh, Notterman, and Schoenfeld, human subjects were taught to lift their index fingers from a key on signal to avoid receiving a shock. Of course, they learned to do this very well, automatically lifting the finger when the signal went on. When shock was discontinued, they kept lifting their fingers at the signal and they kept having strong autonomic reactions. To get them to stop the avoiding reaction, the index fingers of half the subjects were tied to the key. When that was done, most of them extinguished — that is, stopped avoiding — and a conditioned cardiac response was extinguished also. Subjects who had not had their fingers tied down kept on avoiding.

Rationale

This brings us to the rationale for Implosive Therapy. Rationales for extinction in general have to do with the Pavlovian or classical model of learning. In the well-known example of Pavlov's dogs, a tone, the conditioned stimulus (CS) shortly precedes the presentation of food powder, the unconditioned stimulus (UCS). After a number of pairings of the tone and the food powder the dog's salivation response, which is the natural or unconditioned response (UCR) to food, occurs to the tone as well as to the presentation of food powder.

Another example, more analogous to the development of clinical anxiety or fear, finds the pairing of a buzzer (CS) with shock (UCS) given to animals, generating the withdrawal and arousal associated with shock (UCR) to the buzzer as well (CR).

Now, two factor theories of how neuroses develop include another step. First, there is the Pavlovian or classical conditioning of fear by repeated pairing of some cue with a painful stimulus. Then defensive behaviors develop on an instrumental or operant conditioning basis; that is, successful avoidance of the fear-producing situation is rewarded through the reduction of fear.

This theoretical explanation of the development of fear may be clearer in a clinical example. Many phobic individuals are afraid of specific items or situations. An explanation of a phobic's development of a fear of elevators might go something like this. Some painful, unpleasant, or traumatic event (UCS) occurs in the presence of an elevator (CS), and the phobic associates the anxiety of the unpleasant situation (UCR) with the elevator and begins to avoid elevators (CR). Each time the phobic encounters an elevator, he avoids it and thus reduces his fear. The association of the elevator with something painful is classical conditioning. The fear reduction resulting from avoidance of the elevator is operant conditioning. (The avoidance may continue for such a long time that the phobic no longer remembers why he fears elevators.)

Stampfl's belief is that the fear must be extinguished by repeated presentations of the conditioned stimulus. Though this initially generates considerable anxiety and discomfort, it is in this way that the client can learn that the conditioned stimulus is no longer followed by or paired with the unconditioned stimulus. The elevator phobic described above, if forced to ride the elevator rather than avoid it, would discover that there was no longer any connection between elevators (CS) and unpleasant experiences (UCS). Stampfl points out that in desensitization approaches, one is often dealing with stimuli other than the original conditioned stimuli. For example, if one had become anxious due to a critical rejecting mother, other critical women or other authority figures may serve as approximations to the original stimulus (stimulus generalization). Thus, a story will be visualized with women criticizing and humiliating the individual.

Stampfl's explanation of what occurs in Implosive Therapy has not gone unchallenged. Other theoretical rationales have been offered. It has been suggested that Implosive Therapy may function as negative practice. That is, the client is satiated with the repeated presentations of the noxious stimulus and abandons the fear through exhaustion. Other theorists suggest that Implosive Therapy works because clients are reassured or given courage when they discover that they don't fall apart when they become fearful.

The Technique

Now, how is Implosive Therapy done? First, Stampfl recommends two evaluative interviews with the patient. The first interview is generally exploratory, with some history taking. This is facilitated by having the patient take home a life history questionnaire to fill out. Then the focus in the initial interview can be on the genesis of the particular fears that the patient has — what things the patient is afraid of, what are the specifics of these fears, when did they start, and how have they affected his or her life.

In the second interview Stampfl recommends further investigation of fears to obtain as much detailed information about the patient's fears as possible. Inferences are made about these fears from what the therapist knows about the patient's history and his general behaviors or modes of adapting to life situations. Core conflicts are inferred and the therapist formulates them in ways that are often somewhat psychoanalytic, such as castration anxiety or an Oedipus complex. The therapist can formulate core conflicts in other ways in terms of early childhood learning experiences, repetitive ways of relating to the mother or father, for example. For example, did the patient have a very punitive father or rejecting mother, or did the mother discourage certain kinds of behavior by belittling the patient?

Stampfl makes the inferences from the information he gets from the patient for his own conceptualization of the problem, and he uses these inferences directly in the story he then presents for the patient to imagine. For example, for a patient with a fear of heights, the therapist might hypothesize a fear of bodily injury in general. He might tell the patient, "Imagine climbing the stairs in a tall building; look down, and notice how frightening it is and how small things are as you go further and further up the tall building and look over the top. Now imagine getting pushed, or jumping off. Feel the wind against your face; see the windows going by; experience the splatter on the concrete, and bones breaking, and guts falling out."

An instrument I give to the patient in the first interview is something called the Fear Survey Schedule (Wolpe, 1969), which lists 122 things that a person might be afraid of, such as dead people, automobiles, open spaces, heights, birds, insects, being criticized, feeling foolish, feeling rejected, and being disapproved of. A person checks "Not at All," "A Little," "A Fair Amount," "Much" or "Very Much." The completed schedule serves as the focus for the interview; inquiries can be made regarding all the items in the "Much" or "Very Much" categories, focusing on specifics — e.g., "What about this is frightening to you?" and "When does it happen?"

Next a story is concocted, using the therapist's imagination and the data at hand. In the telling of this story, Stampfl starts out with the relatively milder fears or the relatively peripheral ones in his opinion — the more immediate or obvious kinds of fears, not the most disastrous — and then goes into things that are more related to core conflicts. It is thus more and more catastrophic as it goes along. In contrast to the systematic desensitization method, one builds up to the most frightening material as rapidly as possible. When the story is presented to the patient, that person must visualize it intensely. Stampfl often has the patient first imagine a neutral scene to see how well he can use his imagination to get the patient accustomed to visualizing a scene. It is important to check how well the patient is visualizing. The patient can be asked from time to time, "Are you seeing this clearly?" and "How are you feeling?" to check on how much anxiety is experienced. Instead of relaxing, the patient is encouraged to experience as much fear and anxiety as possible. As a matter of fact, part of the description might be, "Now your heart is beating very fast, your palms are sweating, and you're gasping for breath," suggesting some autonomic consequences that will increase the experience of fear.

The story must continue for forty-five minutes to an hour; research evidence suggests that shorter stories are less effective. Stampfl often goes for an hour and a half, which requires real talent and imagination.

Thus, the Implosive Therapist "floods" his subjects to exhaustion. They are usually drained and feel relaxed after having gone through so much stress and strain. In my therapy I do something that Stampfl does not do—I add a relaxation procedure which consists of about ten minutes of relaxation instructions that are really quite effective. Done only at the end of the story, this serves as a reward for cooperating in the procedure and shows the contrast between the frightening fantasies and reality, that really there is nothing that can hurt one in the safety of the office. Relaxation also serves to do away with any residual tension that might be present.

The same story is repeated until the patient is bored with it and reports no more fear. Then a new part of the story, or a whole new story may be added.

When the patient is really cooperative, the therapist may ask him to practice at home. He is instructed to visualize the whole story and time it, make it last at least forty-five minutes, and make it as vivid as possible. Some patients will do this and some will not. Before he goes home to practice, the patient should go through and tell the story himself in the first person, present tense, as though it is happening right now, picturing it as he tells it. The therapist can fill in any gaps that the patient leaves out. Another technique that is worthy of attention is the preparation of tape recordings of the story, which the patient can play at home each day.

You will note that, as in systematic desensitization, Implosive Therapy desensitizes the patient to imagined or fantasy stimulus situations. We count on some generalization from the imaginal presentation of frightening stimuli or events to real-life situations in which frightening stimuli are present. People will probably experience more reduction of their fears to the imaginal than to the actual stimuli, but this will allow them to deal with frightening stimuli in real life, to have a little less fear so they can approach closer before they become frightened. Then perhaps some *in vivo* desensitization will take place as they deal with the stimuli with no aversive consequences. Studies such as one that found improved college grades resulting from Implosive Therapy for test-taking anxiety (Prochaska, 1971) support my hope that fear reduction can be generalized.

Wolpe criticizes Implosive Therapy as a dangerous technique which might make the patient worse, and Morganstern (1973) also questions its safety. I know of no evidence to support their views. It appears that if a patient does the extensive visualization repeatedly, he or she will get better. However, there is some suggestive evidence that some people will report an increase in their fears after the first session or two, especially between the first and second sessions. Kotila (1969) noted a temporary increase in fear after one Implosive session. Barrett (1969) reports that two subjects displayed increased fear after the first Implosive Therapy treatment, but both returned for a second session and had a successful outcome. So, I have come to the view recently that it is important to do the first two or three sessions in quick succession, perhaps on successive days. Some Implosive therapists (e.g., Ollendick and Gruen, 1972) warn their patients of the fear they may experience after the first session.

Implosive Therapy has been related by some to *covert sensitization,* a technique in which the patient is asked to imagine eating feces or imagine other sickening things while smoking or carrying out some other behavior he or she wants to control. This is done to teach repugnance and avoidance of the behavior. The difference is that in Implosive Therapy one has the person imagine things that he is really afraid of; he is not conditioned to fear them more nor to fear or be repelled by new things. However, Implosion might put him in touch with those fears and break down his defenses some, so that he feels increased fear and panic at first. The relaxation at the end of the session may help minimize this fear.

Stampfl usually advocates ten to fifteen sessions for Implosive Therapy. Much of the research has involved ten sessions or less. One patient I worked with had markedly good results in five sessions. However, she went home and practiced the story every day for several weeks so that there were perhaps a total of thirty sessions. In other cases I have done up to thirty sessions in the office.

Illustrative Case

The first implosion, which I did collaboratively with a student, Kent Herbert, was a patient we shall call Jane. Jane was 25, married, and reported an extreme lack of self-confidence, stomachaches, headaches, shortness of breath, and choking sensations. She stayed home most of the time and cried. A classic example of agoraphobia (fear of leaving home), Jane had strange fears of a violent death with prolonged periods of pain and agony; she said that sometimes she felt as though there were slush in her head. She was afraid of driving and afraid of going into stores. She had frightening fantasies that a plane would crash into her home. On the Fear Survey Schedule, she indicated fears of falling, dead people, being teased, sirens, feeling angry, people in authority, sudden noises, bullying people, dead animals, fighting, sick people, angry people, being criticized, blood, being ignored, darkness, and losing control.

Here is an outline of the story we prepared for her: She is walking down the street and noting the color of the lamp poles and the green leaves on the trees. As she steps out into the street, a car runs over her toe. Then she steps back and starts out again and gets knocked down by a bus. This bruises her, and she is feeling some pain and is struggling to get up when her hand is run over by a motorcycle, severing several fingers. A truck crushes her ribs. Her lungs fill with blood. She is dying and people gather around and do not help in any way. They just scoff at her and laugh at the ugly sight. This is one of the things that bothers her — people not helping and criticizing her by saying, "That's no loss to the world anyhow." The ambulance comes. People cover her with a white sheet. She dies. At this point we had Jane visualize being in the morgue on a cold slab, then being buried. The coffin is lowered, she hears the sound of the dirt on top of the coffin, the sound gradually becomes duller, and her body is rotting and being eaten away by ants, worms, maggots, and rats.

After we presented the story a second time, we had her repeat the story and we filled in any omissions. She did a very good job of repeating it and experiencing the fear, visualizing vividly. She went home and started practicing, first once a day and then twice a day. In three weeks she found this story boring. She would see herself lying in the street and drawing designs on the pavement in her blood. So we gave her another story. She was afraid of suffocating, did not like smog, and disliked crowds so we had her picture herself in downtown Los Angeles on a very smoggy day. In this story it is very crowded, and she is starting to suffocate from the heat and smog. Then there is an air raid warning and hydrogen bomb blast; people are screaming and dying and defecating. There are piles of bodies and dogs eating at her and urinating on her, with other details to render the scene as miserable as we could make it. Two weeks later she reported that this story was boring to her and she wanted to quit. We had her bring in her husband

and talked to him. He said there had been a remarkable change in her. She was working now and going to stores, had enrolled in school and was driving the car. The change was a little hard for him to adapt to, but it was rather nice. He was not accustomed to having such an independent wife.*

The Minnesota Multiphasic Personality Inventory (MMPI) was given to Jane before and after treatment. On the first profile, the scores on schizophrenia, depression, hypochondriasis, and hysteria were considerably deviant (above 90). A high F score indicated that she was exaggerating her symptoms. But, after five weeks of Implosive Therapy, all her scores were in the normal range (below 70), and further, Jane was able to respond to the world and to the therapists without defensiveness or trying to look good.

Evidence of Effectiveness

Morganstern (1973), in a review of Implosive Therapy (flooding), questioned the effectiveness of the technique, but much of the evidence he considered involved very few and very short sessions. Taking number and duration of treatment sessions into consideration, a case can be made that Implosive Therapy is a promising and effective technique. Reviewing all of the available literature reveals that in all studies in which at least four sessions of forty-five minute duration or more were employed, Implosive Therapy resulted in significantly more improvement than did untreated control groups or groups treated with conventional psychotherapy. Hogan (1966) found that with an average of 4.88 months of once-a-week Implosive Therapy, as compared to 8.21 months of conventional psychotherapy, eighteen of twenty-six imploded schizophrenic patients but only eight of twenty-four psychotherapy patients were out of the hospital at a one-year follow-up. Sessions were apparently an hour long. Levis and Carrera (1967) gave 10 hour-long sessions of implosion to a group of psychiatric outpatients who were compared with two conventional therapy groups and a waiting-list control group. Significantly more favorable MMPI changes were observed in the Implosive Therapy group. Marks, Boulougouris, and

---

*After hearing the details of how Implosive Therapy is conducted, some people have remarked on the similarity of Implosion to the conditioning techniques used in the movie "A Clockwork Orange." The two approaches are *not* the same and should *not* be confused. Before beginning Implosive Therapy, the therapist describes the procedure to the client and obtains his/her voluntary consent. The behaviors to be changed are selected by the client in consultation with the therapist. The scenes presented to the client are to be visualized in his/her imagination. Finally, the therapist is cautious that the client leave the session with the anxiety under control. Contrast this with the hero of "A Clockwork Orange" who was the *unwilling* participant in a treatment which bombarded him with "real" unpleasant stimuli and "actual" physical pain.

Marset (1971) saw significant improvement in phobics with 8 one-hour sessions of implosion. Improvement was maintained over a one-year follow-up (Boulougouris, Marks, & Marset, 1971). Using 10 hour-long sessions, Jacobson (1970) found that implosion led to significantly greater reduction of fear of snakes than was observed in therapy control or no-treatment control groups. Watson and Marks (1971) observed significant reduction of fears with 8 sessions of flooding. With an average of 11.7 hour-long sessions of implosion, Boudewyns and Wilson (1972) found that Implosive Therapy with depressed, anxious in-patients led to greater improvement than did the standard hospital treatment, and that it was maintained better at six months and five years follow-up (Boudewyns, 1975) than was true for patients who had been treated with a free-association desensitization technique. Rachman, Hodgson, and Marks (1971) and Hodgson, Rachman, and Marks (1972) found flooding significantly better than a relaxation control procedure for obsessives, with improvement maintained on a three-month follow-up.

Although there are methodological difficulties in some of these studies, the results are quite consistent. They can quite easily be interpreted as showing that implosion is a promising technique worthy of serious consideration and further investigation.

Several studies of Implosive Therapy with less than four sessions or less than 40 minutes per session have found this method to be effective. Prochaska (1971), using three sessions of 46 minutes each, found that implosion was followed by significant reduction of test-taking anxiety as compared with no-treatment controls. Barrett (1969) found that two 50-minute sessions of Implosive Therapy led to marked reduction in fear of snakes.

The success in only one treatment session of Kirchner and Hogan (1966) with rat phobics, and of Hogan and Kirchner (1967) and Hogan and Kirchner (1968) with snake phobics (about two-thirds of the subjects picked up the animal after only one session) may have been due in part to the demand characteristics of the situation. A study that used a "therapy" control group of subjects who experienced a brief talk session found that four of ten of those "eclectic therapy" subjects also picked up the snake. Using four one-hour sessions, Borkovek (1970) found implosion, like other desensitization procedures, to be effective with snake phobics, but also found that an expectancy manipulation (expectancy of no change) could substantially reduce the effect.

All of the studies failing to find Implosive Therapy effective have used less than five sessions or sessions of thirty minutes or less. Carek (1969) used three 50 to 60-minute sessions. DeMoor (1969) used four 20-minute sessions. Fazio (1970) employed three 29-minute sessions. Hekmat (1973) used two 40-minute sessions, each consisting of separate brief presentations of fifty different scenes. Hodgson and Rachman (1969) used one 40-minute session, or one 30-minute session and one 10-minute session. Kotila (1969) used one 40-minute or two 20-minute sessions. Layne (1970) also used only one session. McGlynn (1968) used five 30-minute sessions. Rachman (1966) reports using ten sessions, each consisting of ten 2-minute exposures. Dee (1972) questioned the efficacy of "standardized, taped" Implosive Therapy in discussing the results of a study using four sessions each consisting of two 15-minute implosive scenes.

What are the indications and contraindications for implosion? Where multiple fears are present and systematic desensitization may be prohibitively time-consuming, this technique is often successful. Agoraphobics are generally people with severe multiple fears, and Marks, Boulougouris, and Marset (1971) report superiority of the implosion method over systematic desensitization particularly for agoraphobics. Obsessives, who tend to avoid strong feelings and also find it difficult to relax, are good candidates for Implosion Therapy or flooding. Levis and Carrera (1967) found that the MMPI scales lowered most by implosion were those associated with obsessiveness. Rachman and Marks (1972) found flooding particularly effective in obsessive-compulsive neurosis. When fear of losing control and/or fear of one's own impulses is the problem, implosion can be an effective and feasible means of desensitizing the fear. Research evidence suggests that when *in vivo* desensitization with modeling is practicable, it may be the most effective and efficient approach, but this is often not the case due to the nature of the problem.

Where the patient persistently avoids visualizing the implosive story, Implosion Therapy is much less likely to work, though some people seem to get favorable results with dramatic storytelling and little visualization. Some hysterics, who assiduously avoid discomfort; some resistant passive-aggressive patients, whose mistrust, lack of persistence, and poor motivation interfere with cooperation; and some schizophrenics are among patients I have found to avoid implosive visual imagery.

I have even used implosion with borderline schizophrenics, and it had no bad side effects whatsoever. I also had them practise at home. In some cases, if the story is too frightening, the patient resists such practising sessions. It is very important for the therapist to provide an atmosphere of encouragement and support to get the person actually to experience the scenes and feel the anxiety, and to be willing to practise. Part of getting the person to cooperate is convincing him or her that it is a worthwhile effort; the therapist must be enough of a reinforcer so the person wants to please him or her.

There is some evidence that clarity of visualization rather than intensity of the anxiety aroused is associated with success in implosion. Thus, encouraging clear visualization and asking the patient about the clarity of his images may be important.

Comparison of Implosion with Systematic Desensitization

The results of comparing therapeutic techniques may depend on the skill with which the techniques are used, the therapists' characteristics, and characteristics of the subject group. Morganstern, for example, overlooks the possibility that systematic desensitization may be more appropriate for certain kinds of problems or people with certain characteristics while implosion may be more appropriate for others.

Three studies comparing implosion or flooding with systematic desensitization have used 40 minutes or more per session and four or more sessions of Implosion. Jacobson (1970) found that college students who were afraid of snakes showed equal reduction of their fear with both techniques. In contrast, Marks, Boulougouris, and Marset (1971), working with clinically significant phobias, achieved better results with flooding (which they also called implosion) than with systematic desensitization. Flooding was especially superior for agoraphobics, who had multiple fears and were more severely handicapped by their symptoms than were the specific phobics. Crowe, Marks, Agras, and Leitenberg (1972) found implosion techniques slightly but not significantly better than systematic desensitization for phobics, but apparently consistently better for agoraphobics. They found *in vivo* desensitization significantly superior to systematic desensitization but not significantly superior to implosion. Boudewyns and Wilson (1972) found implosion significantly more effective than a free-association desensitization technique.

Considering studies that used fewer or shorter sessions, we find that Barrett (1968) successfully treated snake phobics with Implosive Therapy in 45 percent of the time required for systematic desensitization. Apparently two sessions of 50 minutes each were considered sufficient for implosion. However, at follow-up, results were less stable for Implosive Therapy than for systematic desensitization. Mealiea and Nawas (1971) found systematic desensitization significantly better than implosion, which was largely ineffective, but their five implosion sessions were only 30 minutes each.

Considering the available evidence, there can no longer be any reasonable doubt that Implosive Therapy can be effective. The remaining questions have to do with how, when, for whom, and with what. When should implosion be used and when would systematic desensitization, *in vivo* desensitization, or assertiveness training—or perhaps no formal desensitization approach at all—be more appropriate. For whom is implosion most effective—i.e., for what kinds of problems and what patient or client characteristics is it most suitable? What are the indications and contraindications? What are the effective components of Implosive Therapy, and how do they work? Is there a way of preparing audiotapes of implosive stories that are effective (is a library of tapes for different problems a possibility)? With what other therapeutic modalities can implosion be combined for more effective alleviation of human problems, and how best can this be done? When we can choose and combine therapeutic approaches on the basis of sound scientific information about their modes of action and their interactions with patient and therapist characteristics, we will more fully realize the potential of such promising treatments as Implosive Therapy.

REFERENCES

BARRETT, C. L. Systematic desensitization versus implosive therapy. *Journal of Abnormal Psychology*, 1969, *74*, 587-592.

BAUM, M. Extinction of avoidance responding through response prevention (flooding). *Psychological Bulletin*, 1970, *72*, 276-284.

BERSH, P. J., NOTTERMAN, V. M., & SCHOENFELD, W. N. Some relations between acquired autonomic and motor behavior during avoidance conditioning. *School of Aviation Medicine*, USAF Report No. 56-80, 1956.

BORKOVEC, T. D. The comparative effectiveness of systematic densensitization and implosive therapy and the effect of expectancy manipulation on the elimination of fear. (Unpublished doctoral dissertation, University of Illinois, 1970.)

BOUDEWYNS, P. A. Implosive therapy and desensitization therapy with inpatients: a five-year follow-up. *Journal of Abnormal Psychology*, 1975, *84*, 159-160.

BOUDEWYNS, P. A., & WILSON, A. E. Implosive therapy and desensitization therapy using free association in the treatment of inpatients. *Journal of Abnormal Psychology*, 1972, *79*, 259-268.

BOULOUGOURIS, J. C., MARKS, I. M., & MARSET, P. Superiority of flooding to desensitization for reducing pathological fear. *Behaviour Research and Therapy*, 1971, *9*, 7-16.

CAREK, R. G. A comparison of two behavioral therapy techniques in the treatment of rat "phobias." (Unpublished doctoral dissertation, University of Iowa, 1969.)

CROWE, M. J., MARKS, I. M., AGRAS, W. S., & LEITENBERG, H. Time-limited desensitization, implosion, and shaping for phobic patients: a crossover study. *Behaviour Research and Therapy*, 1972, *10*, 319-328.

DEE, C. Instructions and the extinction of a learned fear in the context of taped implosive therapy. *Journal of Consulting and Clinical Psychology*, 1972, *39*, 123–132.

DEMOOR, W. Systematic desensitization versus prolonged high intensity stimulation (flooding). *Journal of Behavior Therapy and Experimental Psychiatry*, 1970, *1*, 45–52.

FAZIO, A. F. Treatment components in implosive therapy. *Journal of Abnormal Psychology*, 1970, *76*, 211–219.

GUILANI, B. The role of competing response and manner of presentation of the aversive stimulus in the modification of avoidance behaviour. (Unpublished doctoral dissertation, University of California, Los Angeles, 1970.)

HEKMAT, H. Systematic versus semantic desensitization and implosive therapy. *Journal of Consulting and Clinical Psychology*, 1973, *40*, 202–209.

HODGSON, R. J. & RACHMAN, S. An experimental investigation of the implosion technique. *Behaviour Research and Therapy*, 1970, *8*, 21–27.

HOGAN, R. A. Implosive therapy in the short-term treatment of psychotics. *Psychotherapy: Theory, Research and Practice*, 1966, *3*, 25–32.

HOGAN, R. A., & KIRCHNER, J. H. Preliminary report of the extinction of learned fears via short-term implosive therapy. *Journal of Abnormal Psychology*, 1967, *72*, 106–109.

HOGAN, R. A., & KIRCHNER, J. H. Implosive, eclectic verbal and bibliotherapy in the treatment of fears of snakes. *Behaviour Research and Therapy*, 1968, *6*, 167–171.

JACOBSON, H. A. Reciprocal inhibition and implosive therapy: a comparative study of a fear of snakes. (Unpublished doctoral dissertation, Memphis State University, 1970.)

JONES, M. C. A laboratory study of fear: the case of Peter. *Pedagogical Seminary*, 1924, *31*, 308–315. (a)

JONES, M. C. The elimination of children's fears. *Journal of Experimental Psychology*, 1924, *7*, 382–390. (b)

KAHN, M., & BAKER, B. Desensitization with minimal therapist contact. *Journal of Abnormal Psychology*, 1968, *73*, 198–200.

KIRCHNER, J. H., & HOGAN, R. A. The therapist variable in the implosion of phobias. *Psychotherapy: Theory, Research and Practice*, 1966, *3*, 102–104.

KOTILA, R. R. The effects of education and four varieties of implosive therapy on fear of snakes. (Unpublished doctoral dissertation, Washington State University, 1969.)

LANG, P. J., MELAMED, B. G., & HART, J. A. Psychophysiological analysis of fear modification using an automated desensitization procedure. *Journal of Abnormal Psychology*, 1970, *76*, 220–234.

LAYNE, C. C. The effect of suggestion in implosive therapy for fear of rats. (Unpublished doctoral dissertation, Southern Illinois University, 1970.)

LEITENBERG, H., AGRAS, W. S., BARLOW, D. H., & OLIVEAU, D. C. Contribution of selective positive reinforcement and therapeutic instructions to systematic desensitization therapy. *Journal of Abnormal Psychology,* 1969, *74,* 113–118.

LEVIS, D. J., & CARRERA, R. Effects of ten hours of implosive therapy in the treatment of outpatients: a preliminary report. *Journal of Abnormal Psychology,* 1967, *72,* 507–508.

LONDON, P. *The modes and morals of psychotherapy.* New York: Holt, Rinehart and Winston, 1964.

MARKS, I., BOULOUGOURIS, J., & MARSET, P. Flooding versus desensitization in the treatment of phobic patients: a crossover study. *British Journal of Psychiatry,* 1971, *119,* 353–375.

MCGLYNN, F. D. Systematic desensitization, implosive therapy, and the aversiveness of imaginal hierarchy items. (Unpublished doctoral dissertation, University of Missouri, 1968.)

MEALIEA, W. L., JR., & NAWAS, M. M. Systematic desensitization versus implosive therapy. *Journal of Behavior Therapy and Experimental Psychiatry,* 1970, *2,* 85–94.

MILLER, B. V., & LEVIS, D. J. The effects of varying short visual exposure times to a phobic test stimulus on subsequent avoidance behavior. *Behaviour Research and Therapy,* 1971, *9,* 17–21.

MORGANSTERN, K. P. Implosive therapy and flooding procedures: a critical review. *Psychological Bulletin,* 1973, *79,* 318–334.

PAUL, G. L. *Insight vs. desensitization in psychotherapy.* Stanford, Cal.: Stanford University Press, 1966.

PAUL, G. L. Two-year follow-up of systematic desensitization in therapy groups. *Journal of Abnormal Psychology,* 1968, *73,* 119–130.

PROCHASKA, J. O. Symptom and dynamic cues in the implosive treatment of test anxiety. *Journal of Abnormal Psychology,* 1971, *77,* 133–142.

RACHMAN, S. Studies in desensitization. II. Flooding. *Behaviour Research and Therapy,* 1966, *4,* 1–6.

RACHMAN, S., HODGSON, R., & MARKS, I. M. The treatment of chronic obsessive-compulsive neurosis. *Behaviour Research and Therapy.* 1971, *9,* 237–247.

STAMPFL, T. G., & LEVIS, D. J. Essentials of implosive therapy: a learning-theory-based psychodynamic behavioral therapy. *Journal of Abnormal Psychology,* 1967, *72,* 496–503.

STONE, W. R., JR. Individual and group implosive therapy. (Unpublished doctoral dissertation, University of South Dakota, 1971.)

WATSON, J. P., & MARKS, I. M. Relevant and irrelevant fear in flooding—a crossover study of phobic patients. *Behavioral Therapy,* 1971, *2,* 275–293.

WILLIS, R. W., & EDWARDS, J. A. A study of the comparative effectiveness of systematic desensitization and implosive therapy. *Behaviour Research and Therapy,* 1969, *7,* 387–395.

WOLPE, J. *Psychotherapy by reciprocal inhibition*. Stanford, Cal.: Stanford University Press, 1958.

WOLPE, J. *The practice of behavior therapy.* New York: Pergamon Press, 1969.

WOLPIN, M., & RAINES, J. Visual imagery, expected roles and extinction as possible factors in reducing fear and avoidance behavior. *Behaviour Research and Therapy,* 1966, *4*, 25–37.

10

Behavior Modification: Operant Approaches To Therapy

Virginia Binder

HISTORY OF OPERANT APPROACHES

The idea that the consequences of an individual's behavior influence recurrences of similar behavior is anything but new. Certainly B. F. Skinner did not originate the notion of the carrot and the stick. In fact, for thousands of years parents have been training their children by giving rewards and punishment. Similarly, in the legal system, consequences (usually punishment) are designed to cut down on illegal activities. Even in a therapeutic context, consequences of behavior have been systematically used to change behavior. In the Roman era one of the recommended treatments for alcoholism was to place eels in the bottom of the drinker's glass (Ullman and Krasner, 1975) — a unique form of punishment.

Because the application of reward and punishment has been a part of our culture for so many years, what then is unique about the approach offered by therapists adopting principles from the operant conditioning laboratory? The major distinctions between the use of rewards and punishment in daily life and the treatment methods advocated by operant therapists stem from the systemization of the treatment methods and the verification of the success of the method through research.

"Behavior Modification: Operant Approaches to Therapy," by Virginia Binder, Ph. D. © 1976 by Virginia Binder. This article appears in print for the first time in this volume.

Virginia Binder is Associate Professor of Psychology at California State University, Long Beach. She has also worked as a psychologist at Metropolitan State Hospital, Norwalk, California and served as consultant at the Veterans Administration Hospital, Long Beach and the Ballymun Child Guidance Clinic in Dublin, Ireland.

The actual attempt to apply contingency principles systematically in the treatment of human problems has been prevalent primarily during the last twenty years. Many of the early attempts were of short duration and mainly designed for demonstration purposes. For instance, one of the earliest reported cases applying reward contingencies (Isaacs, Thomas, & Golddiamond, 1960) describes a long-term chronic schizophrenic who was encouraged to speak when receiving gum was made contingent on his speaking. He had been mute for many years. First, the schizophrenic was rewarded with gum by merely attending to the psychologist. Next, he was rewarded for vocalization and for lip movement. As the treatment progressed, he was only rewarded by gum for actual words, and later, for sentences and requests. (This process of successive approximations is called *shaping*.) This demonstration was one of the early illustrations showing that socially desirable behavior could be brought under the control of the therapist.

Other early demonstrations were designed to show that anti-social or deviant behavior is also under the control of its consequences. If such is the case, then one could treat the anti-social behavior by directly attacking the problem rather than searching for some underlying cause. When Ayllon and Haughton (1964) kept accurate records of the frequency of the delusional language of a hospitalized woman, it became readily apparent that the number of times she described herself as the Queen clearly related to the attention she received from bystanders. When people left or ignored her during her delusions, the frequency of her delusions was minimal.

OPERANT THERAPY PRINCIPLES

Stated in the simplest terms, operant therapy follows the principle that behavior that is rewarded will increase in frequency and behavior that is extinguished (ignored) or punished will decrease in frequency. Thus, one should systematically determine the behaviors that are considered desirable and reward them; and ignore or punish those behaviors that are considered undesirable.

Although the principles themselves are straightforward and easy to understand, their actual application becomes much more complex. For example, while it is known that reward will increase the frequency of behavior, how often should reward be given? How soon after a behavior occurs should a reward be given? How do you determine what will be rewarding to a given individual? It is this type of information that has been studied in the laboratory through the years. So now it is possible to apply the principles that have emerged from research rather than using intuitive guesses as to the timing and frequency of reward.

Partial Reinforcement

If one wants to establish a new behavior, it is desirable to reward each occurrence of the behavior immediately. (In practice this is only approximated.) However, if the reward should cease once the behavior has been developed and the termination of the reward is abrupt, the occurrence of the new behavior may cease equally abruptly. Thus, some provision must be made to allow continuance of the behavior without continual immediate reinforcement. A gradual shift, then, to partial reinforcement (reward on a ratio or interval basis) would help to maintain behavior once it has been learned.

Immediate vs. Delayed Reinforcement

Another example of the application of laboratory principles involves the use of immediate and delayed reinforcement. Again, during the learning of a new behavior, immediate reinforcement is important. However, in the practical, real-life situation, people are not immediately rewarded for the acts they perform. For the average worker, tangible material reward may come a week or a month, rather than seconds after the performance of his actions.

Primary vs. Secondary Reinforcement

Although a number of the examples just discussed involve tangible reward, it is important to remember that material rewards are not the only types that can work successfully. For many people, social reinforcement, such as recognition, appreciation, and friendly conversation, can be as rewarding as food, cigarettes, sleep, and opportunities to engage in sexual activity.

Premack Principle

In fact, one important principle, established by Premack (1959) in the laboratory has become a mainstay of those who are limited in the number of reinforcers they have available to offer to patients. The Premack principle, derived from systematic research, is actually used intuitively by many parents daily. Basically, Premack observed that those behaviors in which the organism engages frequently can serve as reinforcers for rarer behaviors. In everyday terms, this means that eating chocolate cake, a highly likely behavior, can serve as a reward for eating spinach, a less likely event. Thus, many parents successfully utilize the principles "You can't have dessert until you finish your vegetables" or "You can't go out to play until you finish your homework."

THERAPEUTIC PROGRAMS

An operant therapist whose name became a household word in the early 1960s was Ivar Lovaas. The autistic children with whom he worked were self-destructive, showed little or no recognition of the outside world, rocked, twisted their hair, rotated objects, and repeated words as if they had no meaning. With considerable patience and astute and creative applications of laboratory principles, Lovaas (1965, 1966b, c) was able to teach these children to speak and engage in social interaction through the shaping procedure. His monumental feat paved the way for other operant conditioning programs.

It should be noted that the nature of the problems, the type of clients, and the approach used by operant therapists has broadened from that developed by Lovaas. The shift in the nature of the problem and the type of clientele has ranged from the early work done primarily with extremely severe behavior disorders (like those of the autistic children) to current work with people having day-to-day problems in self-management or raising children. When the operant therapists were working primarily with more severe problems (often institutionalized individuals), the operant therapists themselves designed the reinforcement systems and, along with their assistants, delivered the reinforcements. In order to make operant therapy more readily available to the public, operant therapists have begun to serve recently as consultants to parents, teachers, and probation workers. In their role of consultant, they have basically trained parents and teachers to use operant methods. Thus, the delivery of the reinforcement has shifted from delivery by the operant therapist himself to delivery by someone easily available in the natural environment of the person with the problem (Tharp & Wetzel, 1969). Even more recently, operant therapists have been attempting to teach their clients to reinforce themselves for the behavior that they desire (for example in weight control, drinking control, sleep problems, and stopping smoking).

A Token Economy—Mental Health Professionals as Therapists

The first behavior modification program with which I worked was a "token economy" at a state hospital. A token economy program defines appropriate and inappropriate behaviors for selected patients and then rewards the appropriate behaviors with tokens and fines the patients for inappropriate behavior. The tokens are then exchangeable for a wide variety of goods, services, and the finer things of life.

Patient Population. The first token economy was in Illinois (Ayllon & Azrin, 1968b) with chronic schizophrenic patients who had been hospitalized for a long time. Other early programs were with retarded children and delinquents. Our program began with only nine women whose reputations distinguished them as the most assaultive and abusive women in the hospital. Thus they were constantly shifted from ward to ward — no one wanted to work with them. As examples of the behaviors we observed, one woman was recorded (before coming to us) as hitting or attempting to hit somebody 22 times every hour. Another one of the women had been lobotomized twice and was still assaultive. Still another had had over 400 electric shock treatments.

Demographic data revealed an age range of 25 to 55 years. The patients had been hospitalized from five to twenty-two years. The most educated patient had a year and half of college, but the average education was about tenth grade. Seven of the women were diagnosed as schizophrenic, one was labeled brain-damaged, and one was labeled retarded.

Planning and Organization of the Program. Before the establishment of the token ward, two weeks were devoted to training the staff and getting the patients ready. During the training period the staff kept a baseline record of the behaviors in which the women engaged, so that we would know specifically what the problems were and how often they occurred.

The program was set up so that each woman would have individualized contingencies. Many of the other token economies, obviously because they have a larger number of patients, define the behaviors to be rewarded similarly for a large number of patients. On some of the token economies we visited, all patients showing up at a meal on time received the same number of tokens. If they made their beds, they all received the same number of tokens. We tried to pick out the most important changes needed by each patient. There were also some things that were rewarded for all individuals, but the patients were at such varying stages of ability that it would have been hard to ask everyone to do the same things in the same way.

The first week was set aside to allow the tokens to acquire value. This was accomplished within a couple of days with little difficulty. If patients are given tokens and then required to give them back in order to get meals, a bed, or an opportunity to watch television, they learn very rapidly that the tokens have meaning — like money. Also, each time a token was given, we tried to spell out the reason to the patient. As noted earlier, one of the things that is very important is immediate reinforcement. When we saw something that was desirable for a particular patient we would try to reward it promptly. Again, this differs from programs having a larger number of patients. Each member of the staff carried around a pocketful of tokens to spend whenever a patient was doing anything that was "appropriate."

Selection of Goals. People always ask, "How do you decide what is appropriate behavior?" On different token economy programs the goals for patients vary. In Ayllon and Azrin's program, the goal was for schizophrenic patients to return to their home communities. For the retarded, the goal is often to learn to be self-sufficient. Unfortunately, a few token economy programs seem to have been set up to reward the staff rather than the patients—in such cases the goal may be a quiet and neat ward rather than individual concern for the patients.

Because we had such severely disturbed patients, our goals were limited. We wanted to get the patients out of the hospital into board and care homes. (Board and care homes are run by community people who provide food and shelter for former patients. In some board and care homes there may be only one guest and no organized programs, while others may have a dozen or more guests and offer recreational activities and medical attention.)

Results of the Program. After four or five months, the hospital budget office objected to the high patient-staff ratio and considered disbanding the program. We decided to bring in additional patients, at which point we switched to a platoon-like system as they do in many other token economy programs. Patients at different stages of progress were entitled to varying amenities, comparable to the lower, middle, and upper socioeconomic classes. Patients with the most "normal" behavior lived in private rooms, had the most freedom, and ate in very dignified surroundings. Each patient could work her way up by improved behavior. One of the saddest things for me was that though we had seen so much improvement in the initial group of women, when the new patients were added, most of the original group were still placed in the lowest category. It should be noted, though, that the new patients were chosen to be less difficult in order to keep up staff morale.

Five of the original nine patients were either placed in a board and care home or placement plans were made within the first year. Of the remaining four, two were transferred for medical reasons and two remained in the hospital.

Problems Encountered with a Token Economy. Many people ask the important question regarding what happens to patients when they leave a token system. It is very easy for patients to discriminate between hospital staff who deliver reinforcement and people in the community.

Thus it is necessary to work toward generalization of improved behaviors outside the hospital. We tried to have the staff avoid uniforms, have volunteers come into the hospital, and to have the patients leave the ward and move into the community for activities. We also tried to work with the people at the board and care homes to teach them some of the principles of reinforcement. We wanted them to continue the policy of praising the patients for acceptable behavior. It is very easy to take acceptable behavior for granted. In addition, we attempted to move the patients from primary reinforcers like food to social reinforcers like enjoying the opportunity to do things with other people. In the beginning, each time we gave a token, we said something like, "That was very good" or "You're doing so well." We didn't continue to give tokens immediately nor extremely frequently. We hoped to bridge the gap, so that by the time a patient was ready to leave our program she might be earning tokens on a weekly basis as one would do with a paycheck. Eventually it was expected that the social companionship of the staff and other patients would become meaningful.

A final difficulty had to do with the limited number of reinforcers available in a state institution. Most of the early token-economy programs relied on the exchange of basic hospital commodities for the tokens. Within the last several years, however, champions of patients' rights have pointed out that hospitalized patients should be entitled to all hospital comforts and should not have to earn them. Court decisions have supported this point of view. Thus those who now hope to operate token economies in public institutions must offer rewards beyond the normal amenities available to all patients in the hospital (Martin, 1975).

Although we did utilize the basic hospital commodities (food, comfortable bed, etc.) as basic reinforcers, we designed the program so that all patients should be able to achieve at least the minimum comforts. In addition, we opened a ward store to provide extra items for which tokens could be exchanged. The store also served as a research tool and research funds were used to set it up. We kept track of the items purchased by the patients. At first they primarily purchased candy and cigarettes, but we expected them to become interested in books, clothing, and grooming aids as they improved. Though there was no noticeable shift in items purchased for the original patients, we did observe that the patients who joined the program later and whose behaviors were more adjusted did buy a wider range of items.

Modification of Children's Behavior— Parents as Therapists

Overview of the Program. The second program took place in a college clinic rather than an institutional setting. Parents whose children presented problems which they could not handle were referred to the clinic by schools, physicians, and social workers. The program, while designed to assist parents, was also intended to teach advanced undergraduates and graduate students behavior modification skills.

The procedures were borrowed liberally from Martha Bernal (1968), who has done extensive work with the "brat syndrome"; Gerald Patterson (1968, 1971b), who has worked with numerous families and an array of presenting problems; and Tharp and Wetzel (1969), who have worked with parents and others in the natural environment.

When parents were referred to the clinic and had child management problems such as uncontrollable temper tantrums, school disturbances, or fears, they were referred to the behavior modification program. During the initial intake interviews an attempt was made to get very specific details about the family problems in order to avoid such general descriptions as, "My child doesn't seem interested in school; he causes us trouble; she's maladjusted." Instead we asked the parents to pinpoint the problems. For example, rather than stating that the child is uncooperative, the parents were to clarify what they meant—i.e., "When I ask him to do something, he requires at least four or five reminders."

The parents were also informed about the extensiveness of the program and the amount of participation required of them. They were asked to observe and record behavior, permit observers to enter the home to view family interactions, and implement the major changes themselves at home.

Working with the Parents to Design the Treatment Plan. Parents who were interested in continuing in the program were asked to read one of two books by Patterson—either *Living with Children* (1968) or *Families* (1971b). It should be noted that both books are short, teach some general principles of behavior modification in a programmed manner, and provide illustrative solutions to family problems. Thus, on the parents' return visit, the student clinicians went over in a general way some of the principles covered in the books and attempted to stress the importance of reward and the role of the parents as models. At this session target behaviors were selected by the parents and/or the clinicians. As noted earlier, it is important to specify precisely the behaviors to be changed in order that they can be accurately observed, recorded, and reinforced. The behaviors should also be specifically defined so that the child will know exactly what is expected and when he will be rewarded. Thus, such target behaviors as playing with a sibling without fighting or coming directly home from school were selected. The clinicians also screened the appropriateness of the target for the age of the child. Occasionally, parents wanted to modify behavior which irritated them, but which fell within the normal activities of children. In such cases the clinicians discussed this with the parents.

While selecting target behaviors, the parents, clinicians, and the child attempted to determine suitable reinforcers. Small children were asked about things they liked. Older children were given an open-ended questionnaire in which they could spell out those things they liked best — both materially and socially. For very young children, parents either provided the information about potential reinforcers or the students making home observations made suggestions. In most cases the biggest reinforcer was the attention of the parents.

Once target behaviors were selected, the parents were asked to keep a baseline record of the frequency of the target behavior(s) each day and to bring the records to the next session. They were also asked to develop a contingency system which they could implement. The clinicians were then able to go over the records, give the parents support for keeping records, and approve, modify, or improve upon the plan of the parents. If the family reported that there was also a school problem, the student clinicians would go to the school, observe, and discuss strategy with the teacher.

After the behavior-change plan was implemented, programs were monitored over a period of weeks. With a single target behavior, some change usually occurred within a week or two. With a multitude of problems, changes would occur more slowly — sometimes over a period of months. If through home observations, phone contacts, or the report of the parents in the weekly sessions, it was apparent that the presenting problem was decreasing in frequency, the clinicians gradually cut down on the number and frequency of sessions with the parents. If it appeared that the program was not working, they attempted to revise it.

Difficulties with Parents as Therapists. While the procedures we followed seem straightforward, certain problems arose. First, the program seemed to involve more effort than a number of parents expected. Often the presenting problem disappeared spontaneously when the parents became aware of the extent of their part in the program. In fact, we had several rapid cures. Tharp and Wetzel (1969) also report the phenomenon in which the treatment may be more trouble for the parents than the original problem.

A second problem was that the parents, despite their reported enthusiasm, often didn't keep records. We utilized the same system for the parents that we were teaching them for their children — i.e., we provided reinforcers for accurate records. The reinforcers included babysitting, trading stamps, and a monetary rebate at the conclusion of the program.

Sometimes an older child in the family was asked to keep records and was rewarded for doing so. Martha Bernal (1970) has designed a tape recorder which is enclosed in a suitcase and activated by a timing mechanism. Although the family is aware they will be recorded, they do not know when. Thus she gets a sample of the interactions going on in the home.

Another dilemma was that parents claimed they understood the principles to be followed, but their behavior was sometimes not consistent with the principles. In these cases the student clinicians acted as models and demonstrated how and when to deliver reinforcement. Some of the parents were asked to interact with their children in a structured setting and then watched a videotape playback of their actions. The clinician then reviewed the session, pointing out to the parents the good and bad aspects.

A final problem was the parents' ethical qualms about bribing children. Many parents believed children should behave appropriately because it is the thing to do, or it is expected. Others parents were quite willing to punish for inappropriate behavior but unwilling to offer reward for appropriate behavior.

Evaluation. Both the parents and the student clinicians independently assessed the success of the program. Our initial follow-up data revealed that we had the most success with families with the most severe presenting problems. Apparently they had the motivation to carry out the treatment program. The most successful cases also had the highest rate of clinician-family contact. We were unable to tell whether the high rate of communication motivated the clients, or whether the families' enthusiasm motivated the students to keep in touch.

Illustrative Cases. One case involved a little boy who was unwilling to go to bed alone because he claimed he was afraid of the dark. Many therapists would view such a problem as stemming from underlying dynamic causes, but a careful analysis of the situation indicated that the boy was only afraid of the dark at home. He had no fear when he stayed with his relatives. His parents' attention to the fear seemed to be maintaining it. The clinicians prescribed a simple program in which the parents agreed to spend time playing on the following evening (which they did not ordinarily do) each time the boy went to sleep without crying or fussing. The darkness phobia disappeared within a week.

A more complex case involved a 9-year-old boy who had been very ill in his early years. He was quite demanding and threatened to hold his breath (at times he actually passed out) if his parents did not give in. Because the parents were so frightened of causing any physical damage to the boy, they always gave in to his requests. We were concerned about his physical problems and his parents' resulting apprehension if we advised them to ignore his demands. Hence, we decided to focus on reward for changing behavior rather than extinction. Although we had no control to rule out the effects of novelty or a change in the parents' attitudes, once a point system was set up so that the boy could earn through good behavior the same sorts of things for which he had disrupted the household, the family returned to normal within several months.

Treatment of Day-to-Day Problems— Clients as Their Own Therapists

People who have "undesirable habits" which they would like to change may now seek the consultation of an operant therapist rather than engage in a lengthy, five or six-year analysis. Therapists offer clients information about operant conditioning and other behavioral techniques to help them design a plan which they must implement on their own. Successful cases have been reported in the literature for some time (Ferster, Nurnberger, & Levitt, 1962; Goldiamond, 1965; Stuart, 1967). Representative cases include attempts to work with obese individuals, attempts to set up drinking and smoking clinics, and programs intended to reduce marital conflict.*

Many of the approaches to solving such problems are unique, but one could present two overall strategies for training clients to modify their own behavior. First, clients can change the environment. They can pinpoint the event(s) precipitating the problem behavior so they can alter the situation to reduce the likelihood of its occurrence. Several examples of how the environment can be changed will be taken from Stuart's (1967) work with obese clients. First the clients were instructed to remove excess food from the house, retaining only food that required preparation. Thus they could not easily reach a hand into a bag of potato chips, but instead had to bake or heat or peel something. It was suggested that the clients restrict their eating to specific areas so that they did not eat while reading, watching television, or chatting with friends. They were also to cut down on the rate of eating so that they could chew the food more thoroughly and pause occasionally to observe their own control over the situation. Clients were also shown how they could engage in other rewarding activities at such times as they might ordinarily snack. For example, they could telephone a

*Dr. Carl E. Thoresen of Stanford University has edited a number of books written for the layman that explain how to use these self-management techniques for self-control of smoking, drinking, insomnia, fear reduction, and sexual dysfunction. See the bibliography section at the end of this chapter for specific titles.

friend in preference to nibbling. Variants of this plan are now widely used and often described in the popular media.

In the second strategy the clients administer consequences to themselves — either rewards or punishments. For example, a woman may agree to buy herself a new dress after she has lost a designated amount of weight, or a smoker may inhale a noxious odor after each cigarette. Both strategies may be combined and the client must record the frequency of his selected "target" behaviors and observe his own progress.

This whole area of working directly with clients — teaching them to analyze and revise their own behavior — is referred to as training in self-control or self-management. A thorough review of the wide variety of behavioral techniques utilized can be found in Goldfried and Merbaum (1973) and Thoresen and Mahoney (1974). Self-control is a term widely used by the lay person, but it has interested operant conditioners only recently. The other techniques described earlier, in which the therapist or someone in the environment delivers the reinforcement, impose outside control on the client. In self-control training the client must reinforce himself. Thus there is a certain amount of motivation required of the client which is not needed in the earlier programs. Although it is not difficult to teach clients how to analyze their own behavior, operant therapists encounter the same difficulties as other therapists in trying to keep up the motivational level of their clients.

RESEARCH EVALUATING THE EFFECTIVENESS OF OPERANT PROGRAMS

In addition to the fact that operant therapists attempt to apply laboratory principles to human problems, the second distinguishing characteristic noted was the research interests of the therapists. Thus one can find numerous journal articles describing the outcomes of operant programs. While many articles have been written on the number of difficulties involved in evaluating the effects of psychotherapy, operant therapists have been in the forefront of those attempting to *solve* some of the problems. For instance, one of the difficulties is in the definition of improvement resulting from psychotherapy. For many therapists, improvement is viewed as better ego functioning, improved insight, or self-actualization. It is often difficult for outside observers to notice such changes in a therapy client. The operant therapist defines improvement based on the designated target behaviors. One can gain consensus about whether weight reduction has occurred, arguments in the home have decreased, fewer notes have been sent from school, or less fighting occurs on a ward. Operant therapists, then, have been able to offer tangible records (an integral part of the treatment plan) to show the concrete changes in behavior.

Considerable research has been conducted on token-economy systems (Atthowe & Krasner, 1968; Ayllon & Azrin, 1968; Cohen, 1968; Girardeau & Spradlin, 1964; O'Leary & Becker, 1967; Schaefer & Martin, 1968) and parent treatment methods (Bernal, 1969; Berkowitz & Graziano, 1972; Patterson, 1971a; Tharp & Wetzel, 1969). These approaches are widely recognized and accepted in the mental health areas. The work in self-control, which includes operant techniques as well as other behavioral techniques, requires considerably more research both in judging the effectiveness of the methods and in designing improved means of implementation.

ETHICAL CONCERNS IN OPERANT PROGRAMS

Although other psychotherapists and critics of operant therapy generally concede that research has documented the effectiveness of many operant programs, they challenge operant therapy primarily on the issue of its limitation of man's freedom. In fact, Rogers and Skinner (1956) debated just this point. The criticism is made primarily by therapists such as Rogers who feel that human beings should control their own destiny and if given the proper support will find their own direction. Skinner (1971) contends, on the other hand, that there are few, if any, circumstances in which people are really free, and that any therapist who believes that he or she does not influence the ideas and behavior of the client is deluding him/herself. As for the evidence that the therapist can refrain from influencing a client, there is little. In fact, Truax (1966) has shown that Rogers himself differentially reinforces certain classes of client responses, and Bandura (1961) has pointed out that clients tend to learn the values and language of their therapists. While operant therapists do not deny that they are setting up situations in which they attempt to change the behavior of their clients, they believe they are doing so in an honest and direct manner, rather than in the subtle fashion of some other therapists. Thus a client who is aware of attempts to change his behavior is better able to exercise choice than a client who does not think he is influenced by his therapist. Operant therapists believe that they are shaping and teaching clients new behaviors so the clients may then have more behavioral alternatives from which to choose when confronting a new situation. This greater range of responses can only increase rather than decrease the relative "freedom" of the client.

Despite the beliefs of most operant therapists that their approach and goals can enhance the freedom of their clients, skepticism by other therapists, the courts, and the public continues. Recently, behavior modifiers are considering steps to assure that the best interests of their clients are served. Among suggested steps are professional and peer review boards to evaluate operant programs (Martin, 1975).

Operant therapists are also criticized because they are seen as cold, distant, mechanistic, and materialistic, whereas other therapists offer warm personal attention to their clients. It is certainly true that some operant therapists tend to be more systematic in setting up programs for their patients, and are concerned about data collection and research. But there is nothing about operant therapy that requires the therapist to be distant and mechanistic. In fact, when a therapist is rewarding a client he is far more effective if he pairs social reinforcement (warmth and praise) with material rewards. His goal generally is to eliminate the need for material rewards as soon as possible. Thus a warm, friendly operant therapist should actually be more successful with his clients. To the surprise of some critics of behavior therapy, a recent study (Staples, Sloane, Whipple, Cristol, & Yorkston, 1975) found behavior therapists to be rated by their patients to be as warm as more traditional therapists. In addition, they found that behavior therapists scored higher on the dimension of accurate empathy than did the traditional therapists. Furthermore, it is interesting to note that operant therapists have worked with patients whose problems are so severe that they have been ignored by other therapists. Operant therapists would seem, then, at least as humanitarian as other psychotherapists.

REFERENCES AND BIBLIOGRAPHY

ATTHOWE, J. W., & KRASNER, L. A preliminary report of the application of contingent reinforcement procedures (token economy) on a "chronic psychiatric ward." *Journal of Abnormal Psychology,* 1968, *73,* 37–43.

AYLLON, T., & AZRIN, N. H. *The token economy: a motivational system for therapy and rehabilitation.* New York: Appleton-Century-Crofts, 1968.

AYLLON, T., & HAUGHTON, E. Modification of symptomatic verbal behavior of mental patients. *Behaviour Research and Therapy,* 1964, *2,* 87–97.

BANDURA, A. Psychotherapy as a learning process. *Psychological Bulletin,* 1961, *58,* 143–159.

BERKOWITZ, B. P., & GRAZIANO, A. M. Training parents as behavior therapists: a review. *Behaviour Research and Therapy,* 1972, *10,* 297–317.

BERNAL, M., DURYEE, J., PRUETT, H., & BURNS, B. Behavior modification and the "brat syndrome." *Journal of Consulting Psychology,* 1968, *32,* 447–455.

BERNAL, M. *Personal communication,* 1970.

COHEN, H. L. Educational therapy: the design of learning environments. In Schlien, J. M. (Ed.), *Research in psychotherapy.* Washington, D.C.: American Psychological Association, 1968.

FERSTER.. C. B., NURNBERGER, J. I., & LEVITT, E. E. The control of eating. *Journal of Mathetics,* 1962, *1,* 87–109.

GIRARDEAU, F. L. & SPRADLIN, J. E. Token rewards in a cottage program. *Mental Retardation,* 1964, *2,* 345–351.

GOLDFRIED, M. R., & MERBAUM, M. *Behavior change through self-control.* New York: Holt, Rinehart and Winston, 1973.

GOLDIAMOND, I. Self-control procedures in personal behavior problems. *Psychological Reports,* 1965, *17,* 851–868.

HERMAN, J., LoPICCOLO, L., & LoPICCOLO, J. *Becoming orgasmic: a sexual growth program for women.* Englewood Cliffs, N.J.: Prentice-Hall, 1976.

ISAACS, W., THOMAS, J., & GOLDIAMOND, I. Application of operant conditioning to reinstate verbal behavior in psychotics. *Journal of Speech and Hearing Disorders,* 1960, *25,* 8–12.

JEFFEREY, D. B., & KATZ, R. *How to help yourself lose weight.* Englewood Cliffs, N.J.: Prentice-Hall (in press).

KRUMBOLTZ, J. & KRUMBOLTZ, H. *Changing children's behavior.* Englewood Cliffs, N.J.: Prentice-Hall, 1972.

LOVAAS, O. I., BERBERICH, J. P., PERLOFF, B. F., & SCHAEFFER, B. Acquisition of imitative speech by schizophrenic children. *Science,* 1966, *151,* 705–707.

LOVAAS, O. I., FREITAG, I., GOLD, V. J., & KASSORLA, I. C. Experimental studies in childhood schizophrenia: analysis of self-destructive behavior. *Journal of Experimental Child Psychology,* 1965, *2,* 67–84.

LOVAAS, O. I., FREITAG, G., KINDER, M. I., RUBENSTEIN, B. D., SCHAEFFER, B., & SIMMONS, J. Q. Establishment of social reinforcers in two schizophrenic children on the basis of food. *Journal of Experimental Child Psychology,* 1966, *4,* 109–125.

MARTIN, R. *Legal challenges to behavior modification.* Champaign, Ill.: Research Press, 1975.

MILLER, W. & MUÑOZ, R. *How to control your drinking.* Englewood Cliffs, N.J.: Prentice-Hall, 1976.

O'LEARY, K. D., & BECKER, W. C. Behavior modification of an adjustment class: token reinforcement program. *Exceptional Children,* 1967, *33,* 637–642.

PATTERSON, G. R. Behavioral intervention procedures in the classroom and in the home. In Bergin, A. E. & Garfield, S. L. (Eds.), *Handbook of psychotherapy and behavior change.* New York: Wiley, 1971. (a)

PATTERSON, G. R. *Families.* Champaign, Ill.: Research Press, 1971. (b)

PATTERSON, G. R., & GUILLION, M. E. *Living with children: new methods for parents and teachers.* Champaign, Ill.: Research Press, 1968.

PREMACK, D. Toward empirical behavior laws. I. Positive reinforcement. *Psychological Review*, 1959, *66*, 219–233.

ROGERS, C. R., & SKINNER, B. F. Some issues concerning the control of human behavior. *Science*, 1956, *124*, 1057–1066.

ROSEN, G. *Don't be afraid: a guide to dealing with your fears.* Englewood Cliffs, N.J.: Prentice-Hall (in press).

SCHAEFER, H., & MARTIN, P. *Behavioral therapy.* New York: McGraw-Hill, 1968.

SKINNER, B. F. *Beyond freedom and dignity.* New York: Knopf, 1971.

STAPLES, F. R., SLOANE, B., WHIPPLE, K., CRISTOL, A. H., & YORKSTON, N.J. Differences between behavior therapists and psychotherapists. *Archives of General Psychiatry*, 1975, *32*, 1515–1522.

STUART, R. B. Behavioral control of overeating. *Behaviour Research and Therapy*, 1967, *5*, 357–365.

THORESEN, C. E., & COATES, T. *How to Sleep Better: a Drug-Free Program for Overcoming Insomnia.* Englewood Cliffs, N.J.: Prentice-Hall (in press).

THORESEN, C. E. & MCALISTER, A. *How to Become an Ex-Smoker.* Englewood Cliffs, N.J.: Prentice-Hall. (in press).

THORESEN, C. E., & MAHONEY, M. J. *Behavioral self-control.* New York: Holt, Rinehart and Winston, 1974.

TRUAX, C. B. Reinforcement and non-reinforcement in Rogerian psychotherapy. *Journal of Abnormal and Social Psychology*, 1966, *71*, 1–9.

THARP, R. B., & WETZEL, R. J. *Behavior modification in the natural environment.* New York: Academic Press, 1969.

ULLMAN, L. P., & KRASNER, L. *A psychological approach to abnormal behavior* (2nd ed.). Englewood Cliffs, N.J.: Prentice-Hall, 1975.

11

Assertion Training

Sherwin B. Cotler

WHAT IS ASSERTION TRAINING?

Assertion Training is primarily concerned with two major interpersonal goals: *anxiety reduction* and *social skill training.* From a conceptual standpoint, Assertion Training involves a multiple set of procedures (primarily behavioral) aimed at enhancing an individual's self-dignity and self-respect. Behaviorally speaking, an individual who is assertive can verbally and nonverbally express a wide range of both positive and negative feelings, emotions, and thoughts; can make decisions and free choices in life; can comfortably establish close interpersonal relationships; can protect him/ herself from being "victimized" and taken advantage of by others; and can successfully satisfy interpersonal needs. These are to be accomplished without experiencing undue amounts of anxiety or guilt and without violating the rights and dignity of others in the process.

"Assertion Training," by Sherwin B. Cotler, Ph.D. © 1976 by Sherwin B. Cotler. This article appears in print for the first time in this volume. Appreciation is expressed by the author to Dr. Julio Guerra, with whom he has conducted many of his assertion groups and workshops and who is responsible for many of the ideas and procedures described in this chapter. Appreciation is also expressed to Dr. John Flowers for his editing and constructive comments on this chapter.

Sherwin B. Cotler is a psychologist in private practice in Huntington Beach, California and is also on the staff on the North Orange County Child Guidance Center. He holds several academic appointments and for the past several years has taught courses, written papers, and consulted in the area of behavior modification. Most recently, he has co-authored a book on assertion training entitled *Assertion Training: A Humanistic-Behavioral Guide to Self-Dignity.*

166

Assertiveness is very closely associated with a humanistic model in the sense that it supports the individualized recognition of self as an important living being who is entitled to thoughts, emotions, and feelings which need not be sacrificed or negotiated away in a relationship with someone else (regardless of whether or not the relationship is an intimate or superficial one). We believe (see Cotler & Guerra, 1976) that you must not only know yourself but also you must learn to feel comfortable with yourself. The most important thing in your life is *you* — only if you respect and take care of yourself will you be able to nourish others. In doing Assertion Training, we have come to recognize a continuum of assertive behaviors and response styles ranging from the nonassertive individual on the one end of the continuum to the aggressive individual on the other end. The nonassertive individual, because of high levels of anxiety, guilt, and/or deficits in social skills, tends to bottle up emotions. As a result, this individual may experience difficulty in being able to ask for some need to be satisfied; socialize comfortably with other people; speak up in a discussion; express feelings to friends; return some merchandise to a store; and/or accept a compliment from someone else without refuting or demeaning it. In addition, nonassertive individuals are often "victimized" by others in the sense that they cannot say "No" to unreasonable requests (e.g., refusing a friend who wants to borrow a highly valued car; or saying "No" to a pushy salesperson) and/or are unable to verbally protect themselves when someone is criticizing or nagging them unfairly. Nonassertive individuals are often depressed, have a poor self-concept, and see themselves as being at the mercy of the world around them.

At the other end of the continuum, there is the aggressive individual who does get more of his (or her) needs met — but often at the expense of someone else's dignity and self-respect. (This person may also have high anxiety, guilt, and/or deficits in social skills.) The aggressive individual is someone who may verbally explode at the slightest provocation and may even be prone to physical fighting when angry; or who embarrasses and puts down others by name calling or obscenities when his (or her) needs are not met. (For example, at a restaurant an aggressive individual may scream at the waitress when the food is not served to his/her liking, whereas a nonassertive individual would be more likely to eat the food and say nothing.) The aggressive person dominates all conversations without letting others talk; and continues to "attack" and criticize people even after they have tried to back away from the situation. Whereas the nonassertive individual is frequently "victimized" by others and consequently may tend to avoid other people, the aggressive person is in turn avoided by others in his or her environment. The end result is the same in the sense that those on the extreme ends of the nonassertive — aggressive continuum have few meaningful relationships with other people. One of the basic goals, then, of Assertion Training is to help the individual find the middle assertive area between nonassertion and aggression where it is possible to relate more effectively and successfully with other human beings and, at the same time, acquire more personal needs and feelings of self-worth. Assertion Training is not aggression training! Nor is it a set of procedures aimed at making the person less responsive to others! On the contrary, it is a set of procedures aimed at making the person more open and honest with his/her own feelings and needs as well as the constructive feelings and needs of others. In this sense, anger may be a very appropriate emotion as long as it is not expressed in a destructive manner.

An important distinction in Assertion Training involves *anxiety reduction* versus *skill training.* Most of us can recall instances in which we thought of what to say only after the opportunity to say it had already passed. Examples of this include being complimentary (and, therefore, potentially more attractive) to someone on a date, being able to disagree with someone in a conversation, remembering important points to make during a discussion with the boss, and/or asking someone to do a favor. Whereas a certain amount of tension may be beneficial to alertness and performance at one end of a behavioral continuum, if the anxiety and tension level becomes too high, successful performance of this activity may actually be impeded. Assertion Training, in conjunction with other behavioral procedures (such as relaxation training and systematic desensitization), can be used to keep the anxiety level below the point at which it interferes with optimum interpersonal interactions. Joseph Wolpe (1958, 1969, 1970), who has made some of the major contributions to Assertion Training, describes this technique as one of the major procedures by which a person can reciprocally inhibit and eliminate interpersonal anxiety. In Assertion Training with highly anxious individuals, a desensitization model is typically followed whereby the therapist attempts to keep anxiety at a minimum, gradually shaping and increasing the desired performance.

On the other hand, there are those individuals who, even when their anxiety levels are low, do not know what to say or do in interpersonal situations. For these people, Assertion Training involves *skill training* so that they are better able to obtain their needs. Dr. Julio Guerra and I spent a year training high school and college-age students in a free clinic how to engage in more satisfying interpersonal relations with members of the opposite sex. Many of these young people knew what to say or do when in the company of the opposite sex; however, their high anxiety levels prevented them from carrying out these actions. Others in the same group did not know how to go about making a date with someone else, how to start or maintain a conversation, or what behaviors the opposite sex generally considered to be complimentary and satisfactory. In most cases it has been our experience that individuals in Assertion Training require *both* anxiety reduction and skill training in being helped to reach desired goals.

Who can utilize Assertion Training principles? It is our belief that each and every one of us can benefit from being assertive. Likewise, people who work with others, especially in a supervisory or training capacity (e.g., therapists, teachers, parents, and training managers), are in a excellent position to teach others assertive behaviors — both by what they model themselves and by some of the systematic procedures described in this chapter. Thus far, we have used Assertion Training with hospitalized patients, out-patients, couples, women's groups, children, adolescents, school administrators, factory workers, business people, and students. The content and focus of what is taught may differ from group to group; however, the overall theme of enhancing a person's self-worth and ability to better survive in a socialized society remains the same.

When can and should assertive responses be made? As we have said, assertive behaviors may be appropriate when a person is attempting to reduce interpersonal anxiety; promote more open and successful communications; acquire additional social skills; and enhance feelings of self-dignity and self-worth. Whereas previous writers have placed a great deal of emphasis on the individual's ability to protect himself from being taken advantage of by others, we feel it is equally important to teach people how and when to express love, affection, and/or praise to others in the environment (Lazarus, 1973, has also emphasized this). However, in responding assertively (both in approach and protective situations), every attempt should be made to avoid harsh, punitive consequences to assertive behavior. If this punishment occurs, a person will be less likely or willing to act assertively in the future. You may know how to respond assertively in a specific situation and *deliberately choose not to do so* if you feel that such a response will lead to the termination of a job, marriage, relationship, etc. that you do not wish to end. On the other hand, you may choose to take this risk, hoping to achieve a better relationship, if you feel that retaining your self-dignity and self-respect is more important than maintaining the relationship as it presently stands.

Two final points before moving on to the next section. There appear to be two myths in our society today to which Assertion Training is directly opposed. The first is the "myth of modesty" and the second is the "myth of the good friend." For some reason, many people in our society today (from the time they are young children) are taught to be modest about their abilities and achievements. One unfortunate result of this modesty, when taken to extreme, is that a person is unable graciously to accept compliments and praise from others and, in some cases, is not even able to acknowledge admirable qualities to himself. As a result of constantly refuting the compliments of others (e.g., "I think your house looks really nice." "That's only because the cleaning lady was here today") the individual is less likely to be complimented in the future. When the compliments then fail to occur, that person often begins to feel rejected and has a poor self-concept. Although Assertion Training does not attempt to turn people into boastful braggarts, it does attempt to help them acknowledge their own positive attributes and accept the compliments and praise given by others.

With respect to the "myth of the good friend," we often assume that if another person *really* cared for us, that person would know what we are really thinking or feeling (e.g., "He should have known I would be angry about his leaving the house to go fishing this weekend when my sister was visiting us"). Being a good friend, or spouse, or parent, or boss does not mean that person has the ability to read minds. If you want people to know what you are thinking or feeling, you have the responsibility to tell them!

DETERMINING THE NEED FOR ASSERTION TRAINING

Given that no individual acts assertively 100% of the time and that we do not always get what we want even when we do act assertively, determining the need for some Assertion Training becomes a matter of analyzing *how often* and *under what circumstances* a person responds in a nonassertive or aggressive manner. As Alberti and Emmons (1970, 1974) have indicated, some people may respond in a nonassertive or aggressive manner in specific situations or with specific individuals in their environment whereas others may respond in this manner over a wide variety of situations and with a greater number of people. Also, as we have indicated in our book on Assertion Training (Cotler & Guerra, 1976), individuals may be differentiated in terms of *request* and *refusal* situations that occur with *intimate* versus *superficial* relationships. The extent and the circumstances of these nonassertive and aggressive responses can usually be obtained through an in-depth interview and a number of self-report, paper-and-pencil measures. In conducting the interviews, it is important to determine how the clients see themselves, how much value they place on their own importance, what are their therapeutic goals and aspirations, what other persons are important in their lives, how they interact with others, and what the typical consequences are of these interactions. By carefully listening and questioning the clients as they describe these interactions (or lack of certain interactions), one can often detect clear evidence of anxiety, the absence of certain social skills, and specific nonassertive/aggressive behaviors.

In addition to the in-depth interview, there are several paper-and-pencil, self-report measures which may be useful in determining the need for some Assertion Training (see Cotler & Guerra, 1976, for a listing of these). Although these questionnaires can serve as a useful adjunct to the initial screening process, there are certain limitations and precautions to their use which should be taken into consideration so as to prevent the collection of misleading information (Cotler & Guerra, 1976).

GROUP VERSUS INDIVIDUAL
ASSERTION TRAINING

Although Assertion Training procedures were originally carried out on a one-to-one basis (Salter, 1949; Wolpe, 1958), increasingly more attention has been given to the use and value of "assertion groups" (Lazarus, 1968; Hedquist & Weinhold, 1970; Alberti & Emmons, 1970, 1974; Fensterheim, 1972; Booraem & Flowers, 1972; Bloomfield, 1973; Cotler, 1973, 1975; Flowers & Guerra, 1974, Shoemaker & Paulson, 1973). In conducting assertion groups in various types of settings, we have generally found that the group model is much more effective and appropriate than teaching assertive behaviors on a one-to-one basis. By utilizing the group setting, the client can obtain the much-needed support and encouragement from others as he or she tries out new behaviors. There is also the advantage that the individual can learn and profit from watching others acquire competence in their own assertive behaviors. Other advantages include the availability of feedback from different people in the group; the opportunity to practise assertive behaviors and do behavioral rehearsal with individuals of different sexes, ages, and backgrounds in the group; the greater variety of situations and assertive solutions to work with; and the opportunity for the client to "coach" others in becoming more assertive. Regarding this last point, Flowers and Guerra (1974) found that people who had the opportunity to serve as "coaches" learned assertive behaviors significantly better than those who did not get this practice as part of their training.

SETTING UP AN ASSERTION TRAINING GROUP

In most cases, assertion groups meet weekly for one and a half to three hours each session. The group can be time-limited (six to twelve weeks) or can be open-ended with new members constantly coming in and other members "graduating" from the group. (Lazarus, 1968, prefers to close the group after the third session and states that most of the learning takes place within the first fifteen to twenty sessions.) Group size generally ranges from six to twelve clients with two to four therapists and/or "visitors" being present at any given time.

After having run several assertion groups, we feel that having at least two trained therapists present at any given time (preferably a man and a woman) offers a distinct advantage to the single therapist model. To begin with, Assertion Training tends to be a very active and potentially draining experience for the therapist; consequently, an additional therapist (or two) allows for recuperation and time to observe the group process. In addition, the coaching and behavioral rehearsal aspects of Assertion Training function much more smoothly and effectively with two or more therapists present. Finally, therapists often rely on different assertive response styles in dealing with the same situation; consequently, having more than one therapist present gives the participants the opportunity to view alternative ways of dealing with the same situation.

Whereas our groups are, in most cases, roughly similar with respect to the absence of psychoses, there may be broad variations with respect to socioeconomic status, education, age, marital status, and sex. This heterogeneity of group membership has been found to be extremely valuable in providing the participants with the opportunity to try out their assertive skills with a broad spectrum of other individuals. It is also beneficial, whenever possible, to have clients from both ends of the nonassertive/ aggressive continuum present in the same group. This broad spectrum allows individuals on both sides of the continuum more easily to find the anchoring points and the "middle ground" between nonassertion and aggression.

In setting up an assertion group, we have found it useful to have a supply of "canned" situations available which describe events that are frequently handled in a nonassertive or aggressive manner (e.g., telling a friend that he or she is doing something that bothers you, resisting a strong sales pitch, or requesting the return of an item that was borrowed from you). The canned situations are especially helpful in providing examples for behavior rehearsal during the early sessions.

Also, in setting up an assertion group, the use of feedback equipment has been found to be very helpful. An audio recorder can be played back to the individual after he or she practices some assertive behavior in order to give feedback as to voice intonation, volume, and firmness (Wolpe & Lazarus, 1966; Lazarus, 1968; McFall & Marston, 1970; McFall & Lillesand, 1971; Cotler, 1973). However, as Alberti and Emmons (1970),

Melnick (1973), and Eisler, Miller, Hersen, and Alford (1974) have indicated, the use of a videotape may be even more effective. The utilization of audio and video equipment may not only be important in providing important feedback information to the client, but in addition, as O'Connor (1969) demonstrated with young children in altering social interactions and Rathus (1973) demonstrated with college women, it may be possible to train individuals in assertive skills by having them view (or listen to) others who can successfully assert themselves.

CONDUCTING AN ASSERTION TRAINING GROUP

The first order of business in an assertion group is to go over the general philosophy of self-dignity and its relationship to assertive behaviors. Case examples of nonassertive, aggressive, and assertive behaviors are given together with some of the ways of dealing with various problem situations. The behavioral goals of the group are discussed together with what types of procedures will be employed. It is explained that the group is designed to keep stress, anxiety, and embarrassment at a minimum; consequently, it is not an "encounter" or "sensitivity" type of group wherein the anxiety level can deliberately be kept quite high for extended periods of time. It is also noted that in becoming more assertive, people will probably not be able (or requested) to deal with those situations which initially evoke high levels of tension. Instead, clients are gradually directed, coached, and given practice in working with increasingly more difficult situations, starting with the least anxiety-producing situation and moving forward in a step-by-step manner. Group participants are also cautioned as to the potential punishing consequences of their assertive actions, and from the beginning of the group process, discrimination training is given as to when asserting oneself versus taking some other form of action is most appropriate.

Two of the first procedural steps covered in the group are the use of "SUDS" and the "no apology rule." "SUDS" stands for the Subjective Units of Discomfort Scale, and is utilized to determine just how anxious a group member feels at any given point. The scale is derived from Wolpe's (1969) concept of the Subjective Unit of Disturbance (SUD). The SUD scale we use ranges from 0 to 100 with 0 representing a state of no anxiety and complete calmness (the feeling you have just before you fall asleep, or after taking a hot bath) and 100 representing an extremely high state of anxiety and tension (the feeling you might have when you are on a large airplane and see the engines suddenly catch fire). Throughout the sessions, the participants are asked to give a subjective score from 0 to 100 as to how relaxed or anxious they feel. This information is used by the group leaders, who determine the pacing and the direction of assertion practice. Because we adhere to a "desensitization model" (Wolpe, 1958) rather than to an "implosion model" (Stampfl & Levis, 1967) in doing Assertion Training, every effort is made to gradually "shape" the individual to handle increasingly more stressful situations while, at the same time, keeping the SUDS level low. (See chapter 9 for a comparison of the two models.) This procedure of a gradual progression from one item (or part of an item) to the next is not unique to us, and it can be found in the writings of others as well (Wolpe, 1969, 1970, 1973; Lazarus, 1968; Geisinger, 1969; Alberti & Emmons, 1970; Fensterheim, 1972; Booraem & Flowers, 1972).

With respect to the "no apology rule," it is explained that many nonassertive individuals tend to be overly apologetic and say "I'm sorry" a great deal of the time. In some cases, they apologize to the point of excusing themselves for taking up oxygen or space when they are in the same room with other people. We explain that although an apology may be very appropriate at certain times, the words, "I'm sorry" are too often used by nonassertive persons to get them out of anxiety-producing situations ("I would like to show you our new Herbee Big Mouth vacuum." "I'm sorry, I already have a vacuum." Note: There is no reason to say, "I'm sorry" if one does not want or need another vacuum). Consequently, for the purposes of the group, no one (including the therapists and the members with aggressive behaviors) is to say, "I'm sorry" during the session. (They can, however, make an apology using other words if they feel that is appropriate.) If the "I'm sorry" statement is made during the session, it is pointed out to the individual, and he or she is asked to rephrase the statement. For example, if someone comes into a meeting late and is questioned about his or her tardiness, a high frequency response is, "I'm sorry, I didn't mean to disrupt anything." This response, which assumes blame and sometimes guilt, is often all that is needed to shift the attention and reduce the anxiety for that individual. But if a woman client, for example, believes she has a good reason for being late or just does not wish to apologize, she may be coached to say something like: "I had something very important to do before I came here" (note: she need not go into details if she does not wish to do so), or "I apologize for being late and I will try to be here on time for the next meeting" or "Because these meetings never seem to start on time, I didn't rush to get here; however, if we will agree to start on time, I will be here at the appointed hour next week." Initially, one of the group leaders may model how walking in late to a meeting without saying "I'm sorry" might be handled (with the other therapist and group members acting as the protagonists). Then the clients receive practice and some coaching as they role-play this same situation until they can comfortably respond in an assertive manner (with the anxiety levels constantly monitored).

We feel that the coaching role is one of the most integral parts of our

Assertion Training groups. It is also one of the most difficult roles to teach others (including other therapists). The job of the coach is actually three-fold. One aspect involves giving the "asserter" specific words to say in an interaction that is being practiced when the asserter cannot think of what to say next and/or when that person's anxiety becomes too high to allow him/her to think clearly. A second function of the coach is to give constant feedback (especially positive feedback) to the assertor as he or she is role playing and practicing a specific situation. The third function is to constantly monitor the client's anxiety level so as to pace and direct the flow of the interaction. The role of the coach is an extremely active one, and it is one that requires a considerable amount of practice. At the same time, however, it may be one of the most important aspects of successful Assertion Training.

In working with specific assertive skills, the group is often divided into triads with one individual taking the role of the "asserter," one person acting as the "coach," and the third person assuming the "recipient" or "protagonist" role. The participants then role-play various situations (either canned or real) and alternate roles so that each person has the opportunity to be the asserter, coach, and recipient. Until the group members can role-play the different roles comfortably, the group leader(s) often take the role of the recipient; however, within a short period of time, the other group members can begin taking this role as well as the role of the coach.

In addition to the assertive questionnaires used in the initial assessment of the individual, there are a number of other self-report, paper-and-pencil measures that we use throughout the training process. One such measure is the Assertive Goal Scale, which provides information as to the individualized short-and long-range assertive goals of each group member, the weighted importance of each of these goals, the anticipated anxiety level in completing the goals, and the length of time the individual thinks it will take to successfully complete each goal (Cotler & Guerra, 1976). This scale is first given during one of the early sessions and then again at various times throughout the training process. The participants are also asked to keep a record of their assertive, nonassertive, and aggressive behaviors outside the group in an Assertion Training Diary (a similar practice has been followed by Wolpe, 1958; Fensterheim, 1972; Shoemaker & Paulson, 1973). This Assertion Training Diary is used to record the assertion-related situation, the person's anxiety level in the situation, the outcome (i.e., what happened and how the person felt), and the person's future goals related to this or similar situations. This diary constitutes many of the situations that are discussed, role-played, and coached during the group sessions. In reporting on these outside experiences, it is extremely important that clients receive praise and support for their successful behaviors as well as discussing their failures.

Closely related to the record keeping is the utilization of homework assignments (Salter, 1949; Wolpe & Lazarus, 1966; Lazarus, 1968; Neuman, 1969; Alberti & Emmons, 1970; Fensterheim, 1972; Booraem & Flowers, 1972; Guerra & Horskey, 1973; Shoemaker & Paulson, 1973; Cotler, 1973, 1975; Cotler & Guerra, 1976). As a person begins to make progress in becoming more assertive, he/she is asked to complete certain assignments outside the group. These assignments are recorded on a Homework Diary Sheet and their outcomes are discussed during the next group session. In making these assignments, it is very important that they be arranged in a hierarchical order with the least stressful tasks being assigned first so that the probability for success is maximized. The first assignment may be one that does not require any personal interaction, such as reading a book on Assertion Training (e.g., Alberti & Emmons, 1974; Phelps & Austin, 1975). Depending upon the individual's goals, anxiety level, and progress, additional assignments can include tasks such as asking the telephone information operator for a phone number, going to a gas station and asking for some special service such as checking battery water after buying $2 worth of gas, returning a previously purchased item to a store, complimenting the service given in a restaurant, starting a conversation with someone, and so on. The clients are asked to record their SUDS level in performing each of these tasks, and gradually they are asked to complete more difficult assignments and ones that relate specifically to life situations in which they would like to become more assertive. (For a more detailed list of homework assignments, refer to Cotler & Guerra, 1976.)

In teaching assertive behaviors, an assortment of various procedures are frequently used (e.g., behavior rehearsal, shaping, modeling, coaching, homework assignments). Like others before us (Wolpe, 1958, 1969, 1970, 1973; Lesser, 1967; Lazarus, 1968; Wilson & Smith, 1968; Geisinger, 1969; Piaget & Lazarus, 1969), we also incorporate relaxation training and systematic desensitization into the Assertion Training process. Consequently, during some of the early sessions, participants are taught how to produce a state of relaxation in themselves. This training is carried out using imagery, deep-breathing exercises, and, in some cases, biofeedback equipment. In later sessions, the last ten to fifteen minutes of the session is sometimes spent in doing some relaxation exercises or other activity that allows the group to end in a warm, congenial manner.

Whereas Alberti and Emmons (1970) have indicated that they wish to avoid anything resembling "gamesmanship" when teaching assertive skills, we believe that certain "gamesmanship techniques" may be very appropriate to have in one's repertoire when another person may not honor or listen to an honest, direct, and clearly worded communication. These "protective techniques" can be utilized, for example, when a person continues nagging after you have asked him or her to stop; in saying "No" to a pushy salesperson or friend who is trying to impose wishes that do not agree with your feelings; when someone persists in unfairly criticizing and verbally attacking you. Several of these "protective techniques" have been given descriptive names such as "Broken Record," "Time-Out," "Sorting Issues," and "Disarming Anger" (Cotler, 1973; Cotler & Guerra, 1976) and these protective procedures are discussed, modeled, and practiced during the sessions. In utilizing these techniques, it should be recognized that there may be a temporary break in the interpersonal relationships (whether they are intimate or superficial) involved until the clients can acquire a more equitable method of communication. In some cases, the other person may not wish to adopt a more equitable relationship; consequently, there may be a more permanent break (resulting in a divorce, loss of friendship, or loss of a job). Because of this possibility, it is very important that people be aware of the possible consequences of their actions. In some cases, they may view the dissolution of a relationship as a rewarding outcome if they can acquire greater self-respect and dignity. It should also be noted that in many cases a break in the relationship can be avoided by working with both of the concerned parties (e.g., bringing the spouse into therapy and telling the client what to expect and how to foster a more equitable relationship) and/or teaching the client how to work out mutually regarding agreements through "contingency contracts."

An equally important aspect of Assertion Training is teaching people how to become closer and more intimate with others in their environment. Whereas some may have more trouble in protecting themselves from being "used" by others, others will experience greater difficulty in being able to express feelings of tenderness, praise, respect, and/or appreciation for other human beings. Examples of approach behaviors can include starting and maintaining enjoyable conversations, being able to compliment and praise others, being able to accept compliments given by others, communicating feelings using "I" statements, and being able to contract with someone else for mutually satisfying needs and desires. For example, in working with starting and maintaining more enjoyable conversations, we systematically teach others how to ask open-ended questions (i.e., those questions that tend to promote more discussion from the other person); how to listen for and follow up on "free information" (i.e., information volunteered but not asked for); how to make self-disclosures and give out free information about one's feelings, opinions, and experiences; how to tell stories and use humor; and how to give out compliments whenever they seem appropriate. We even teach how to terminate conversations, recognizing that an individual may not risk getting involved in the first place unless there is a way to back off if so desired. As with the protective skills, these approach behaviors are taught through discussion, role playing, coaching, homework assignments, and other assertion-related procedures (Cotler & Guerra, 1976).

In teaching these protective and approach skills, we also focus a considerable amount of time and attention on the nonverbal aspects of communication (Salter, 1949; Wolpe & Lazarus, 1966; Booraem & Flowers, 1972; Eisler et al., 1973; Guerra & Horskey, 1974; Eisler et al., 1974, have also done work in this area). Our intent here is to have people's nonverbal messages match and complement what they are attempting to communicate verbally. So we work with factors such as eye contact, voice characteristics, body space, facial expressions, timing, and touching (Cotler & Guerra, 1976). We have found that positive physical contact is one of the more difficult nonverbal behaviors to teach others (including therapists), and yet this can be one of the most rewarding and meaningful (assertive) behaviors in a relationship.

EVALUATING THE OUTCOME
OF ASSERTION TRAINING

Wolpe and Lazarus (1966) have indicated that improvement appears to follow a similar pattern for people receiving Assertion Training, especially those who are seen over a three- to six-month period. Initially the client becomes aware of the extent of her/his nonassertive or aggressive behaviors and the negative repercussions to these behavior patterns. Next comes an appreciation for the potential of assertive behaviors; this is followed by a tentative and sometimes clumsy attempt to act in an assertive manner. After the person has ironed out some of the rough spots in acting assertively and standing up for his/her rights, there may occur a stage in which the formerly nonassertive individual's responses are modified by the negative environmental consequences and the feedback received in the group. Then the newly acquired assertive skills begin to be used in a much more appropriate manner; the client expresses feelings and stands up for his or her rights more consistently while, at the same time, discriminating under what circumstances the assertive responses may be inappropriate or unadaptive. Finally, there is a stage of development in which the client becomes aware of a growing mastery of various interpersonal situations, and with this awareness, a better self-concept with greater self-respect emerges.

Changes occurring as a result of Assertive Training can be evaluated across three major dimensions: self-report measures, behavioral changes, and physiological changes. With respect to the self-report, paper-and-pencil measures (which are probably the most common type of measure used at this time), we are currently using the number of goals completed on the Assertive Goal Scale, the number of homework assignments completed successfully, changes in anxiety levels as reported on the various SUD scales, and changes in the questionnaires that are administered before and after training is completed. With respect to behavioral changes, most of these measures concern behaviors that occur within the group. As such, eye contact, frequency of touching, the number of self-disclosures, body space, etc. are all within the realms of measurement and statistical evaluation. Outside the group setting, there has been some limited use of the contrived situation, in which, for example, a confederate of the therapist calls the client and tries to persuade him/her to do something (e.g., buy magazines, volunteer time); however, this has only been reported thus far with student populations (McFall & Marston, 1970; McFall & Lillesand, 1971.) An evaluation criterion that has not as yet been reported involves the use of portable, biofeedback equipment that could be carried unseen into the portable, biofeedback equipment that could be carried unseen into the client's environment and used to record and monitor anxiety levels as that person encounters various interpersonal situations. There has been some attempt to measure physiological changes within the Assertion Training session (McFall & Marston, 1970), and it is probably just a matter of time before physiological measures are given more evaluative attention both within and outside the group sessions.

CONCLUSION

It may be too early as yet to assess the impact and value of Assertion Training to the behavioral therapies or to psychotherapy in general. Certainly there have been several additions made to the early Assertion Training procedures described by Salter (1949) and Wolpe (1958). These additions have included the utilization of group methods; work with hospitalized patients; the use of tokens to provide feedback and effect changes occurring within groups, and the use of multiple therapists in conducting group Assertion Training. Assertion Training procedures have been shown to be useful in a wide variety of settings and with various target populations. As therapists become more knowledgeable and skilled in the area of Assertion Training, the range of application and the innovations are likely to expand even further. It is our belief that Assertion Training will have its greatest impact over the next few years with adolescents, young adults, and women, because these are three populations that are actively seeking to obtain more freedom, recognition, and equality in our present society. As evidenced by the number of books that have recently been published in this area (Alberti & Emmons, 1975; Cotler & Guerra, 1976; Fensterheim & Baer, 1975; Lazarus & Fay, 1975; Phelps & Austin, 1975), Assertion Training is rapidly gaining increasingly more attention in the therapy literature. Perhaps we are now just beginning to recognize the full impact and utility of these procedures to enhance self-dignity and to satisfy more interpersonal and intrapersonal needs.

REFERENCES

ALBERTI, R. E., & EMMONS, M. L. *Your perfect right: a guide to assertive behavior.* San Luis Obispo, Cal.: Impact, 1970.

ALBERTI, R. E., & EMMONS, M. L. *Stand up, speak out, talk back!* New York: Pocket Books, 1975.

ALBERTI, R. E., & EMMONS, M. L. *Your perfect right* (2nd ed.). San Luis Obispo, Cal.: Impact, 1974.

BLOOMFIELD, H. H. Assertive training in an outpatient group of chronic schizophrenics: a preliminary report. *Behaviour Therapy,* 1973, *4,* 277–281.

BOORAEM, C. D., & FLOWERS, J. V. Reduction of anxiety and personal space as a function of assertion training with severely disturbed neuropsychiatric inpatients. *Psychological Reports,* 1972, *30,* 923–929.

COTLER, S. B. *A cassette tape on relaxation training.* Huntington Beach, Cal.: Continuing Education Seminars, 1976.

COTLER, S. B. Assertion training: a road leading where? *The Counseling Psychologist,* 1975, *5,* 20–29.

COTLER, S. B. *How to train others to do assertion training: a didactic group model.* Paper presented at Western Psychological Association meetings, Anaheim, Cal., April, 1973.

COTLER, S. B., & GUERRA, J. J. *Assertion training: a humanistic-behavioral guide to self-dignity.* Champaign, Ill.: Research Press, 1976.

EISLER, R. M., MILLER, P. M., & HERSEN, M. Components of assertive behavior. *Journal of Clinical Psychology,* 1973, *3,* 295–299.

EISLER, R. M., MILLER, P. M., HERSEN, M., & ALFORD, H. Effects of assertion training on marital interaction. *Archives of General Psychiatry,* 1974, *30,* 643–649.

FENSTERHEIM, H. Behavior therapy: assertive training in groups. In Sager, C. J., and Kaplan, H. (Eds.), *Progress in group and family therapy*. New York: Brunner/Mazel, 1972.

FENSTERHEIM, H., & BAER, J. *Don't say yes when you want to say no*. New York: David McKay, 1975.

FLOWERS, J. V., & GUERRA, J. The use of client-coaching in assertion training with large groups. *Community Mental Health Journal*, 1974, *10*, 414–417.

GARLINGTON, W. K., & COTLER, S. B. Systematic desensitization with test anxiety. *Behaviour Research and Therapy*, 1968, *6*, 247–256.

GEISINGER, D. L. Controlling sexual and interpersonal anxieties. In Krumboltz, J. D., and Thoresen, C. E. (Eds.), *Behavioral counseling: cases and techniques*. New York: Holt, Rinehart and Winston, 1969.

GUERRA, J., & HORSKY, D. *The use of "graduated" clients as role models in an assertion training group at a free clinic*. Paper presented at Western Psychological Association meetings, Anaheim, Cal., April, 1973.

HEDQUIST, F. J., & WEINHOLD, B. K. Behavioral group counseling with socially anxious and unassertive college students. *Journal of Counseling Psychology*, 1970, *17*, 237–242.

LAZARUS, A. A. Behavior rehearsal vs. nondirective therapy vs. advice in effecting behavior change. *Behaviour Research and Therapy*, 1966, *4*, 209–212.

LAZARUS, A. A. Behavior therapy in groups. In Gazda, G. M. (Ed.), *Basic approaches to group psychotherapy and group counseling*. Springfield, Ill.: Charles C. Thomas, 1968.

LAZARUS, A. A. On assertive behavior: A brief note. *Behavior Therapy*, 1973, *4*, 697–699.

LAZARUS, A. A., & FAY, A. *I can if I want to*. New York: William Morrow & Co., 1975.

LESSER, E. Behavior therapy with a narcotics user: a case report. *Behaviour Research and Therapy*, 1967, *5*, 251–252.

MCCALL, R. M., & MARSTON, A. R. An experimental investigation of behavior rehearsal in assertive training. *Journal of Abnormal Psychology*, 1970, *76*, 295–303.

MCCALL, R. M., & MARSTON, A. R. Behavior rehearsal with modeling and coaching in assertion training. *Journal of Abnormal Psychology*, 1971, *77*, 313-323.

MELNICK, J. A comparison of replication techniques in the modification of minimal dating behavior. *Journal of Abnormal Psychology*, 1973, *81*, 51–59.

NEUMAN, D. Using assertive training. In Krumboltz, J. D., and Thoresen, C. E. (Eds.), *Behavioral counseling: cases and techniques*. New York: Holt, Rinehart and Winston, 1969.

O'CONNOR, R. D. Modification of social withdrawal through symbolic modeling. *Journal of Applied Behavior Analysis*, 1969, *2*, 15–22.

PHELPS, S., & AUSTIN, N. *The assertive woman.* San Luis Obispo, Cal.: Impact, 1975.

PIAGET, G. W., & LAZARUS, A. A. The use of rehearsal-desensitization. *Psychotherapy: Theory, Research, and Practice,* 1969, *6,* 264–266.

RATHUS, S. A. Instigation of assertive behavior through videotape-mediated assertive models and direct practice. *Behaviour Research and Therapy,* 1973, *11,* 57–65.

SALTER, A. *Conditioned reflex therapy.* New York: Creative Age Press, 1949.

SHOEMAKER, M. E., & PAULSON, T. L. *Group assertion training for mothers as a family intervention in a child out-patient setting.* Paper presented at the Western Psychological Association meetings, Anaheim, Cal., April, 1973.

STAMPEL, T. G., & LEVIS, D. J. Essentials of implosive therapy: a learning-theory-based psychodynamic behavioral therapy. *Journal of Abnormal Psychology,* 1967, *72,* 496–503.

WILSON, A. E., & SMITH, F. J. *Counterconditioning therapy using free association: a case study.* Paper presented at the American Psychological Association meetings, San Francisco, Cal., Sept. 1968.

WOLPE, J. *Psychotherapy by reciprocal inhibition.* Stanford, Cal.: Stanford University Press, 1958.

WOLPE, J. *The practice of behavior therapy.* New York: Pergamon Press, 1969.

WOLPE, J. The instigation of assertive behavior: transcripts from two cases. *Journal of Behavior Therapy and Experimental Psychiatry,* 1970, *1,* 145–151.

WOLPE, J. Supervision transcript: V. Mainly about assertion training. *Journal of Behavior Therapy and Experimental Psychiatry,* 1973, *4,* 141–148.

WOLPE, J., & LAZARUS, A. A. *Behavior therapy techniques: a guide to the treatment of neuroses.* New York: Pergamon Press, 1966.

IV

THERAPIES EMPHASIZING
BIOLOGICAL PROCESSES

Part II of this volume dealt with therapies directed toward improving the client's self-understanding through cognitive and emotional processes. Part III was concerned with behavioral therapies that were less concerned with self-understanding than with overt improvement. We come now to the two concluding therapies, both of which have biological emphases. The first, LSD Therapy, integrates the use of a biochemical agent into a psychological framework (usually psychoanalysis), while Megavitamin Therapy focuses entirely on the client's biological functioning. Many recent advances in psychobiology and psychopharmacology have stimulated renewed interest in biological approaches to the understanding and treatment of mental illness.

Cohen, in his chapter on LSD Therapy, postulates that the client, under the influence of LSD, may undergo a reshaping of his perceptual and cognitive structures such that he sees himself, present and past, in a new light. So graphic, in fact, is Cohen's description of the client's LSD experience that the term "a new light" seems much too weak. The use of LSD for any purpose has become exceedingly controversial since the unfavorable publicity about its dangers and misuses. However, some controlled research has continued and there have been promising reports about the use of LSD with terminally ill clients.

Rimland, in his chapter on Megavitamin Therapy, relies on biochemistry rather than psychological experience to bring about change in the client. His perspective, philosophy, and assumptions are radically different from those of other contributors to this book. Rimland insists that research does not support the widely held belief in psychogenic mental illness, nor in psychotherapeutic treatment for such disorders. He believes the treatments of the future will come largely from the biochemistry laboratory; but, unlike Cohen, he holds out for the use of substances normally present in the human body.

12

The Use of Psychedelics as Adjuncts to Psychotherapy

Sidney Cohen

Before judging whether a drug like LSD has any value as a therapeutic adjunct, we should examine the effects of this agent on human psychic functioning. Perhaps some of the effects can be exploited in intensifying or accelerating the unlearning and learning processes we call psychotherapy. Certain effects which do not seem to be associated with the psychotherapeutic process are not considered at this time.

THE PSYCHEDELIC STATE

The Freudian topography of the psyche is not the most accurate one, but it is widely known, and I shall use it. Those who prefer some other model will be able to translate what is said into programming theory, learning theory, behavior theory, Jungian, Adlerian, or even Zen theory.

What I shall emphasize is psychedelic psychotherapy. This is the use of a high dose (300–1000 mcg) of d-lysergic acid diethylamide (LSD) to produce a maximal experience. Psycholytic psychotherapy is a technique that employs small amounts of LSD (25–150 mcg) to enhance conventional psychotherapeutic methods. Occasional LSD experiences are interspersed in a series of non-drug sessions in the expectation that otherwise inacces-

Sidney Cohen is director of the Council on Alcohol and Drug Abuse, UCLA. He is author of *The Beyond Within—The LSD Story, Psychochemotherapy: The Physician's Manual,* and co-author of *LSD.* He is also consultant to the National Institute of Mental Health.

sible unconscious material will be retrieved, and the emotional working through of significant problem areas will occur during the LSD session and during subsequent interviews. Table 12-1 compares some aspects of psycholytic and psychedelic therapy.

TABLE 12-1
Comparison of the Major Approaches to LSD Therapy

	Psycholytic Psychotherapy	Psychedelic Psychotherapy
Dose	Low (25–150 mcg).	High (300–1,000 mcg).
Frequency	Multiple sessions with numerous non-drug interviews for working through LSD sessions.	A single or very few LSD experiences.
Goal	Retrieval of unconscious material, reduction of defensiveness, intensification of transference, regression, insight, abreaction. Personality maturation through fuller understanding of oneself.	An out-of-the-body transcendental or mystical state; a psychological death-rebirth experience. A new beginning with the letting go of old, destructive behaviors.
Indications	Patients in conventional psychotherapy who are not making progress. May include neurotics, psychopaths, and psychosomatic problems.	Existential or situational problems: drug addiction, alcoholism, excessive grief reactions.

The Id

Little can be said about the effect of LSD on the id except that drives are generally diminished. Libidinal energies are channeled into other areas of the psyche. Unless situational cues or the explicit intent during the LSD experience are erotically directed, sexuality is reduced during the period of drug activity.

The Ego

Ego functioning is markedly altered. As loss of ego controls occurs during the LSD state, defensiveness initially increases in an effort to maintain ego integrity. In the full-blown state, ego intactness is markedly disrupted or completely lost. That aspect of ego functioning known as the observer self is usually in abeyance. In the absence of a critical self, incoming sensory information or recalled data are received with an overwhelming feeling of validity. This absence of the critical or monitoring function accounts for the "realer than real" declarations of the subject. Without the critical function of the ego, the subject thus becomes intensely suggestible to sensory cues. This hypersuggestibility can be exploited in the therapeutic process.

The loss of ego controls also produces an intensification of the patient-therapist interaction. Because the patient's reality-testing ability is in abeyance, the therapist becomes a most important object occupying a central, even enveloping role in the patient's fantasies. Rapport is ordinarily heightened, but the opposite occasionally occurs. The therapeutic biases of the therapist are picked up by the patient with great sensitivity. Patients of Freudian therapists report Freudian visual symbolism. Patients of Jungian therapists tell of archetypes and spectacular details from the collective unconscious.

In a therapeutic session the well-known visual alterations produced by LSD may be helpful. The imagery projected from unconscious material may be vividly displayed in polychromatic symbols. The retrieval of repressed material is seen rather than imagined. Sometimes it may be so vivid that it becomes terrifying and overpowering. At this point the therapist must actively support and reassure his patient. The working-through of the recalled information can be so painful that the therapist's function is to keep the patient from utilizing his repertoire of evasive tactics to escape from facing up to the grueling task of conflict resolution.

The peculiar synesthesias, a crossing-over of feelings and thought, also may come to serve a therapeutic function. The patient might not only be seeing his problems but also hearing and feeling them, indeed thoroughly reliving them. His memories achieve a multidimensionality that is rarely experienced in sober existence. Ancient memories are retrieved with startling clarity and veridicality. The recall of long-lost details can be greatly enhanced. Patients speak of actually re-experiencing the remembered event.

The emotional response is also exaggerated. It may vary from panic to ecstasy. The intense feelings engendered by the surge of unconscious material can be a powerful and shaking event. If emotional abreaction and emotional insight into these repressed matters is of therapeutic value, then LSD-assisted therapy is quite capable of providing them.

One frequently expressed reservation about LSD-engendered insights is whether they may be of a fictitious nature due to the toxic effect of the drug and without particular relevance to the patient's problems. Furthermore, the hypersuggestible nature of the condition makes some wonder whether the insights are not therapist-initiated from his verbal or nonverbal cues. In fact, this issue is one appropriate to ask of all insight therapy. No careful study has been done to validate LSD-derived insights. Perhaps such a study is not possible. One completely negativistic view is that an insight is that which the patient and his therapist believe. If they both thoroughly believe in the truth of the insightful experience it can be used to generate changes in neurotic styles, and the resultant change is the important part of the transaction. Even if it is assumed that drug-induced and therapist-induced components of the insight occur, some aspect of it must fit the patient's needs, or it will be rejected immediately or upon further working-through.

The Superego

It is in the area of the superego that the more important alterations of functioning occur while the patient is under the influence of LSD. These are the changes that I believe are the primary sources of behavior change when it occurs.

By the very nature of the high-dose LSD state, many acquired attitudes, beliefs, and goals become less significant. Feelings of shame and guilt are recognized as trivial or absurd. Ideas of self-depreciation and low self-esteem are set aside in view of the perceived "all-rightness" of the universe. The total or almost complete loss of ego boundaries results in strong feelings of universal relatedness. Existence is conceived as meaningful. However tiny one's part in the scheme of things is felt to be, somehow it is essential. The depersonalization also induces a fusion with all things and people since the "I" no longer exists but fuses into a union with everything.

Obviously one's value system undergoes great transformations. Many of the cultural and provincial taboos and personal aspirations recede. Values assume a more eternal and cosmic quality. Indeed, at the height of the reaction, strong feelings of omnipotence and omniscience can develop, and these require therapeutic assistance. At any rate, day-to-day and pedestrian troubles and problems seem insignificant in the midst of the transcendent experience. This temporarily altered perspective may be helpful for those people who are overwhelmed by the magnitude of their ordinary problems. If the old superego constraints were much too rigid and too demanding, they might remain relaxed after a transient exposure to the new frame of reference with its more cosmic values.

It can be inferred from what has been said that drastic chages in one's attitude toward one's personal death would occur. The life-death dichotomy disappears. Some patients report an absolute inability to distinguish between existence and nonexistence during the high-dose state. Ordinary fears of one's obliteration are set aside. The dissolution of ego boundaries can be considered a form of psychic death, with psychic rebirth occurring as the boundaries re-establish themselves. This psychological death can be conceptualized as a discontinuity of experience that may permit a new beginning unburdened by many of the old difficulties.

SOME ISSUES

In view of the potentially favorable therapeutic aspects of the controlled LSD state, we must examine a number of issues that arise. First of all, can a lifetime of ineffectual, destructive behavior patterns be changed by one or a few exposures to a psychedelic drug? It is evident that fundamental character structure can hardly be expected to undergo revision from a single event, no matter how unique it is. Some of the characterological matrix is genetically determined, other elements are deeply ingrained by a lifetime of conditioning. What seems to change following single dramatic events, whether they be chemically or experientially caused, are attitude, value, and belief systems. These qualitites are well-known to be amenable to sudden shifts. Religious conversion, maximal political indoctrination (brainwashing), and extreme emotional events are other methods of inducing alterations in these superego functions. Feelings of alienation and excessive fear of death are particularly amenable to the sort of transformation that LSD can produce. This has been exploited by me in a study of anguished, terminally ill cancer patients over the past decade. The favorable findings have been confirmed by Grof and Kast (discussed in edited volume of Gamage and Zerkin, 1970). In addition to the decrease in agitation over one's impending death, a reduction in the need for analgesics is generally observed. This, too, can be thought of as a shift in a person's attitude toward pain. It seems that the grim meaning of the pain requires large amounts of narcotics. When dying and death become more acceptable, the overwhelmingly fearful significance of the pain also is reduced.

Assuming that rapid changes in one's frame of reference occur, why is it that they do not "wash out," with the patient reverting back to his earlier behavioral patterns? In fact, this is precisely what tends to happen. More than one alcoholic who has been treated with psychedelic psychotherapy — has "seen the light," seen why he was destroying himself, and resolved never to drink again — has slipped back to his excessive drinking patterns after a period of time. It may be that we should think of the unique LSD event as providing the possibility for change rather than assuming that it will inevitably induce change. What is too often ignored is that a vast re-educational process must be provided during the post-LSD period. The established ineffective ways of responding to life stress must be converted into more effective coping mechanisms. Appropriate behavior must be rewarded, retrogressive activity must be examined and never rewarded. Without a suitable period of relearning (or reconditioning), it seems inevitable that the older defenses will prevail.

From what has been said, it is evident that some high-dose LSD states can produce a condition similar to the spontaneously occurring transcendental experience. Such qualities as ineffability, feelings of mystical union, perceptual brilliance, elation, and awe are mentioned by more than half of those who are given the drug under conditions conducive to a peak or religious experience. Whether the chemically induced transcendental state is identical to or merely mimics the naturally occurring state does not need to be resolved in this discussion. What is important is that the episodes of self-transcendence, whether chemically or spontaneously acquired, can result in altered personality, attitudinal, or behavioral changes that may be desirable or undesirable.

Such transformations following momentary religious experiences are well-documented. Individuals have made abrupt, sustained alterations in themselves and in their culture as the result of transcendental events. It is important to point out that the alterations happen much less frequently than one would hope. Large numbers of people have been overwhelmed by these extra-ordinary, shaking experiences, felt that henceforth their lives must be transformed, and found that after a short "honeymoon" period they slid back to their earlier levels of functioning. For some, the situation may have been worse than before the transcendent experience because the burden of guilt was added after one had finally seen the light and failed it.

INDICATIONS AND CONTRAINDICATIONS

It is the selected, severe, problem alcoholic who has been a prime target for psychedelic psychotherapy. He is often alienated from society, a "lost" person without sustaining faiths or beliefs. It is said that most problem drinkers must "hit bottom" before they can rehabilitate themselves. This "hitting bottom" seems to consist of a number of factors. It consists of the long-delayed acknowledgment that one is a drunk, that one's drinking is out of control, that help is needed, and that the situation is catastrophic. An LSD experience may provide some of these insights. The alcoholic's self-esteem tends to be low and his destructive life is obvious. Furthermore, his subsequent behavior can be an easy measure of success or failure. The initial reports by Osmond, Hoffer, and others were generally favorable. Some remarkable individual results were obtained. The later controlled studies tended to show that over a longer follow-up period, the group of alcoholics receiving LSD did not do significantly better than the group that received similar treatment without LSD. The lack of an intensive educational after-care program for both the LSD and control groups has been an almost universal defect in the design of these studies.

Other areas of treatment include impotence and frigidity, certain types of neuroses, drug addiction, and psychopathic personalities. Although individual investigators have reported successful results, the procedure has not been generally accepted. Lauretta Bender has studied some autistic children under daily doses of LSD. She reported improvement with increased contact with the environment. It is not clear whether the improvement was due to the psychedelic effects of the drug, since methysergide, a nonhallucinogenic LSD analogue, also gives good results. The improved contact may have been due to the increased central sympathetic stimulation which both compounds evoke.

Favorable indications for psychedelic psychotherapy include a high level of motivation to change, a history of past achievement with fairly good and not overly rigid ego defenses, an adequate level of intelligence, and an openness to the out-of-the-body state which LSD can produce. Those who have a serious situational problem with which they are unable to cope or those with a behavioral disturbance that is destructive are favorable candidates. Certain depressed patients do well. Family understanding and support of the procedure is a definite asset.

Paranoid personalities and borderline individuals are best not treated with LSD. In the former instance, the paranoid mechanism may become reinforced; in the latter instance the individual could be precipitated into a prolonged psychotic break. Inadequate, unstable, immature personalities do not make significant progress with psychedelic psychotherapy and may be harmed by it. Very rigid individuals will fight the reaction and fail to benefit from the experience. The treatment of schizophrenic reactions with LSD is not considered a satisfactory procedure. No one believes that mental deficiency will be improved.

THERAPIST BREAKDOWN

I would like to close by mentioning one complication of LSD therapy that has hardly been mentioned in the literature. This is the therapist breakdown. I have witnessed an unexpected number of psychedelic therapists who have developed overt psychotic breaks, excessive paranoid states, severe depressions, or blatantly anti-social behaviors. There are a number of possible explanations for the surprisingly high casualty list. First of all, whenever a novel and spectacular treatment procedure appears, it is the marginal therapist who is most attracted to it. He has not done well with conventional techniques and readily embraces something new in the hope that the method will compensate for a lack of training or some interpersonal inadequacy. Psychedelic psychotherapy has a special hazard for the psychotherapist with paranoid trends. The patients are so vulnerable, the state is so overpowering, that the therapist may become more grandiose than usual. His ability to provide the unique experience reinforces private notions of omnipotence. A few have become so convinced of their Godlike power that they acted out these ideas. A few therapists became unhinged in the course of personally taking LSD too often and without proper guidance. Finally, doing psychedelic psychotherapy is a stressful experience. The hours of work are long, and the therapist's skill and energy are often strained to the utmost. The responsibilities are great, for without knowledgeable guidance and assistance, the defenseless patient can become overwhelmed and act out and hurt himself or fall apart and not be able to recoup.

SUMMARY

It is regrettable that the attention to the misuse of LSD caused a decrease in the number of human investigations with this interesting agent. Its evaluation as a psychotherapeutic adjunct remains incomplete. It is my impression that when the current anxieties about LSD abuse have subsided, we will resume its evaluation as an accelerator of psychotherapy. Surely, more skillful methods of reinforcing and perpetuating the attitudinal shifts which LSD can generate will be devised. Even more important, perhaps, is that this agent still has much to teach us about the nature of human thinking.

REFERENCES AND BIBLIOGRAPHY

ABRAMSON, H. A. (ED.). *The use of LSD in psychotherapy.* Josiah Macy, Jr. Foundation transactions. Madison, N.J.: Madison Printing Co., 1960.

ABRAMSON, H. A. (Ed.). *The use of LSD in psychotherapy and alcoholism.* New York: Bobbs-Merrill, 1967.

COHEN, S. *The beyond within: the LSD story.* New York: Atheneum, 1967.

The Use of Psychedelics as Adjuncts to Psychotherapy   **193**

COHEN, S. *The drug dilemma* (2nd ed.). New York: McGraw-Hill, 1976.

HOFFER, A., & OSMOND, H. *The hallucinogens.* New York: Academic Press, 1967.

LING, T. M., & BUCKMAN, J. *Lysergic acid and ritalin in the treatment of neurosis.* London: Lambarde Press, 1963.

PAHNKE, W. N., KURLAND, A. A., UNGER, S., SAVAGE, C., & GROF, S. The experimental use of psychedelic (LSD) psychotherapy. In Gamage, J. R., and Zerkin, E. L. (Eds.). *Hallucinogenic drug research.* Beloit, Wis.: Stash Press, 1970.

13

Psychological Treatment Versus Megavitamin Therapy

Bernard Rimland

Although my primary mission is to discuss the role of high-dosage vitamins in treating mental disorders, I feel I can do so most effectively by first discussing the conceptual basis underlying certain of the competitors to megavitamin therapy, most of which I regard as being, to put it kindly, obsolete.

THE VALIDITY OF CONCEPTS UNDERLYING PSYCHOTHERAPY

Most forms of treatment of mental disorder are based on the idea, and I believe it to be a demonstrably fallacious idea, that mental disorders are caused, partially or totally, by the patients' adverse experiences in the psychosocial environment. More specifically, most forms of psychotherapy are based on the concept that the patient has been damaged psychologically by faulty interactions with other people, usually his mother or other family

"Psychological Treatment versus Megavitamin Therapy," by Bernard Rimland, Ph. D. © 1976 by Bernard Rimland. This article appears in print for the first time in this volume.

Bernard Rimland is director of the Institute for Child Behavior Research, San Diego, and author of the book *Infantile Autism*. He has also contributed many articles on Megavitamin Therapy to journals and books.

members, and that he is thus suffering from only a "functional" problem. It is believed that there is nothing physically wrong with his brain, or his other bodily organs, that causes his psychological discomfort or his odd behavior. He is, in a word, "maladjusted" rather than physically impaired.

This idea is so pervasive and so widely accepted that I often find audiences incredulous when I tell them, quite frankly, that I believe it will in a decade or two be relegated to the realm of mythology.

Although it embarrasses me to confess my gullibility, I must admit that for some years I too believed in the "psychogenicity" or "functionality" of mental disorder. I was taught psychogenesis as a student, and subsequently taught it to my students when I became an instructor. It annoys me that the textbooks did not (and still do not) admit that they were presenting only theories — we students were led to believe that it was *known* that psychosocial factors not only *could* but *did* cause mental illness. Careful study of this problem convinces me that the authorities are wrong in this matter, just as authorities throughout history frequently have been proven wrong on other matters.

Since many readers will doubt that the concept of psychologically caused mental illness is even open to question, let me quote for you from the writings of others in support of my own position on the matter. (My position is not that it is *proven* that psychological factors cannot produce mental illness, but that there is at present no scientific evidence that indicates that they can — and I doubt that such evidence will be found.)

One authority who attempted to find evidence for the psychogenicity of mental illness is psychiatrist Ian Stevenson. Here is what he said:

> If the experiences of childhood importantly influence the later personality, we should expect to find some correlation between such experiences and the later occurrence of mental disorders. In fact, no such correlations have ever been shown. (Stevenson, 1957, p. 153)

Here are quotes from several other sources which will, I hope, help shake your conviction in the validity of what you may have believed heretofore about the psychogenicity of "mental" disorder:

> There are no data to prove that . . . there is a class of "functional" mental illness that is produced by emotional disturbance alone and susceptible of cure only by talking to the patient or allowing the patient to talk. (Hebb, 1949, p. 271)

> There seems to be no clearly demonstrated instance of either a cultural or social factor being known to be a predisposing factor in mental illness . . . The absence of clear-cut evidence does not show that the hypothesis is incorrect but only that it has not been demonstrated even once. (Milbank Memorial Fund, 1961, p. 379)

Psychologists have reasoned that the experiences the individual has in his early life at home . . . are major determinants in . . . the development of psychopathology. A review of the research of the past forty years failed to support this assumption. No factors were found in the parent-child inter-action of schizophrenics, neurotics or those with behavior disorders which could be identified as unique to them or which could distinguish one group from the other or any of the groups from the families of the controls. (Frank, 1965, p. 19).

If it is true, as I'm sure you may by now be willing to acknowledge, that the psychogenic viewpoint is less well-established scientifically than we have been led to believe, perhaps you are wondering, as I have been for the past fifteen years, why the belief in psychogenesis is so widely held, by both professionals and lay people. It is an intriguing question, and I have sought answers for it in many ways. I can only mention a few of the reasons at this point, but if you are interested in the problem you may wish to read a more comprehensive treatment of the subject in my paper "Psychogenesis versus Biogenesis" (Rimland, 1969).

In brief, here is my analysis of a few of the more important reasons for the peculiarly widespread belief in psychogenesis.

Negative Medical Tests

When medical tests fail to find a physical defect or problem known to be able to cause behavior disorders, the disorder is labeled "functional." Such illogic! Each human brain contains about 9 billion neurons — three times as many neurons as there are human beings on Earth! No one — not one of us 3 billion human beings now living — understands how even the simplest of these neurons work. Our knowledge about how the brain operates is very close to zero. (It may even be less than zero, in that much of what we think we know may prove to be wrong.) This being so, how can anyone be so arrogant as to say that a given brain is organically sound — that the person's problems stem from faulty upbringing? Since, according to the quotations cited above, there is no scientific evidence that poor upbringing *can* cause mental disorder, arriving at the conclusion that Mary Smith's problem is "functional" clearly involves some tenuous reasoning.

The "Self-Evident" Argument

According to some authorities, it is self-evident that faulty experiences bring about mental disorder, even though some of us may be more pre-disposed than others to become mentally disordered. I simply don't sub-scribe to such "evidence." It was self-evident for centuries that the earth was flat, that heavier-than-air devices could not fly, that heavy objects fall faster than light objects, that the atom is indivisible, etc. No, I prefer to base my beliefs on empirical evidence, and as the research studies quoted earlier show, there is no evidence that psychological factors can cause or contribute to the production of mental disorders.

Case Histories

At the root of much psychogenic thinking are the plausible and convincing case histories that we have all read in our textbooks and in novels, and seen on movie and television screens. Those stories in the small print on the pages of the textbooks were usually much more interesting and memorable than the technical discussions. It's too bad that they were used to illustrate points that were probably untrue. It is very easy for a textbook author to discuss a mentally abnormal patient, then go through the family history (sibling rivalry, foster mother, alcoholic father, etc.) to show very neatly how these adverse experiences caused the problem. The trouble is that *all of us* have had experiences in our childhood which could be trotted out if we became deranged. Think about it: suppose you secretly took a drug that produces aberrant behavior. Would a textbook author, unaware of the cause of your disorder but looking for interesting case material, be able to construct a good story from what he could find out about you? Of course he could.

Some years ago, at the University of California at Berkeley, a psychiatrist and a psychologist interviewed 100 normal young men of above-average intelligence (Renaud & Estess, 1961). They reported that they were surprised to find just as many supposedly "pathogenic" (disease-causing) circumstances in the lives of these men as in any group of "sick" patients they had seen. Their finding didn't surprise me, since research had made it obvious for some time that the relationship between adverse family/social environments and mental illness was purely coincidental, not the neat cause-and-effect one that had long been accepted.

I have mentioned only three of the many reasons I have uncovered for what I believe to be the erroneous belief that mental illness is ever or frequently of psychological origin, rather than being caused by biogenic factors. Some of the other reasons, such as "The Continuum Fallacy," "the Diagnostic Issue," and the "Unhappiness Error," are discussed in my previously mentioned paper "Psychogenesis versus Biogenesis" and will be treated more fully in a book now in preparation. Space limitations prevent further presentation of them here. My purpose for going into this matter was to instill a properly skeptical attitude toward the claims of the psychotherapists.

I am sometimes asked, "If you don't think the psychosocial environment contributes to mental illness, how do you account for the effectiveness of psychotherapy (or psychoanalysis) in helping patients with "mental" disorders? This question, as many readers probably know by now, has a very obvious answer: There is no scientific evidence whatever that psychotherapy does help the mentally ill (psychotics or neurotics), despite the numerous studies that have attempted to show its beneficial effects.

In 1949, in his celebrated book *The Organization of Behavior*, D.O. Hebb briefly reviewed the evidence on the effectiveness of psychotherapy and psychoanalysis and concluded flatly: "There is no body of fact to show that psychotherapy is valuable" (p. 271). A few years later, H. J. Eysenck made a more intensive review and came to the same conclusion (see Eysenck, 1966, and Rachman, 1971 for more recent reviews). The literature on the effectiveness of child psychotherapy has been separately reviewed by several authors (Levitt, 1963; Lewis, 1965) with similar findings. Levitt, basing his conclusion on nearly sixty controlled studies involving thousands of children, said the conclusion was "inescapable" that psychotherapy could not be claimed to be effective.

The studies that claim that benefits are derived from psychotherapy seem to be largely those in which no control group is used, and in which anecdotal and testimonial evidence make the findings scientifically useless. These are the kinds of studies that medicine (except for psychiatry) wisely learned to ignore long ago.

Space limitations prevent our reviewing the massive research literature on the efficacy of psychotherapy. It is possible only to note briefly that the proponents (usually practitioners) of psychotherapy have fought back vigorously, but their claims are peculiarly small. Pointing to what they regard as technical shortcomings in the research, they say, for the most part, "Psychotherapy has not been proven useless — it simply has not been proven useful" (Astin, 1961). They have also, as Astin noted, de-emphasized the "cure" aspects and have instead suggested rather nebulous general benefits, such as self-actualization or, perhaps, happiness, but again proof of efficacy is lacking.

The burden of proof of usefulness traditionally rests on the advocates of any treatment. Be that as it may, the failure of psychotherapy (and I do think it is a failure, to put the matter bluntly) to ameliorate mental disorder in children and adults is precisely what one would expect because the "insight" psychotherapy is intended to provide is of no relevance with regard to the cause of the disorder.

Since anyone questioning the claims of the psychotherapists is probably considered even more anti-humanitarian than one who questions psychogenesis, let me attempt to redeem myself by adding, as an aside, that I am in general agreement with the position taken by Schofield in his book *Psychotherapy: The Purchase of Friendship* (1964). Most people feel a desire to talk to a sympathetic person about their problems, and they should be given an opportunity to do so. To pretend, however, in the face of existing evidence, that such conversation has curative powers, or that the listener needs to be highly sophisticated in psychology or psychiatry, is quite unjustified.

I have been discussing primarily the "insight" forms of psychotherapy. The other class of psychological treatments for behavioral disorders is sometimes called, in contrast, "action therapy" or behavior therapy and involves training (or retraining) the patient so as to control the most obvious or disturbing of his symptoms. Unlike (insight) psychotherapy, there does seem to be some evidence that the action therapies often are effective. Because behavior modification tends to work, many people (including some rather sophisticated ones who should know better) claim that their success constitutes proof that the disorder was psychosocially caused. This is clearly nonsense — it would make as much sense to say that the usefulness of aspirin in treating a headache shows that a deficiency of aspirin caused the headache. It would be like saying that the usefulness of operant conditioning (a form of "action therapy") in training Helen Keller to write and speak proved that she had not been blind and deaf at the beginning of the treatment.

Since space limitations do not permit us to discuss these matters in any further detail, I will just have to assert that I believe that in coming decades it will become increasingly clear that the causes and treatments of behavior disorders will be better understood as our understanding of biochemistry increases, and that our present preoccupation with "psychological" causes will quickly fade into well-deserved obscurity.

THE MEGAVITAMIN TREATMENT: AN EXPERIMENT WITH PSYCHOTIC CHILDREN

My experience with the megavitamin approach is based largely on work with children, although most of the work in this field by others has been with adult patients.

One of the functions of the Institute for Child Behavior Research in San Diego is to serve as an information clearinghouse for parents and professionals around the world who are interested in research on the causes and treatment of severe behavior disorders in children. Each year we at the

Institute receive letters and phone calls from thousands of people asking for information and telling us what has and has not worked to help their child or the children with whom they are concerned. An amazing variety of ideas has been tried out — ranging from music and shadow therapy through psychotherapy and operant conditioning to colonic irrigations, spinal adjustments, and "rage reduction therapy." It doesn't take long to develop a skeptical attitude about most of these "breakthroughs."

In the mid-1960s, I began to hear from various parents who had started to experiment on their own mentally ill children, using quite large amounts of certain harmless, water-soluble vitamins. These unhappy people would write to me about the bitter disappointment and discouragement they had experienced with the usual treatment method, such as psychotherapy or psychoanalysis, which have repeatedly been found to be useless, yet which continue to be practiced, at great expense to the families. They would then tell me they had read articles in the *New York Times* and elsewhere about the work of Drs. Abram Hoffer and Humphry Osmond, who were reporting good results when they used massive dosages of certain vitamins on adult schizophrenics, and had decided to experiment on their own after determining there was no danger.

At first I was quite skeptical about the reports that some of the parents sent me about the improvement they saw in their sick children. As you may know, these children spurt ahead or fall apart periodically for no discernible reason, and whatever treatment is being used at the time gets the credit, or the blame. But as the letters accumulated, I became more interested in the reports. For one thing, the parents were often reporting changes in behavior that were clearly tied to the raising or lowering of the dosage level of one or more of the vitamins. Also, even though few of the parents were acquainted with each other and each was trying quite a variety of vitamins, the same small group of vitamins was being mentioned again and again. As the number of parent-experimenters grew, it began to include more parents whom I knew personally to be intelligent and reliable people. At that point I contacted a number of doctors in California and on the East Coast who had been experimenting with vitamin therapy. The combined information from the doctors and parents convinced me that I could not, in good conscience, fail to pursue this lead. I was of course aware that my working on the vitamin approach would create much hostility against me among many medical authorities who were totally and irrevocably convinced that the use of vitamins would not be helpful.

Before going on to describe the vitamin study itself, let me discuss a few important related points.

First, there is the often-voiced concern about safety. With the exception of vitamins A and D, which can be harmful for some people if taken in very large doses for an extended time, there is little or no danger in taking large quantities of vitamins. Most vitamins are soluble in water, and the body merely excretes what it doesn't use. The vitamins are immeasurably safer than the drugs that are routinely given to children. A recent report has shown, for example, a relationship between medically administered amphetamines and the later occurrence of Hodgkin's disease (Newell, Rawlings, Kinnear, Correa, Henderson, Dworsky, Menck, Thompson, & Sheehan, 1973).

Second, the commonly held belief that everyone gets all the vitamins he needs by eating a normal diet should be recognized as sheer nonsense. Most of us can get along reasonably well, apparently, without supplementing our vitamin intake, but even among normal, well-functioning people there is an enormous range of individuality in vitamin needs. A range of 2,000 percent in vitamin requirements from one healthy person to another is not uncommon, as biochemist Roger Williams (1956) has pointed out in his book *Biochemical Individuality* and elsewhere. Additionally, there are well-known disorders that stem from just such differences between people in vitamin requirements. These are called vitamin-dependency conditions, as differentiated from the vitamin deficiency condition of a normal person on a poor diet. Every physician is acquainted with vitamin D-resistant rickets, where the child sometimes needs hundreds of times as much vitamin D as the normal child. Since 1954, about sixteen inherited diseases have been discovered which require massive dosages of one or another vitamin as the major form of treatment (Rosenberg, 1970). Who can say, in the absence of contrary information, that any one of us, or any sick person, is not the victim of just such a genetic vitamin dependency?

Third, and again contrary to widespread belief, there is a sizable body of scientific literature, including both control-group studies of vitamin effectiveness and laboratory studies on vitamin metabolism, which demonstrate beyond any doubt that at least some forms of what is called mental illness are closely linked to biochemical errors in the body. For those interested in learning more about these matters, let me recommend the recent book *Orthomolecular Psychiatry*, edited by David R. Hawkins and Linus Pauling. My chapter in that book (Rimland, 1973) provides not only a more comprehensive report of the ICBR vitamin study than can be presented here but also presents an extensive review of the scientific literature on vitamin therapy of mental illness, especially as it pertains to children. If anyone tells you that there is no scientific basis for believing that high dosages of vitamins may be useful in treating mental illness, he is simply admitting that he has not done his homework. There is by now a substantial and impressive body of data on the subject.

After deciding to investigate the problem, I sent a questionnaire to the approximately 1,000 parents and professionals then on the Institute mailing list to locate as many people as possible who had tried the vitamin approach. By analyzing the data from the 57 parents and 7 physicians who responded in detail, we evolved the selection of vitamins and dosages used in our study.

After consulting several nutritionists, biochemically oriented psychiatrists, and biochemists, we decided to start with a potent multiple-B-vitamin tablet plus several grams per day of vitamin C. After two weeks, two B-vitamins, niacinamide and pyridoxine, were added, each in quantities several hundred times the usual dosage. Finally, after two more weeks, megadose amounts of pantothenic acid (another B-vitamin) were added. The actual dosage levels used were determined by the weight of the child. The subjects of the study were the children of the several hundred parents from various parts of the U.S. and Canada who indicated, in response to our mail survey, that they would like to participate, and could find a local physician willing to cooperate.

The study took about four and a half months per child. After three months on the vitamins, a "no-treatment" period was scheduled so that any changes resulting from discontinuance of the vitamins could be observed. The vitamins were than reinstated briefly as the final stage in our design. The parents completed a simple one-page form describing the child's status every two weeks, and every month a similar form was completed by the child's physician. The parents also completed a more intensive questionnaire at the conclusion of their child's participation in the study.

Although all the vitamins used were well-established as being nontoxic, even in large quantities, we required the parents to obtain the participation of a physician of their choice, both to guard against the possibility of an adverse reaction and also to provide an independent opinion on the child's response to the vitamins.

The findings I will report are based on the first 191 children for whom we received complete data, including the final report. There is a large amount of information for every child in the study: detailed, periodic doctor and parent ratings on speech, eating, sleeping, tantrums, alertness, and so forth, as well as an extensive tabulation of positive and negative side effects. These data occupy some twenty IBM cards per child. To analyze them will require a great deal of time and effort. Our initial analysis was based on only a single two-digit score, ranging from a possible

99 (indicating phenomenal improvement) to a possible 10 (indicating great deterioration of behavior). These overall improvement scores were assigned and independently checked by two judges, after intensive study of all parent and doctor reports for each child. Discrepant or ambiguous ratings were resolved by discussion or excluded from the analysis.

Before giving you the results of the statistical analysis, I must tell you the rationale underlying our rather unusual experimental design.

Our decision to use a design other than the traditional control-group-and-placebo design has attracted a good deal of criticism from people who do not realize that there may be better alternatives. There are many reasons for deciding against the traditional design. My chapter in *Orthomolecular Psychiatry* discusses some shortcomings of the double-blind. The most important reason is that this design presupposes that the subjects constitute a homogeneous group.

I am firmly convinced that very little progress may be expected in finding cause and treatment for mental illness in children until the total group of children now loosely called "autistic," "schizophrenic," "psychotic," or "severely emotionally disturbed" can be subdivided in a scientific way into smaller homogeneous subgroups (Rimland, 1964; 1971). Leo Kanner, the man who discovered and named "infantile autism," has pointed out that for centuries medicine could make no progress against the disease known as "the fevers." It was not until "the fevers" were broken down into separate syndromes or disease entities such as malaria, diphtheria, tuberculosis, cholera, etc. that progress could be made toward finding causes and cures. Mental retardation provides an example closer to home—until it became possible to fractionate the mass of "retardates" into smaller groups such as PKU, cretinism, galactosemia, and mongolism, it was hopeless to try to devise means of prevention or treatment.

I believe the children loosely called "autistic" or "schizophrenic" actually represent a dozen or more different diseases or disorders, each with its own cause (Rimland, 1971). It is essential that we develop the means for finding the various subtypes of autistic-type children. I have been involved in research on this problem for many years. Computer technology is beginning to provide useful ways of approaching the problem of classification.

For each child enrolled in the vitamin study, we had required the completion of several research questionnaires by the parents, including our diagnostic questionnaire, Form E-2. Form E-2 consists of over 100 detailed questions, to be completed by the parents, covering the child's medical and birth history, symptomatology, and other information. E-2 was designed for computer analysis. Our hypothesis in the vitamin study was that only certain subgroups of the children would be helped, while other subgroups, because the cause of their problem was not related to their vitamin requirements, would show no benefits. We assumed that the information on Form E-2, while by no means exhaustive, was sufficient to permit a computer to classify the children into clusters that would show differential response to the vitamins.

I will not trouble you here with the many details of the statistical analysis. Briefly, through the use of highly sophisticated computer programs, various collaborating researchers were able to identify subgroups of children helped by the vitamins. For instance, using his computer program *Normix*, John H. Wolfe of the Naval Personnel and Training Research Laboratory in San Diego was able to classify the 191 children into six homogeneous subgroups or clusters. The clusters were formed *without* information of how well the children had responded to the vitamins. Only *after* the clusters were formed were the vitamin improvement scores entered into the computer so that the mean improvement score for each cluster could be determined.

The differences between the mean improvement scores for the six groups were found to be significant at the .02 level. That is, there was only one chance in fifty that the group means would be found to be so different if the vitamins did not in fact influence the improvement scores. It may thus be said with a high degree of assurance that the vitamin treatment does in fact importantly influence the behavior of certain children. As predicted, certain subgroups of children responded much more strongly than others.

Similar analyses were performed on our data by Dr. James Cameron of Napa State Hospital in California, and by Drs. Raymond Christal and Janos Koplyay of the Lackland Air Force Base in Texas. These analyses also produced results that were highly significant statistically. There is no reasonable explanation for these findings other than that the vitamins do help some children.

One of the chief advantages of the type of design we used is that now we know that we can take the more than 4,000 E-2 forms on file at our Institute, subject them to computer analysis, and tell with a reasonable degree of accuracy whether each child is or is not likely to benefit if placed on the vitamin regime we used.

The next step in our analysis of the data collected on our group of 191 children will be to do a fine-grained computer analysis of the findings to see if we can determine which vitamins were most helpful for each subgroup. Our use of megadose levels of four vitamins was in effect a "shotgun" approach, and now we need to narrow our aim.

The bottom section of Table 13-1 summarizes the findings of the megavitamin study.

TABLE 13-1

Comparison of Parent Ratings of Effectiveness of All Drugs, Best Drug (Mellaril) and Vitamins

Treatment	Total	No Definite Effect	Possibly Helped a Little	Total	Some Improvement	Definitely Helped	Total	Made a Little Worse	Made Much Worse	Total
All Drugs (Average Drug)	1591 100%	402 25.3	324 20.3	726 45.6	202 12.7	238 14.9	440 27.7	209 13.1	216 13.6	425 26.7
Best Drug (Mellaril)	277 100%	60 21.7	61 22.0	121 43.7	57 20.6	44 15.8	101 36.4	31 11.2	24 8.7	55 19.9
High Dosage Vitamins	191 100%	20 10.4	37 19.4	57 29.8	41 21.5	86 45.0	127 66.5	4 2.1	3 1.6	7 3.7

SOURCE: From B. Rimland, "An Orthomolecular Study of Psychotic Children," *Journal of Orthomolecular Psychiatry*, 1974, 3, 371–377.

While the vitamin study was in progress, our Institute was also collect-ing data for an evaluation of fourteen drugs commonly used with autistic and autistic-type children. The data were collected by mail questionnaires from parents in all parts of the U.S. The drugs and dosages were as pre-scribed by each child's physician, and our role was merely to collect and tabulate the child's response, as assessed by the parents. Table 13-1 also presents a summary of the results of the drug study and has been set up to facilitate comparison of the drugs and the vitamins.

Inspection of the table shows that the vitamins are not only far more likely to be helpful than the drugs, they are also far less likely to cause any kind of harm — behavioral or physical.

The findings in Table 13-1 are of special interest in view of the criticism of our vitamin study commonly made by people who do not understand the experimental design of the study. Some of our critics have suggested that our findings reflect only wishful thinking — they assert that our positive results might stem from the fact that many parents would be inclined to overrate the vitamins because they want so badly to see their child improve. This criticism is not valid, since parent expectation could not influence the computer grouping, but if it were valid, the same spurious effect should be seen in the parent's assessment of the drugs. It is not. Because there is clearly much more improvement reported for the vitamins than for the drugs, the argument that our vitamin findings reflect only wishful thinking by the parents must be rejected on these additional grounds. Note also that the drugs were specifically prescribed for each child by his own physician, while the vitamins were uniformly given to all the children, the dosage depending solely on body weight.

A quite unexpected side benefit of the vitamins was, in many cases, an improvement in the child's physical well-being. Many parents reported such things as improved skin condition or hair texture, better muscle tone, and the cessation of teeth grinding. But of course, what is of most interest is the behavioral improvement that constituted the basic reason for doing this study. In many children the improvement was striking. It shows up most clearly in contrasting the behavior of the child during the several months he was on the vitamins — during which time there was often a gradual improvement — with his behavior during the no-treatment period when the vitamins were suddenly stopped. Here are a few examples of such changes as reported by the parents:

> Frustration level extremely high without the vitamins. Much yelling and irritability. Has to be given directions three times instead of once. Changes were evident after three days of no vitamins and grew worse each subsequent day. . . . I resumed vitamins on the 14th day.

On August 5th (10th day of no-treatment period) both parents, who had been keeping separate notes, agreed that marked deterioration of behavior had occurred. William seemed to have withdrawn into himself; he no longer exhibited the lively interest in the world around him that had marked the previous month. His newfound willingness to cooperate and to obey such directions as he understood disappeared rapidly. His old repertoire of mannerisms and bizarre hand motions and positions, which had been waning, reasserted itself with a vengence. . . .

Harriet seems to be progressively less social with us. She is starting to retreat to her room for longer periods, as she did before she started the vitamin therapy.

Mary has been off the vitamins for two weeks. Her speech hasn't deteriorated, but all the annoying noises . . . have returned. Her skin tone isn't as good and the slightly bluish transparency to her facial skin is again noticeable. She is having trouble focusing her eyes and the pupils appear dilated and her expression is far off and dreamy, jaw slack. . . .

He stopped taking the vitamins exactly five days ago. I never expected the definite reaction that has gradually shown up without a doubt during these last five days — slowly at first and then increasing at an amazing rate. His doctor is on vacation and we cannot see the substitute doctor until next Thursday. However, I took it upon myself this morning to start him again on the complete dosage. I only hope it will relieve his present symptoms soon, symptoms that cannot be traced to anything short of not having the vitamins for these few days.

He gradually showed improvement in every area on the checklist — even those I may have noted as no behavioral improvement because now in those areas he has badly regressed. He is agitated and crying practically all the time, shaking nervously, hiding under blankets, tapping on things with spoons, getting into things he hasn't been getting into and that he shouldn't get into, eating poorly and away from the family table, making continuous odd noises, and seems to be suffering physically from some internal misery. Without a doubt, I trace his former improvement to the vitamins. He became calmer, seemed normal in public, didn't make noises, and verbalized sensibly, socialized more, was very much, much better.

The foregoing are just a sample of the reports in our files. There are many, many more. Also impressive, beyond the statistical data, are the reports we received from teachers who had documented improvement in their records when the children were on the vitamins and deterioration when the children were taken off the vitamins — *and these were teachers who had no idea whatever that the children were in our study or that the children were on or off treatment at any point in time.* We had asked the parents to keep secret from the school the child's being in the study until it was over.

Earlier I mentioned the fact that some of the children had shown adverse effects from the vitamins. A small number of children became irritable, hyperactive, sensitive to sounds, and enuretic when placed on the vitamins. These effects quickly disappeared when the parents stopped the vitamins. This puzzled us. The professors at the University Medical School were of no help. The answer came in the form of a phone call from the well-known nutritionist, Adelle Davis, who had served as a consultant during our planning sessions. She wanted to know the details of our study so she could include them in her then-in-preparation book *Let's Have Healthy Children* (1972). When I told her what vitamins we were using, and at what levels, she reminded me that she had long before urged that we include the mineral magnesium in our regime: "Where is the magnesium I told you to use?" Somewhat embarrassed, I explained that each child was already taking a whole handful of tablets, and adding magnesium would just add several more to the total. "Well," she said, "you'll have problems if you don't." "What kinds of problems?" I asked. Her reply astounded me: "Irritability, sound sensitivity, enuresis." She was perfectly on target! It seems that certain of the vitamins (B-6 in particular) combine with the magnesium in the body in order to perform their functions, and by adding the B-6 without the supplemental magnesium we were creating a relative deficiency of magnesium. The symptoms the children were experiencing were those of mild magnesium deficiency.

This incident illustrates two points; first, that certain dysnutritional conditions produce highly predictable behavioral manifestations, and second, that the megavitamin treatment can be quite complex, if done correctly. We would no doubt have had even better results from our study had we included magnesium, and perhaps zinc and other trace minerals. Today we know only a little of what there is to learn about the megavitamin approach, but we are learning constantly.

In the several years that have passed since I completed my study, the use of megavitamin therapy, and public interest in the topic, have increased enormously. In the late 1960s there were only two laboratories in the U.S. that marketed vitamin tablets in the megadose range. Today (in 1976) there are at least thirty commercial sources for megavitamins. In the last three years at least a dozen books have been published devoted primarily or entirely to the use of megavitamins in the treatment of mental disorders.

There are a number of reasons for the upsurge in interest in the mega-vitamin approach. One is increasing public disillusionment with both psychotherapy and drugs, the most common treatments for mental disorder. Psychotherapy is falling into disfavor because its general uselessness has begun to become known to larger segments of the public. Drugs are falling into disfavor because they are not only far more dangerous than was first supposed but also it is becoming increasingly evident that they merely suppress some of the most visible symptoms without really making much of a dent in the disorder underlying the patient's disturbed feelings or behavior. It is quite clear that the difference between a schizophrenic and a normal person is not that the schizophrenic has a deficiency of Chlor-promazine. The difference between Jane Doe when she is inexplicably anxious and when she is calm is not that her body is sometimes deficient in Librium.

Earlier in this chapter I referred on several occasions to the book *Orthomolecular Psychiatry*. Ther term "orthomolecular" was coined in 1967 by Nobel Prize winner Linus Pauling. "Ortho" means "corrective" or "reparative," and "molecular" refers to the chemistry of the body. Orthomolecular psychiatry involves the attempt to improve the function of the brain by providing the optimum concentration of substances *normally present* in the human body. Such substances include vitamins, minerals, and hormones; drugs and medicines, which for the most part are foreign to the body, are excluded from the concept. Note that the concept is broad enough to cover the exclusion or removal of substances *not* normally present in the body, such as food additives, mercury and lead, pesticides, and other pollutants that can interfere with brain functioning.

The orthomolecular concept makes very good sense to me, as I think it should to most reasonable people. I have coined the term "toximolecular" to contrast the orthomolecular approach with the one most present-day physicians use. (Did you know that prescription drugs kill more patients each year than does cancer of the breast, and that reactions to prescription drugs account for as many as 50 million hospital-patient-days a year? [Silverman & Lee, 1974].)

In 1972 the several hundred physicians throughout the U.S. who were achieving success with megavitamins and related approaches joined forces and established the Academy of Orthomolecular Psychiatry (AOP). As might be expected, the medical establishment frowned on this innovation (just as it has frowned on virtually every innovation in the treatment of physical and mental illness) and decided to set things right again.

In 1973 the American Psychiatric Association published its *Task Force Report on Megavitamin Therapy*. Space does not permit me to go into any detail about this report and its innumerable shortcomings. Perhaps it will suffice to point out that although there are numerous psychiatrists who are members of both the AOP and the APA, no AOP member was invited to participate in the task force, nor was any AOP member ever consulted, even once, before the publication of the report. Three of the five APA report authors were outspoken critics of the megavitamin approach before they even accepted the assignment, and the other two were at best neutral — they were certainly not pro-vitamin. The outcome was predictable.

The report was widely distributed to the news media, and today one sees frequent reference to it in newspapers and magazines. "The megavitamin treatment was tested and found to be valueless," according to *Consumers Reports*, the *Los Angeles Times* and numerous other publications which have taken the APA report at face value. *Don't you believe it!*

Sooner or later the American Psychiatric Association will have to admit that psychotherapy and drug therapy, the present mainstays of its members, are respectively useless and dangerous. It will have to recognize the outstanding success that the orthomolecular methods have achieved with many patients who had failed to respond to the traditional methods. It will acknowledge that the orthomolecular methods are safer, more effective, and more rational than the methods currently in wide use.

These changes will come. It is only a matter of time.

REFERENCES

ASTIN, A. W. The functional autonomy of psychotherapy. *American Psychologist,* 1961, *16,* 75–78.

DAVIS, A. *Let's have healthy children.* New York: Harcourt Brace Jovanovich, 1972.

EYSENCK, H. J. *The effects of psychotherapy.* New York: Science House, 1969.

FRANK, G. H. The role of the family in the development of psychopathology. *Psychological Bulletin,* 1965, *64,* 191–205.

HEBB, D. O. *Organization of behavior.* New York: Wiley, 1949.

LEVITT, E. E. Psychotherapy with children: A further evaluation. *Behaviour Research and Therapy,* 1963, *1,* 45–51.

LEWIS, W. W. Continuity and intervention in emotional disturbance: a review. *Exceptional Children,* 1965, *31,* 465–475.

MILBANK MEMORIAL FUND QUARTERLY. *The causes of mental disorder.* New York: Milbank Memorial Fund, 1961.

NEWELL, G. R., RAWLINGS, W., KINNEAR, B. K., CORREA, P., HENDERSON, B. E., DWORSKY, R., MENCK, H., THOMPSON, R, & SHEEHAN, W. W. Case-control study of Hodgkin's disease. I. Results of the interview questionnaire. *Journal of the National Cancer Institute,* 1973, *51*(5), 1437–1441.

RACHMAN, S. *The effects of psychotherapy.* Oxford: Pergamon, 1971.

RENAUD, H., & ESTESS, F. Life history interviews with one hundred normal American males. *American Journal of Orthopsychiatry,* 1961, *31,* 786–802.

RIMLAND, B. *Infantile autism.* New York: Appleton-Century-Crofts, 1964.

RIMLAND, B. Psychogenesis versus biogenesis: the issues and the evidence. In Plog, S. C., and Edgerton, R. B. (Eds.), *Changing perspectives in mental illness.* New York: Holt, Rinehart and Winston, 1969.

RIMLAND, B. The differentiation of childhood psychosis: an analysis of checklists for 2,218 psychotic children. *Journal of Autism and Childhood Schizophrenia,* 1971, *2,* 161–174.

RIMLAND, B. The effect of high dosage levels of certain vitamins on the behavior of children with severe mental disorders. In Hawkins, D. R., and Pauling, L. (Eds.), *Orthomolecular psychiatry.* San Francisco: W. H. Freeman, 1973.

ROSENBERG, L. E. Vitamin-dependent genetic disease. *Hospital Practice,* 1970, *5,* 59–66.

SCHOFIELD, W. *Psychotherapy: The purchase of friendship.* Englewood Cliffs, N.J.: Prentice-Hall, 1964.

SILVERMAN, M., & LEE, P. R. *Pills, profits and politics.* Berkeley: University of California Press, 1974.

STEVENSON, I. Is the human personality more plastic in infancy and childhood? *American Journal of Psychiatry,* 1957, *114,* 152–161.

WILLIAMS, R. J. *Biochemical individuality.* New York: Wiley, 1956.

V

CONCLUSION

The proliferation of new therapies within the past fifteen to twenty years is indeed striking. As information about each approach is disseminated, it attracts enthusiasts who testify to its effectiveness. In some cases these testimonials are substantiated by scientific research; in other cases the research evidence is inconclusive, and in still other cases no research is conducted.

The Conclusion focuses on the difficulties involved in trying systematically to assess the value of various therapies. Controversy exists about such things as the appropriate choice of subjects, units of measurement, and research design. The evaluative strategy of each of the therapies presented in this volume is described and it is suggested that (on the basis of the available evidence) it is too early to determine differential effectiveness.

14

Evaluating the Effectiveness of Psychotherapy

Virginia Binder

With so many therapeutic approaches available to the person in need, how does he or she go about choosing the type of therapy suitable to his or her problems? Is there a governing agency or group of therapists who recommend where to go for help? Is there informative guidance to be found in newspaper advertisements or telephone directory listings? Has research clearly established which of the many therapy approaches is best for a given problem?

The answer to the above questions is a resounding NO! People seem to choose their type of therapy and therapist very informally—largely by word of mouth. If they want to consult a therapist, they are likely to ask their physician, teacher, clergyman, or even their friend for a recommendation. They are usually interested in knowing what the therapy is like. Often they may have read about the therapy in newspapers, magazines, or books. If it sounds reasonable to them (as "reasonable" is discussed in Chapter 1), then that is the basis for choice.

Given the above situation, have there been any attempts to determine which therapies are effective, or the relative efficacy of the various therapies? Yes, studies designed to answer these questions are called therapy *outcome* studies. Such studies vary in sophistication ranging from the single-case presentation based largely on anecdotes to a multifactor design that seeks to control numerous variables.

For a good many years the name most frequently associated with outcome research was Eysenck (1952, 1961). He is known for his surveys of the

"Evaluating the Effectiveness of Psychotherapy," by Virginia Binder, Ph.D. © 1976 by Virginia Binder. This article appears in print for the first time in this volume.

literature which conclude that two out of three neurotics treated by psychotherapists show improvement. These figures are impressive until Eysenck points out that two of three neurotics who receive no formal therapy also improve. While Eysenck's methods have been criticized by therapists and researchers alike, his statistics are widely cited. Other researchers (Truax & Carkhuff, 1967; Levitt, 1957, 1971) have come to similar conclusions regarding the overall lack of effectiveness of therapy.

More recently, Meltzoff and Kornreich (1970) have surveyed over 100 studies (all meeting a minimum criterion of having some form of control group) and concluded that the majority of studies support the effectiveness of therapy. Similarly, Luborsky, Singer, and Luborsky (1975) believe evidence exists for the value of therapy.

To understand how different researchers can come to such diverse conclusions while reviewing many of the same studies, it is necessary to consider the problems encountered in trying to conduct outcome studies.

DEFINITION OF SUCCESS

First of all, it is necessary to determine what constitutes successful therapy. In other words, what are the goals of therapy? Having now read descriptions of more than a dozen therapies, you are well aware that the goal of most therapies is to help the client improve his functioning in some way. But the type of functioning considered important for therapeutic change varies widely. For someone like Cohen, whose LSD Therapy is used as an adjunct to psychoanalysis, the goals could be to "retrieve inaccessible unconscious material, to alter superego functioning, or to have the client's value system assume a more eternal and cosmic quality." In contrast, the Behavior therapists usually have a specific goal such as the elimination of fear as in Implosive Therapy or a decrease in a child's tantrums as in Operant Therapy. Other approaches prescribe goals that may fall somewhere along the continuum from the very general, abstract type of change prescribed by Cohen to the particular, well-defined change of the behaviorists. For example, the Gestalt therapist, Yontef, strives for "Awareness" in his clients; Karle, Woldenberg, and Hart hope to have clients live from their feelings; Glasser encourages a successful identity; Ellis desires the elimination of disordered thinking; Cotler helps clients assert their rights; and Runciman aids clients as they strive for adequate and/or more pleasurable sexual functioning—moving roughly from the general to the specific.

MEASUREMENT OF SUCCESS

Though the goals of therapy may be generally stated, actual outcome studies require the assigning of a number so that differential change in clients can be assessed. While many therapists may argue that no single number or pattern of numbers can possibly represent the experiences of their clients, even the loftiest of goals like giving a more cosmic quality to a client's value system can be or have been quantified in some way.

Frequently Used Measures

Rating scales. The most common way of assigning a number to therapeutic change is to use a rating scale allowing for numbers from, say, 1 to 5 to represent varying degrees of improvement. The therapist, the client, or some outsider like an employer or relative may complete such a scale or in some cases more than one person may do so. This method of evaluation was mentioned by Cohen, Rimland, and Glasser. However, self-report measures and therapists' evaluations are generally biased in favor of improvement. How many clients who have invested considerable time and possibly money readily admit that therapy was a waste of time? And it seems equally likely that therapists would interpret any type of change they observe as at least slight improvement.

Psychological tests. Another, seemingly more objective way to measure change is through changes on psychological tests. Both projective techniques like the Rorschach inkblots and personality inventories, a series of statements with which the client must agree or disagree, have been used to assess changes in clients.

The projective techniques, often used by those with a psychoanalytic orientation, are not highly regarded by scientists because the reliability (consistency) and validity (usefulness of the information provided) leave much to be desired. Some personality inventories have much greater reliability and validity than projective devices, but very few of the standard inventories for which reliability and validity coefficients are widely known relate to the specific goals of therapy. Implosive therapists have reported changes in the direction of fewer behavioral deviations on the widely used Minnesota Multiphasic Personality Inventory (MMPI), but such changes are hard to relate to the purpose of the therapy. Objective inventories have also been used by those evaluating the Transcendental Meditation program.

Physiological measures. A still more objective approach in the eyes of some would be the measurement of physiological changes to determine the success of therapy. This measurement technique has been used by systematic desensitization therapists in trying to show a reduction in anxiety through changes in the galvanic skin response (GSR) and heart rate. The Transcendental Meditation program has also been studied in this way. However, physiological changes recorded on even the most expensive and elaborate apparatus are subject to considerable human error in recording and interpretation (Lang, 1971). Though these problems may be minimal compared to the subjectivity of projective test interpretation, physiological measures also suffer from the difficulties noted with the MMPI as a measure. In what way should physiological states change to reflect improvement in therapy? It isn't unreasonable to expect a more relaxed state to accompany reductions in anxiety or fear, but what changes should be expected when physiological measures are used to evaluate a therapy that advocates a change in feeling states like the therapy of Karle, Woldenberg, and Hart?

Behavioral measures. Research methodologists in the area of outcome research often prefer to use behavioral measures that can be unambiguously measured, counted, or tallied. Implosive therapists and systematic desensitization therapists treat phobics and find behavioral measures useful. If the client fears a snake, it is possible to measure the closest distance at which the client will tolerate the snake. If a client is afraid to assert himself with a girl, one could tally the number of dates made. Often, observers are trained so that even naive raters can consistently measure the phenomenon in question. As with all other approaches, behavioral measures also have limitations. Behavior therapists prefer them because they work with observable changes. But for therapists interested in altering ego structure, helping someone intensify feelings, or aiding maturity, one would be hard-pressed to select a measure to observe and count that the therapist would agree captures the essence of his approach.

General Recommendations about Measurement

Thus, it should be readily apparent that there is no single best measure of the effectiveness of therapy. Methodologists (Bergin, 1971; Fiske, Hunt, Luborsky, Orne, Parloff, Reiser, & Tuma, 1970; Green, Gleser, Stone, & Seifert, 1975; Luborsky, Singer, & Luborsky, 1975) have made a number of suggestions regarding the way measures should be collected in psychotherapy studies. First of all, it is quite unlikely, as Kiesler (1966) points out, that all therapy is alike or uniform. To question whether therapy in general is effective, according to Kiesler, is inappropriate. Instead, one should look to see which of the therapies are effective under what conditions; for, as you have discovered, the therapeutic approaches vary considerably. When one designs an outcome study one should include a measure or measures relevant to the therapies being compared. But at the same time it would also be helpful to include measures that might tap areas in which no change is expected. For example, the Implosive therapist could measure anxiety reduction in some way and also measure changes in the value system. In this way it would be possible to determine which of the therapies effect which kinds of changes and to what extent. It is conceivable that a therapy method that theoretically deals only with behavioral changes could also show changes in other spheres. Furthermore, while a number of the measurement techniques described earlier were laden with problems, it might be wise to continue their use in order to provide a basis of comparison between old and new evaluations. To sum up these recommendations then, multiple measures should be collected with particular inclusion of factors relevant to therapy. Bloomfield reports the use of multiple measures by those interested in the Transcendental Meditation program.

Two further suggestions have also been put forth regarding therapy measures. Because none of the currently used measures is completely satisfactory, there is a need for the development of new measures. One type suggested would be the use of unobtrusive measures, also called nonreactive measures, in which clients are unaware they are being observed or studied. Such nonreactive measures help to minimize the biases introduced when clients intentionally or unintentionally try to create certain impressions. Unobtrusive measures have not yet been widely used in outcome studies. In one of my projects I hoped to see whether purchases in a ward canteen would reflect behavioral improvement on a token-economy program (see Chapter 10). It was hypothesized that patients showing the least sociable and most inappropriate behavior would purchase items that were primary reinforcers—like candy. The most sociable patients would purchase items to help improve their appearance—like make-up and clothing—and improve their interaction with others—like games and newspapers. Because the patients were unaware that their purchases were monitored, the relationship found between patients' socialization ability and type of purchases indicates that such unobtrusive measures have promise in assessing behavior change.

The second additional recommendation involves the use of change criterion tailor-made for each individual client. It should be possible to designate the type of changes needed based on the presenting complaint. Thus, the kinds of change desired would be specified for each client before therapy is begun. Cotler's Assertive Goal Scale is an example of such a measure. As yet there are no good research designs that can accommodate such a scheme.

It has been typical of therapists when designing outcome studies to select the measures that best reflect the changes they hope to bring about in clients. Until recently, then, few therapists collected the multiple measures that would be most helpful in answering the question, "What treatment by whom is most effective for this individual with that specific problem and under what set of circumstances?" (Paul, 1967, p. 111).

It seems unlikely to expect therapies in their current state of sophistication to bring about change simultaneously in all possible spheres — cognitive, emotional, and behavioral. It seems more reasonable to expect an approach aimed at cognitive change such as the Rational-Emotive approach of Albert Ellis to produce the most change on intellectual measures, LSD Therapy to show up best on emotional measures, and behavior approaches like that of Assertion Training to show the most change on action measures.

THE NEED FOR CONTROLLED EVALUATION

The majority of successful therapy studies reported in the literature are individual case studies or a collection of case studies. For most of these studies it is impossible to tell whether the change occurring in the clients (assuming the change is real and not a product of the therapist's wishful thinking) is due to the specific characteristics of the therapy itself or to some other factors such as the faith in the treatment and other placebo effects described in the first chapter; or reduction of stress in the client's environment, the acquisition of a good friend, or even the mere passage of time in the client's life. (For a more complete discussion of factors that can account for change other than the treatment itself, see Campbell & Stanley, 1963.)

Since Western therapies present themselves as scientific in form, evaluation of their effectiveness must be done within the framework of scientific method. And the use of a control group is one requirement of the scientific method when treatment outcomes are evaluated. A control group consists of people who do not receive treatment but who are as much as possible like the people who do receive treatment. A control group is necessary because people change for a vast array of reasons over a period of time, and one can be sure that a given change resulted from treatment, rather than some other factor such as those mentioned in the previous paragraph, only when the treated group shows the change and a similar, but untreated group does not.

Two main approaches to the use of control groups can be found in therapy research. In the first, individuals who receive threatment are compared with others who, theoretically at least, are untreated. In the second, individuals are used as their own controls and compared across time. Whether or not this latter approach is an improvement over the old-fashioned case study depends on the nature of the design chosen.

In the psychological laboratory, assigning subjects to treatment and control groups is a straightforward matter. Thus, many academicians assume it should be equally easy in therapy research. However, a stumbling block occurs immediately because many clinicians are unwilling to randomly assign clients in need of help to an untreated control group because of ethical considerations. These clinicians are concerned that people in need will be denied a potentially helpful treatment. Consequently, the type of untreated control groups found in the literature are rarely groups that can be considered comparable to those given treatment. Many therapists seem oblivious to the point that groups being compared should be as similar as possible on all dimensions except for the matter of receiving the treatment. Thus they offer the data from therapy rejects or dropouts as a suitable comparison. The motivation of those who are rejected or who drop out is undoubtedly different from that of the remainers.

In practice, it is extremely difficult to include an untreated control group in an outcome study. In order to obtain the measures needed to assess change, some contact must be made with those in the untreated control group, and so they may receive some help during this contact. The help may come in the form of a cathartic experience during the assessment, the increased attention, and other placebo components that may occur at this initial stage.

Types of Control

Waiting-list control groups. A better approach, from both ethical and design perspectives, is to assign subjects to a waiting-list control group. For those with ethical concerns, the waiting-list group is not denied treatment, but simply asked to wait a given period before receiving treatment. Such a waiting period is common in many therapeutic settings because of the large demand for services. From a design perspective, subjects in the treatment and waiting-list groups can be considered equivalent if they are randomly assigned to their respective conditions and the number of persons in each is large enough. A careful look at some outcome studies indicates that the subjects in the waiting-list control groups are not assigned to the condition randomly. Instead they have been assigned to their groups in a number of ways, such as motivation for treatment or severity of problem, and they may differ from the treated subjects on these variables. Thus they are not suitable subjects for comparison. Just as it is difficult to find an untreated control group, in practice it is also hard to retain subjects in a waiting-list group. It often happens that people in such groups leave the area or seek help elsewhere. Only when the wait is relatively brief does this approach work.

Attention-placebo groups. Another type of control group is also incorporated in the better-designed outcome studies. This group is called an attention-placebo group. As noted in the introductory chapter, much of the success of a new approach may be due to placebo components such as novelty, expectation of help, and enthusiasm of its advocates. A placebo-control group is one in which an attempt is made to provide all the trappings of a therapy except for the actual method the therapist believes is responsible for the change in his clients.

For instance, in an Implosive Therapy study the attention-placebo group may be given instructions, therapeutic attention (actual time with a therapist), a rationale for the procedure, and all other aspects of the treatment, such as equal length and number of sessions. They may even be presented with frightening imagery, but not that which is relevant to their fear. If the attention-placebo group does show improvement, then it is likely that much of the success of the therapy is due to the extra-therapy aspects.

Subjects as their own controls. The types of controls described above are used when one group of subjects is being compared with another. Bergin (1971) has argued that comparisons between groups of subjects often disguise the true effects of therapy. He believes that certain clients may improve, others may get worse, and some may stay about the same. When all their scores are averaged and compared, we may lose considerable information about the specific effects of therapy.

Another major strategy for setting up controls involves using subjects as their own controls. This may be done casually or with attempted precision, and is often the design of choice for Behavior therapists who choose to collect a greater amount of data on fewer subjects. Leitenberg (1973) has described the major types of designs available, but the most frequently used one is called the withdrawal design. Here an Operant therapist might collect base-rate data and then introduce some contingency such as praise for attempts at socialization. When the rate of socialization increases after the praise, the contingency is withdrawn. If the praise is indeed re-

Evaluating the Effectiveness of Psychotherapy   223

sponsible for the change in socialization, then the new performance should decline until the praise is reintroduced. Once again, a design that solves certain problems presents difficulties of its own. With the withdrawal design, therapists may be reluctant to give up the gains obtained — even temporarily. Sometimes it is not possible to withdraw the treatment, such as would happen with LSD Therapy or with a mother who has been trained in reinforcement principles. The design is also inappropriate where specific treatment goals cannot be stated or changes are not expected for a considerable period of time.

The method of using clients as their own controls was used in the study of unobtrusive measures noted in my discussion of the token-economy experiment. A multiple baseline approach was used whereby purchases in a number of categories were continuously recorded. A change in the rate of purchase in a category was expected following the introduction of treatment emphasis on the area. For instance, it was expected that more grooming aids would be bought during the ward emphasis on appearance, and the increase in the purchase of books and records would occur during the ward focus on leisure activities.

While the two major approaches to control noted above are those most widely used, the ability of the computer to handle large amounts of data easily may make statistical control an alternative approach in therapy studies. Rimland has utilized such a strategy in evaluating the usefulness of megavitamins for psychotic children (see Chapter 13).

ADDITIONAL PROBLEMS IN OUTCOME RESEARCH

The problems of measurement and selection of appropriate control groups are the biggest obstacles to definitive outcome research. But numerous other headaches also plague the researcher. A dilemma for the whole field of psychiatric diagnosis raises its ugly head here also. If you want to designate the type of people for whom a certain therapy works best, you need to have some system of labeling or classification. The current system of categorizing people as chronic schizophrenics, depressives, anxiety neurotics, sociopaths, and so forth overlooks considerable individuality in people. The classification scheme has been widely challenged as unreliable, unrelated to cause and effect, and demeaning, but as yet has not been replaced by anything better. Most outcome studies use the labels to describe their client sample. Hence the reader of the research is unsure about the extent to which the findings of a study may be generalized. The more information that is provided about the therapy clients, the better, as far as knowing for whom the therapy works.

More recently, clients have been chosen and described on the basis of their presenting problem rather than their psychiatric label. So a therapy may be known as effective for those with speech anxiety, impotent men, or brats. A person with numerous complaints, vague complaints, or undefined complaints might not know where to turn for help.

Some outcome studies focus on demonstrating the effectiveness of therapy relative to no treatment, while other outcome studies attempt to demonstrate the relative efficacy of a number of therapies. The same problems of measurement, control, and client description remain, but still new ones arise regarding such details as the length of treatment, the frequency of sessions, and the types of therapists to administer the treatment. Therapies of varying duration should be compared in some comparable fashion. But is it fair to allow the same length of time for Gestalt Therapy to produce change as for Assertion Training? Is the personality and charisma of the Gestalt therapist or the Implosive therapist the factor that produces improvement in clients, or is it the method itself? In the ideal therapy design, the same therapists would conduct all the treatments — their own favorite as well as the others being compared. Then, if one approach were clearly superior regardless of its practitioner and his or her enthusiasm, you would have a strong endorsement of the therapy. Often, however, it is difficult to train therapists to conduct a number of therapies as competently as they conduct their own.

In the light of the questions raised about outcome designs, it becomes easier to understand how there could be such divergent opinions about the effectiveness of therapy as those of Eysenck (1952) versus Meltzoff and Kornreich (1970). It is becoming more and more popular to test the efficacy of therapy. Whether you find many studies supportive of therapy depends on your standards for accepting the design of a given study as capable of offering adequate evidence. My own review of many of the studies cited by Meltzoff and Kornreich found far fewer pieces of research that I would classify as adequate for basing conclusions.

Perhaps an encouraging note needs to be sounded at this point. Therapists and researchers have become increasingly aware of the design pitfalls in outcome research and have been proposing some ingenious solutions. The study by Paul (1966) cited in this book by Storms (Chapter 8) was the start of this trend. Paul's study offered solutions for the problems of measurement, choice of controls, selection of clients and therapists, and means of keeping conditions comparable across groups.

CONCLUSION

The therapies described in this book vary in the amount of research available to support their claims. The proportion of each chapter devoted to research reflects this variation nicely. However, one should not automatically assume that a therapy with little or no emphasis on research is ineffective. It is equally likely that the therapy is too new, the therapists less interested in data collection, or the changes desired are elusive to traditional outcome measures. Certainly it is reassuring to many to see a therapist who can document the success rate of his approach, but many are willing to choose a therapist in whom they believe regardless of statistics. Given the current state of knowledge in the field, faith may be an important factor in bringing about change. Thus whether the client bases his faith on facts and figures or on his own gut reactions, his preference and his belief may contribute largely to his outcome.

REFERENCES

BERGIN, A. E. The evaluation of therapeutic outcomes. In Bergin, A. E., & Garfield, S. L. (Eds.), *Handbook of psychotherapy and behavior change.* New York: Wiley, 1971.

CAMPBELL, D. T., & STANLEY, J. C. *Experimental and quasi-experimental designs for research.* Chicago: Rand McNally, 1966.

EYSENCK, H. J. The effects of psychotherapy: an evaluation. *Journal of Consulting Psychology,* 1952, *16*, 319–324.

EYSENCK, H. J. The effects of psychotherapy. In Eysenck, H. J. (Ed.), *Handbook of abnormal psychology.* New York: Basic Books, 1961.

FISKE, D., HUNT, H. F., LUBORSKY, L., ORNE, M., PARLOFF, M., REISER, M., & TUMA, A. H. Planning of research on effectiveness of psychotherapy. *American Psychologist,* 1970, *25*, 727–737.

GREEN, B. L., GLESER, G. C., STONE, W. N., & SEIFERT, R. F. Relationships among diverse measures of psychotherapy outcome. *Journal of Consulting and Clinical Psychology,* 1975, *43*(5), 689–699.

KEISLER, D. J. Some myths of psychotherapy research and the search for a paradigm. *Psychological Bulletin,* 1966, *65*, 110–136.

LANG, P. J. The application of psychophysiological methods to the study of psychotherapy and behavior modification. In Bergin, A. E., & Garfield, S. L. (Eds.), *Handbook of psychotherapy and behavior change*. New York: Wiley, 1971.

LEITENBERG, H. The use of single case methodology in psychotherapy research. *Journal of Abnormal Psychology*, 1973, *82*, 87–101.

LEVITT, E. E. The results of psychotherapy with children: an evaluation. *Journal of Consulting Psychology*, 1957, *21*, 189–196.

LEVITT, E. E. Research on psychotherapy with children. In Bergin, A. E., & Garfield, S. L. (Eds.), *Handbook of psychotherapy and behavior change*. New York: Wiley, 1971.

LUBORSKY, L., SINGER, B., & LUBORSKY, L. Comparative studies of psychotherapies. Is it true that "everyone has won and all must have prizes"? *Archives of General Psychiatry*, 1975, *32*, 995–1008.

MELTZOFF, J., & KORNREICH, J. *Research in psychotherapy*. New York: Atherton, 1970.

PAUL, G. L. *Insight vs. desensitization in psychotherapy*. Stanford, Cal.: Stanford University Press, 1966.

TRUAX, C. B., & CARKHUFF, R. R. *Toward effective counseling and psychotherapy*. Chicago: Aldine, 1967.

Index